A Handbook of Scandinavian Names

D1649038

A Handbook of
Scandinavian Names

Nancy L. Coleman and Olav Veka

NORTHFIELD PUBLIC LIBRARY
210 Washington Street
Northfield, MN 55057

The University of Wisconsin Press

3/11

The University of Wisconsin Press
1930 Monroe Street, 3rd Floor
Madison, Wisconsin 53711-2059
uwpress.wisc.edu

3 Henrietta Street
London WC2E 8LU, England
eurospanbookstore.com

Copyright © 2010
The Board of Regents of the University of Wisconsin System
All rights reserved. No part of this publication may be reproduced, stored in a retrieval system, or
transmitted, in any format or by any means, digital, electronic, mechanical, photocopying, recording,
or otherwise, or conveyed via the Internet or a Web site without written permission of the University
of Wisconsin Press, except in the case of brief quotations embedded in critical articles and reviews.

5   4   3   2   1

Printed in the United States of America

Library of Congress Cataloging-in-Publication Data
Coleman, Nancy L. (Nancy Louise), 1945–
    A handbook of Scandinavian names / Nancy L. Coleman and Olav Veka.
      p. cm.
    Includes bibliographical references and index.
    ISBN 978-0-299-24834-5 (pbk. : alk. paper) — ISBN 978-0-299-24833-8 (e-book)
    1. Names Personal — Scandinavian. 2. Scandinavian languages — Etymology — Names. I. Veka, Olav.
II. Title.
PD1803.C65   2010
929.7′48—dc22
                          2010011535

Contents

Preface   vii

Pronunciation Guide   ix

Abbreviations and Symbols   xvii

Dictionary of Scandinavian Names
    Girls Names   3
    Boys Names   22

A Guide to Scandinavian Naming
    Scandinavian Immigration to North America   53
    Naming Traditions in Scandinavia   69
    Namesakes in the Scandinavian Tradition   80
    Adapting Names in Scandinavian America   85
    Scandinavian Given Names in Historical Perspective   120
    Name Laws   135
    Top Names in Scandinavia Today   139
    Names from Norse Mythology   146
    Name Days   149
    Naming Traditions in the Royal Families   159
    A Scandinavian Name for Your Baby   173

Definitions   183
References   185
Index   189

Preface

A Handbook of Scandinavian Names is both a dictionary of names for girls and boys and a handbook on naming traditions. In our context, Scandinavian names include names used in the countries of Denmark, Iceland, Norway, and Sweden. The languages in these countries are all closely related and belong to the same family of Indo-European languages. Finland is also a Scandinavian country, but it is divided linguistically. There is a Swedish-speaking minority of about 6 percent, and many in this population use Swedish language names. Finnish is the first language of the majority of Finns, however, and Finnish is not Indo-European but part of the Finno-Ugric language group, which also includes Hungarian and Estonian. Immigration from Finland to the United States is an integral part of immigration from the other Scandinavian countries, however. For this reason, a section on Finnish immigration is included.

The languages of the Sámi people, a minority population living in northern Norway, Sweden, Finland, and Russia, belong to the same group as Finnish. Greenland is a part of Denmark, but the native language, Kalaallisut, belongs to still another family of languages unrelated to Indo-European, the Inuit-Aleut family, spoken by Inuits in Alaska, Canada, and Greenland. Finnish, Sámi, and Kalaallisut (Inuit) names will not be treated in this book.

The names of girls and boys are treated in different sections. Each entry gives information about the pronunciation of the name in Scandinavia, in which Scandinavian country or countries the name is primarily used, its origin and meaning, relevant information about its frequency and popularity during the immigration period (ca. 1840–1910), and well-known bearers of the name.

The second section of the book is a handbook containing information on a number of subjects relevant to the context of Scandinavian names and naming traditions in the home countries and the United States.

Both of the authors have a Norwegian background, and most of our research has been on Norwegian names and naming traditions. Our aim is to cover the entire field of Scandinavian names, but in some instances the material has an unavoidable Norwegian slant.

This book should meet the needs of different groups of readers. We hope that all these groups will find something that interests them:

- Readers looking for information on the names used in their own immigrant families
- Readers looking for authentic Scandinavian names for their children
- Readers desiring information about the context of using a Scandinavian name
- Readers with a general interest in names and naming traditions.

Names are part of the broader cultural heritage brought to the United States by immigrants from the Scandinavian countries. Many books have been published in English on other aspects of Scandinavian culture, but until now there has not been a book devoted to Scandinavian names and naming traditions. Naming books are available for other ethnic groups, such as Irish, Scottish, and German.

Some Scandinavian names are popular in mainstream American culture, as can be confirmed by looking at any one of the many name books published for the American market. Unfortunately, some of the information in these books is erroneous or misunderstood in the cultural context, and new books use existing books as sources, so myths about Scandinavian names are perpetuated from book to book.

There are also a good many Web sites where you can find suggestions for Scandinavian baby names. Unfortunately, many of these resources also give unreliable information on which names belong to the Scandinavian naming vocabulary, as well as the meanings.

It is always important to know something about the cultural context of a name, and Scandinavian naming traditions differ from those in the United States, as well as other European countries. It is hoped that this volume will correct misconceptions and be a reliable source for people looking for information on Scandinavian names.

Pronunciation Guide

This pronunciation guide is designed to help you approximate the pronunciation of names in Danish, Norwegian, and Swedish. It is based on the spelling and pronunciation of English according to General American English pronunciation, with occasional references to British English. The system is based on the symbols or phonetics used in phrase books for tourists and some English language dictionaries. Our variant of this system is based on the selection of names in this volume, and it is therefore not comprehensive.

A stressed syllable is shown in bold type. Scandinavian languages normally stress the first syllable in a word, but there are some exceptions. Names borrowed and developed from Latin and other Romance languages typically place the accent toward the end of the word.

Examples for most sounds will be given for both girls names and boys names.

Danish

Written Danish and Norwegian *bokmål* look very similar, but the pronunciation is different. Danish intonation is less "musical" than Norwegian and Swedish, and the glottal stop explained below gives it a guttural character that sounds peculiar to other Scandinavians.

Consonants

Most consonants in Danish are pronounced as in English. Exceptions are noted in the table below.

Letter	Pronunciation Explained	Symbol	Examples	Pronunciation
bj	Both **b** and **j** are pronounced. The j is pronounced like the **y** in 'yet.'	by	**Bjørg** **Bjørn** **Bj**arke	**byoerg** **byoern** **byar**-keh
c	Pronounced like **s** before e, i, and y.	s	Cecilie	say-**see**-lee-eh
c	Pronounced like **k** before a, o, and u, and in the combination ch.	k	Carin Christine Carl Christian	**kaa**-rin kris-**teen**-eh **kaarl** **krehs**-tyaan

Letter	Pronunciation Explained	Symbol	Examples	Pronunciation
d	A final d preceded by a consonant is not pronounced.	—	Ragnhild Svend	**ræng**-nill **svehn**
d	Pronounced like **th** in 'this' at the end of a word or after a vowel, or between a vowel and unstressed e or i.	th	Gudrun Knud	**gooth**-roon **knooth**
j, hj	Pronounced like **y** in 'yet.'	y	Janne Hjørdis Jens Hjalmar	**yæn**-na **yoer**-dees **yehns** **yaal**-mahr
kn	**K** and **n** are both pronounced.	kn	Knud	**Knooth**
ng	Pronounced like **ng** in 'thing.'	ng	Inger Ingolf	**ing**-ehr **ing**-golf
r	Pronounced at the back of the throat, like the French r. Pronounced at the beginning of a word, otherwise often omitted.	r	Rigmor Roald	**reeg**-moor **roo**-al
t	As in English, but like **d** between vowels.	d	Gitte Jytte	**gih**-deh **yewd**-deh
th	Only the t is pronounced.	t	Margrethe Thyra Thor Theis	mar-**gray**-teh **tew**-ra **tohr** **tæis**
w	Pronounced like **v**. Often an alternate spelling (Viggo).	v	Wiggo	**vig**-go

Vowels

Danish often uses a glottal stop in connection with the pronunciation of vowels. This is a short puff of air. The sound is too complicated to include in this pronunciation guide. Leaving it out will not be an impediment to pronouncing the names. The next table provides details of vowel pronunciation.

Note that Danish has three extra vowels: æ, ø, and å. See also page 69 for a comparison of the "extra" vowels in Norwegian, Swedish, Danish, and Icelandic.

Letter	Pronunciation Explained	Symbol	Examples	Pronunciation
a	"Open" a is pronounced like **a** in 'father.'	aa	Karl Lars Karen	**kaarl** **laars** **kaa**-rehn
a	"Flat" a is pronounced like **a** in 'cat.'	æ	Mads Anne	**mæss** **æn**-neh
a	The combination ag is pronounced like the **ow** in 'how.'	ow	Agnes Vagn	**owng**-nehs **vown**

Letter	Pronunciation Explained	Symbol	Examples	Pronunciation
a	Short a is pronounced like **a** in 'about' or **u** in 'cut' (British English). In names used at the end of the word.	a	Anna	**aan**-na
e	Long e is pronounced like **ay** in 'say.' Occasionally written ee.	ay	Margrethe Preben Steen	maar-**gray**-teh **pray**-behn **stayn**
e	Short e is pronounced like **e** in 'let.' Short e may occur in a stressed or unstressed syllable.	eh	Elisabet Gitte Esben Ole	eh-**lee**-saa-beht **gid**-deh **ehs**-behn **oo**-leh
i	Long i is pronounced like **ee** in 'see.'	ee	Ida Ivar	**ee**-da **ee**-vaa
i	Short i is pronounced like **i** in 'sit.'	i	Gitte Niels	**gid**-deh **nils**
o	Long o is pronounced like **oo** in 'soon.'	oo	Lone Tor	**loo**-neh **toor**
o	Sometimes long o is pronounced like **å**.	oa	Tove Morten	**toa**-veh **moar**-tehn
o	Short o is pronounced like **o** in 'lot.'	o	Gorm Viggo	**gorm** **vig**-go
u	Long u is pronounced like **oo** in 'pool.'	oo	Ruth Ulf	**root** **oolf**
u	Short u is pronounced like **oo** in 'foot.'	uh	Uffe Ulrikke	**uhf**-feh uhl-**rig**-geh
y	Pronounced like **ew** in 'few.'	ew	Thyra Tyge	**tew**-ra **tew**-geh
æ	Pronounced like **a** in 'man.'	æ	Lærke	**lær**-keh
ø	Similar to the **u** in 'fur.' Round the lips and try to say **eh**.	oe	Søs Søren	**soes** **soern**
å (aa)	Pronounced like **oa** in 'boat.' Older forms use aa instead of å.	oa	Åse/Aase Åge/Aage	**oa**-seh **oa**-geh

Diphthongs (Vowel Combinations)

Letters	Pronunciation Explained	Symbol	Examples	Pronunciation
ai, aj	Pronounced like the pronoun **I**.	I	Laila Kaj	**II**-la **kI**
ei, ej	Similar to **ai** in 'wait,' but the first part is the **æ** sound.	æi	Theis Ejvind	**Tæis** **ei**-vinn

Norwegian

Most people listening to Norwegian think it sounds musical because it goes up and down. The system of intonation is too complicated to include here, but leaving it out will not be an impediment to approximating the pronunciation of names.

Consonants

Most of the consonants in Norwegian are pronounced as in English. The table below lists exceptions.

Letter	Pronunciation Explained	Symbol	Examples	Pronunciation
bj	Both **b** and **j** are pronounced. The j is pronounced like the **y** in 'yet.'	by	**Bjørg** **Bjørn**	**byoerg** **byoern**
c	Pronounced like **s** before e, i and y.	s	**Cecilie**	say-**seel**-ee-eh
c	Pronounced like **k** before a, o, and u, and in the combination ch.	k	**Christine** Wen**che** **Carsten** **Christian**	kris-**tee**-neh **vehng**-keh **kaar**-stehn **kris**-tee-yan
d	A final d in a name is usually not pronounced.	—	Ragnhild Gudmund	**rag**-nill **gewd**-mewnn
gj, gy	In a name that begins with gj and gy, g is pronounced like **y** in 'yes.'	y	**Gjertrud** **Gy**da **Gjermund**	**yær**-trew(d) **yew**-da **yær**-mewnn
h	Often silent, as in names ending in '-hild.'		Ragnhild Torhild	**rag**-nill **tor**-ill
h	The h is pronounced at the beginning of a name.		Helga Harald	**Hehl**-ga **Hahr**-aald
j	Pronounced like **y** in 'yes.'	y	Janne Johannes	**yaan**-neh yoh-**haan**-nehs
kj, ki	Pronounced like **ch** as in German ich (similar to a breathy h as in 'huge'). In parts of western Norway it is pronounced like English **ch** in Charles.	kh	**Kj**erstin **Ki**rstin **Kj**artan **Kj**ell	**khærsh**-tin **khirsh**-tin **khaar**-taan **khehll**
kn	**K** and **n** are both pronounced.	kn	**Kn**ut	**knewt**
r	In eastern and northern Norway r is rolled using the tip of the tongue. In southern and southwestern Norway it is pronounced as the r in French. (Compare the Danish r.)	r	Randi Runar	**raan**-dee **rew**-naar
rs	Pronounced like **rsh**.	rsh	Kje**rs**tin Ande**rs** Ca**rs**ten no**rs**k	**khærsh**-tin **aan**-dehrsh **kaarsh**-tehn **nohrshk**
w	Pronounced like **v**. Names normally starting with v often have variants beginning with w.	v	**W**enche **W**iggo	**vehng**-keh **vig**-goh

Vowels

Vowels are long in most stressed syllables, but in a word of only one syllable the vowel may be long or short. A vowel followed by one consonant is long (tak—roof, ceiling). A short vowel is followed by a double consonant or two or more consonants (takk—thank you). See the next table for vowel pronunciation.

Note that Norwegian, like Danish, has three extra vowels: æ, ø, and å. See also page 69 for a comparison of the "extra" vowels in Danish, Norwegian, Swedish, and Icelandic.

Letter	Pronunciation Explained	Symbol	Examples	Pronunciation
a	Long a is pronounced like **a** in 'father.'	aa	Arnhild Dag	**aarn**-nill **daag**
a	Short a is pronounced like **a** in 'about' or **u** in 'cut' (British English).	a	Anna Sturla	**aan**-na **stewr**-la
e	Long e is pronounced like **ay** in 'say.'	ay	Lene Even	**lay**-neh **ay**-vehn
e	When followed by r, pronounced like **a** in 'man.'	æ	Gerd Gjermund	**gærd** **yær**-mewnn
e	Short e is pronounced like **e** in 'let.' Short e may occur in a stressed or unstressed syllable.	eh	Irene Endre	ee-**ray**-neh **ehn**-dreh
i	Long i is pronounced like **ee** in 'see.'	ee	Kari Ivar	**kaa**-ree **ee**-vaar
i	Short i is pronounced like **i** in 'sit.'	i	Kristin Sindre	**kris**-tin **sinn**-dreh
o	Long o is pronounced like **oo** in 'soon,' but round the lips more.	oo	Solveig Tor	**sool**-væig **toor**
o	Short o is pronounced like **ou** in 'bought,' or **o** in 'got' (British English).	o	**Otto**	**ot**-to
u	Pronounced similar to the **ew** in 'few.'	ew	Gunnhild Gunnar	**gewn**-nill **gewn**-naar
y	Difficult sound for English speakers, similar to the **u** above. Round the lips and try to say **ee**. We use the same symbol for both u and y.	ew	Yngvill Tryggve	**ewng**-vill **trewgg**-veh
æ	Pronounced like **a** in cat. Rare in names; found in more surnames as an alternate spelling for e.	æ	Sæbjørn Sæther	**sæ**-byoern **sæ**-tehr
ø	Similar to the **u** in 'fur.' Round the lips and try to say **eh**.	oe	Bjørg Bjørn	**byoerg** **byoern**
ø	Typical in dialect forms, see the diphthong **øy** below.		Østen (Øystein) Gønner (Gunvor)	**oes**-tehn **goen**-nehr
å	Pronounced like **oa** in 'boat.' Older forms use aa for å.	oa	Åse/Aase Åge/Aage	**oa**-seh **oa**-geh

Diphthongs (Vowel Combinations)

Letters	Pronunciation Explained	Symbol	Examples	Pronunciation
ai, aj	Pronounced like the pronoun **I**.	I	Kajsa Kai	**kI**-sa **kI**
au	Similar to **ou** in loud.	ou	**Aud** **Gaute**	**oud** **gou**-teh
ei	Similar to **ai** in wait, but the first part is the **æ** sound.	æi	Eivor Einar	**æi**-voar **æi**-naar
øy	Similar to **oy** in boy, but the first part is the **ø** sound.	oey	Veslemøy Øyvind	**vehs**-leh-moey **oey**-vinn

Swedish

Most people listening to Swedish think it sounds musical because it goes up and down. The system of intonation is too complicated to include here, but leaving it out will not be an impediment to approximating the pronunciation of names.

Consonants
Most of the consonants in Swedish are pronounced as in English. Exceptions are listed in the table below.

Letter	Pronunciation Explained	Symbol	Examples	Pronunciation
bj	Both **b** and **j** are pronounced. The j is pronounced like the **y** in 'yet.'	by	Björg Björn	**byoerg** **byoern**
c	Pronounced like **s** before e, i and y.	s	Cecilia	say-**seel**-ee-a
c	Pronounced like **k** before a, o, and u, and in the combination ch.	k	Carina Christian	kaa-**ree**-na **kris**-tyaan
g	Pronounced like **y** before e and ö in a few names.	y	Gertrud Göran	**yær**-trewd **yoer**-aan
j	Pronounced like **y** in yes.	y	Johan Johanna	yoo-**haan** yoo-**haan**-na
kn	**K** and **n** are both pronounced.	kn	Knut	**knewt**
r	Rolled using the tip of the tongue. In southern Sweden pronounced like the French or Danish r.	r	Rolf Ragna	**rolf** **raag**-na
rs	Pronounced like **rsh**.	rsh	Karsten Kerstin	**kahrsh**-tehn **kehrs**-tin

Vowels
Vowels are long in most stressed syllables, but in a word or element of only one syllable the vowel may be long or short. The table below provides details of vowel pronunciation.

Note that Swedish has three extra vowels: å, ä, and ö. See also page 69 for a comparison of these vowel sounds in Danish, Norwegian, Swedish, and Icelandic.

Letter	Pronunciation Explained	Symbol	Examples	Pronunciation
a	Long a is pronounced like **a** in father.	aa	Malin Ingmar	**maa**-lin **ing**-maar
a	Short a is pronounced like **a** in 'about' or **u** in 'cut' (British English).	a	Anna Gösta	**aan**-na **yoes**-ta
e	Long e is pronounced like **ay** in 'say.'	ay	Greta Emil	**gray**-ta **ay**-meel
e	When followed by r and another consonant, pronounced like **a** in man.	æ	Kerstin Bernt	**khærs**-tin **bærnt**
e	Short e is pronounced like **e** in 'let.' Short e may occur in a stressed or unstressed syllable.	eh	Ebba Erik	**ehb**-ba **eh**-reek
i	Long i is pronounced like **ee** in 'see.'	ee	Kristina Idar	kris-**tee**-na **ee**-daar
i	Short i is pronounced like **i** in 'sit.'	i	Birgitta Krister	bir-**git**-ta **kris**-tehr
o	Long o is pronounced like **oo** in 'food.'	oo	Oda Olof	**oo**-da **oo**-loaf
o	Short o is pronounced like **ou** in 'bought,' or **o** in 'got' (British English).	o	Odd	**od**
u	Pronounced similar to the **ew** in 'few.'	ew	Ulla Gunnar	**ewl**-la **gewn**-naar
y	Difficult sound for English speakers. Similar to the **u** above. Round the lips and try to say **ee**. We use the same symbol for both u and y.	ew	Ylva Yngvar	**ewl**-va **ewng**-vaar
ä	Pronounced like **ai** in 'hair, a bit more closed than Norwegian and Danish æ.	æ	Pär	**pær**
ö	Similar to the **u** in 'fur.' Round the lips and try to say **eh**.	oe	Björg Björn	**byoerg** **byoern**
å	Pronounced like **oa** in 'boat.'	oa	Åsa	**oa**-sa

Diphthongs (*Vowel Combinations*)

Letters	Pronunciation Explained	Symbol	Examples	Pronunciation
ai, aj	Pronounced like the pronoun **I**.	I	Kajsa Kaj	k**I**-sa k**I**

Abbreviations and Symbols

D = Danish
N = Norwegian
S = Swedish
b. = born
d. = died
Q ǫ = Old Norse letter, called "o with ogonek" (o with a tail). Pronunciation similar to the letter å in modern Scandinavian languages.
Ð ð = Old Norse and Modern Icelandic letter, called "edh," pronounced as 'th' in this.
Þ þ = Old Norse and Modern Icelandic letter, called "thorn," pronounced as 'th' in thing.
→ = A name with an arrow in front of it has an entry in the dictionary section. Used in lists of name forms, where not all names have an entry of their own.

Dictionary of
Scandinavian Names

Girls Names

The section on girls names contains fewer names than the section on boys names (ca. 550 as opposed to ca. 1,000 boys names). This is due to the fact that naming girls is more susceptible to shifting fashions in naming, resulting in more girls names being imported from other countries than is the case for the boys names. A large number of the imported girls names are not of interest in a book of Scandinavian names, since they primarily belong in an international context. The imported names included here have all been adapted to the Scandinavian environment in spelling and/or pronunciation. For more information on naming fashions, see pages 128–34.

The letter C is mostly used in imported names and loan words in Scandinavian, but in the United States immigrants frequently chose the spelling with C instead of K. Many names starting with W are also spelled with V.

Following the practice of Scandinavian languages, note that names beginning with Æ-, Ä-, Ø-, Ö-, and Å- (which are all separate letters rather than accented vowels) are to be found at the end of the alphabet.

Agata, Agate (D: aa-**gæ**-teh; N: aa-**gaa**-ta, aa-**gaa**-teh; S: aa-**gaa**-ta) From Greek 'good, honorable.' See Agda, Ågot.

Agda (**aag**-da) Swedish form of Agata. See Ågot.

Agnes (D: **owng**-nehs; N/S: **aag**-nehs) From Latin 'pure, holy.' Common in Sweden.

Agneta, Agnete (D: owng-**nay**-teh; N/S: aag-**nay**-ta, aag-**nay**-teh) From Latin, ablative case Agnete, a form of Agnes. Agnetha Fältskog was a lead singer in ABBA, the Swedish pop group active from 1972 until 1982.

Aina (**I**-na) From Finnish Aino, probably meaning 'the only one.' Known from the national epic *Kalevala*. Popular in Scandinavia in the 1970s.

Alberta, Alberte (D: aal-**bær**-teh; N/S: aal-**bær**-ta, aal-**bær**-teh) Feminine form of German Albert.

Alfhild, Alvhild (**aal**-fill; S: **aalf**-hild) Most common in Norway. From Old Norse Alfhildr, a compound of *alf* 'elf, fairy' and *hildr* 'battle.'

Alfrid (**aal**-freed) Swedish; first element *al* either 'all' or 'elf' or 'noble,' last element *fríðr* 'beautiful, fair.' Rare.

Alida (aa-**lee**-da) A Dutch form of German Adelheid, from *adal* 'noble' and *heid* 'gleam, glitter.' Especially common in Norway during the 1860–1910 immigration period.

Alma (D: **æl**-ma; N/S: **aal**-ma) Either from Spanish 'nourishing, good,' or short form of Amalia. Finnish author and historian Alma Söderhjelm (1870–1949).

Alva (**aal**-va) Feminine form of Alv, in Swedish also short form of names beginning with Alf- or Alv-. Swedish politician and ambassador Alva Myrdal (1902–86) received the Nobel Peace Prize in 1982.

Alvilde (aal-**vill**-deh) See Alfhild.

Amalia, Amalie (D: æ-**mæ**-lee-æ, æ-**mæ**-lee-eh; N: aa-**maa**-lee-a, aa-**maa**-lee-eh; S: aa-**maa**-lee-a) From German short form of names with *amal*- 'work, diligent.' The Norwegian author Amalie Skram (1846–1905). The Danish palace Amalienborg is named after Queen Sophie Amalie (d. 1685).

Amanda (D: aa-**mæn**-da; N/S: aa-**maan**-da) From Latin 'lovable' and *amare* 'to love.' Not common, but acquired some popularity from the Norwegian song "Amanda fra Haugesund" (Amanda from Haugesund). Norwegian Oscars given to films are called "Amandas," and the Amanda Ceremony is held in Haugesund. Also popular from the Danish song "Min Amanda var fra Kjerteminde" (My Amanda Was from Kerteminde).

Ambjørg (N: aam-**byoerg**) First element, see Arn-, last element *bjørg* 'protection.'

Amelia (S: aa-**may**-lee-a) Swedish form of Amalia, from French Amélie.

An- A prefix found in several names. See Arn-.

Andrea, Andrina, Andrine (D: æn-**dray**-a, æn-**dree**-neh; N/S: aan-**dray**-a, aan-**dree**-na, aan-**dree**-neh) Feminine forms of Andreas.

Ane (D: **æ**-neh; N/S: **aa**-neh) Common in Norway (Gudbrandsdal) and especially Denmark; a form of Anna or Anne.

Anita (D: æ-**nee**-ta; N/S: aa-**nee**-ta [as in English]) Spanish form of Anna. Popular in Norway and Sweden in the 1960s and 1970s. Swedish actress Anita Ekberg (b. 1931).

Anja (D: **æn**-ya; N/S: **aan**-ya) Russian (pet) form of Anna. Popular in the 1970s and 1980s.

Anna (D: **æn**-na; N/S: **aan**-na) From Hebrew Hannah 'mercy,' name of the mother of Virgin Mary. Together with the variant Anne the most common girls name in all Scandinavia since 1500. Common among immigrants 1850–1900, together with variant forms such as Ane, Ann, Anne. Anne has gradually gained popularity in Norway and Denmark the last fifty years, but Anna is on the rise again today. Anna common

in Sweden. Many variants in several languages: Ane, Anne, Anita, Anja, Ann, Annette, Anniken, Annie, Anny, Nancy, Nanny, etc. The most common name in compound names like Anne Marie and Anne Sofie. The Danish princess Anne-Marie (b. 1946) married Konstantin, former king of Greece.

Anne (D: **æn**-neh; N: **aan**-neh) Norwegian and Danish form of Anna.

An(n)ette (D: æ-**nehd**-deh; N: aa-**neht**-teh; S: aa-**neht**) French diminutive form of Anna. Very popular especially in Norway in the 1980s.

An(n)ika, Anniken (**aan**-ee-ka, **aan**-ee-kehn) Swedish form and Norwegian form, from a German diminutive or pet form of Anna. Annika Hansen (alias Seven of Nine) was a fictional character on the American television series *Star Trek: Voyager*. Swedish golfer Annika Sörenstam (b. 1970).

Anni, Annie, Anny (D: **æn**-nee, **æn**-nee, **æn**-new; N/S: **aan**-nee, **aan**-nee, **aan**-new) English pet forms of Anna. Anni-Frid Lyngstad in ABBA, the Swedish pop group active from 1972 until 1982.

Arn- A common prefix in Norwegian names like Arna, Arnbjørg, Arnhild, Arnlaug, Arnveig. From Old Norse *arn* 'eagle.' Also in the assimilated forms An-, as in Anbjørg, Anlaug, Anveig; and Am- as in → Ambjørg.

As- A common prefix in mostly Norwegian compound names like Asbjørg, → Aslaug, → Astrid. From Old Norse *áss* 'god.'

Aslaug (**aas**-loug) Norwegian, from Old Norse Áslaug, a compound of *áss* 'god' and *laug*, of uncertain origin.

Asta, Aste (**aas**-ta, **aas**-teh) Short forms of Astrid or a pet name for Augusta.

Astrid, Astri (D: **æs**-treeth; N: **aas**-tree; S: **aas**-treed) Mostly Norwegian and Swedish, from Old Norse Ástríðr, a compound of *áss* 'god' and *fríðr* 'beautiful, fair.' Made popular by Princess Astrid of Norway (b. 1932), the famous Swedish author Astrid Lindgren (1907–2002), and Princess Astrid of Sweden, later Queen Astrid of Belgium (1905–35). A well-known Norwegian folk

song is "Astri mi Astri" (Astri My Astri).
Opera singer Astrid Varnay (1918–2006)
was born in Sweden.

Aud, Aud- (**oud**) An independent name or
a first element in some Norwegian names
like Audgunn, Audhild, Audny, from Old
Norse *auðr* 'wealth, prosperity.' All of them
popular in Norway before and after World
War II.

Augusta (ou-**gews**-ta) Feminine form of Latin
August(us) 'the exalted.' Rare today. Also a
more recent feminine form of August.

Beata, Beate (bay-**aa**-ta, bay-**aa**-teh) From
Latin 'happy one.' Used by the Swedish
nobility.

Bente (**behn**-teh) One of the most popular
names in Norway and Denmark the first
decades after World War II, more rare today.
A form of Benedikte, a feminine form of
Latin Benedictus 'blessed.' Swedish forms
Bengta or Benkta.

Bergit (**bær**-git) See Birgit.

Bergljot (**bær**-glee-oat) Norwegian, from Old
Norse Bergljót, a compound of *berg* 'protection' and *ljót* 'bright, shining.' Popular
around 1900, rare today. Known through
the poem "Bergljot" by Norwegian writer
Bjørnstjerne Bjørnson.

Berit (**behr**-it) A form of Birgitte. Very common in Norway with a peak in the 1940s.

Bernardina, Bernardine, Berhardina, Berhar-
dine (behr-naar-**dee**-na, behr-naar-**dee**-
neh, behr-har-**dee**-na, behr-har-**dee**-neh; S:
bær-nar-**dee**-na, bær-har-**dee**-na) A feminine form of Bernhard. Some usage in the
nineteenth century. See Dina.

Berta, Berte (D: **bær**-teh; N: **bær**-ta, **bær**-teh;
S: **bær**-ta) Mostly Norwegian, common
in the immigration period, rarer today.
Either a form of Birgitte or a short form of
various German compounds with *ber(h)t*
'famous, shining.' Berta mostly in western
Norway (Vestlandet), Berte in eastern Norway (Austlandet). Also written Bertha and
Berthe.

Bina (**bee**-na) Swedish short form of names
like Sabina or Jakobina.

Birgit (**bir**-git) A short form of Birgitta.

Birgitta, Birgitte (D: bir-**geed**-deh; N/S:
bir-**git**-ta, bir-**git**-teh) Mostly Swedish, a
transformation of Celtic *brigit* 'the exalted
one,' an ancient goddess. Saint Brigid of
Kildare (450–525) is a patron saint of Ireland. English form Bridget. Bridget Jones is
a fictional character created by the English
writer Helen Fielding. The popularity in
Sweden goes back to Saint Birgitta (1303–
73), but the name is known in Norway
from 1000. Princess Birgitta of Sweden
(b. 1937).

Birte, Birthe (**bir**-teh) Danish short forms of
Birgitte.

Bjørg (**byoerg**) Very common around World
War II in Norway; rare today. From Old
Norse *bjǫrg* 'protection.'

Björk (**byoerk**) A newer Icelandic name
from *björk* 'birch.' Rare as a single name,
but popular today as a second name, ranking number 1 in 2004 in Iceland. For example, Linda Björk, Maria Björk. Rare in
Denmark, Norway, and Sweden. Icelandic
singer, songwriter, and actress Björk
(b. 1965).

Blenda (**blehn**-da) Swedish, of uncertain origin, but associated with the verb *blända* 'to
be blinded by the sun.'

Bodil (**boo**-dill) A Danish form of Bodhild,
in Old Norse Bóthildr, a compound of *bót*
'help' and *hildr* 'battle.' Popular after World
War II. Danish actress Bodil Kjer (1917–
2003) and actress and director Bodil Ipsen
(1889–1964); Denmark's Bodil Award for
film is named after both of them.

Borghild (**borg**-hild, **borg**-hill) Norwegian,
from Old Norse *borg* 'protection' and *hildr*
'battle.' Very popular around 1900 but rare
today.

Brit, Britt (**breet**, **britt**) Both forms common
in Sweden (especially Britt) and Norway
(especially Brit). Short forms of Birgitta.
Swedish actress Britt Ekland (b. 1942).

Brita, Britta (**bree**-ta, **brit**-ta) Common in
Norway ca. 1900. See Brit.

Brynhild(a) (**brewn**-hild, brewn-**hill**-da)
Norwegian, from Old Norse Brynhildr, a
compound of *brynja* 'coat of mail' and *hildr*
'battle.' Norwegian dialect form Brønla, in

the United States written Brynla. A main character in *The Saga of the Volsungs*, based on the related German epic poem *Nibelungenlied*. Made popular by Wagner's operas.
Börta (**boer**-ta) Swedish form of Berta.

Cajsa (S: **kI**-sa) See Kajsa.
Carine, Carina (ka-**ree**-neh, ka-**ree**-na) See Karina.
Caroline (D/N: kaa-ro-**lee**-neh; S: kaa-ro-**leen**) See Karolina.
Carrie (**kehr**-ree [as in English]) Americanized form of the popular Norwegian name Kari. The English pronunciation of Carrie corresponds roughly to the Norwegian name. In English also a pet form of Caroline.
Cat(h)arina, Cat(h)arine (ka-ta-**ree**-na, ka-ta-**ree**-neh) See Kat(h)arina.
Cathrina, Cathrine (D: ka-**tree**-neh; N/S: ka-**tree**-na, ka-**tree**-neh) Common spelling of Katrina, Katrine.
Cecilia, Cecilie (say-**see**-lee-a, say-**see**-lee-eh) See Silje, Sissel.
Christiana, Christiane (D: kris-tee-**æn**-eh; N/S: kris-tee-**aan**-na, kris-tee-**aan**-eh) See Kristiana.
Christina, Christine (kris-**tee**-na, kris-**tee**-neh) See Kristina. Christine Nordhagen, born in Alberta, Canada, in 1971, of Norwegian descent, has won several world championships in wrestling.
Clara (**klaa**-ra) See Klara.

Dag- The first element in several names, especially Norwegian, like Dagfrid, → Dagmar, Dagne, → Dagny, and Dagrun. From Old Norse *dagr* 'day.' None of them are frequently used. See male names with the same first element Dag-.
Daga (S: **daa**-ga) Swedish, feminine form of Dag or pet form of Dagny.
Dagmar (D: **dow**-maa; N/S: **daag**-maar) A Scandinavian (especially Danish) form of Slavic Dragomir, composed of 'beloved' and 'peace,' but reinterpreted as a compound of *dag* 'day, beautiful' and *mar* 'virgin.' Princess Dragomir from Bohemia was married in 1205 to the Danish king Valdemar Sejr.

Dagny (D: **dow**-new; N/S: **daag**-new) From Old Norse Dagný, a compound of *dag* 'day' and *ný* 'new.' Dialect form Dagne.
Dana (**daa**-na [or as in English]) Of unclear origin, but some usage is connected to the first element in Danica. The Old Norse female form Dana corresponds to the male Danr. Not common in Scandinavia, but some usage in Scandinavian America, perhaps to mark Danish ancestry.
Danica, Danika (**daan**-ee-ka) Not common in Scandinavia, but some usage in North America. First element *dan* from Daniel or Old Norse *danr* 'dane,' followed by a diminutive suffix, similar to Annika. Reinforced usage from the ethnic meaning 'person from Denmark,' like Svea (Sweden) and Norman (Norway). Actress and writer Danica McKellar (b. 1975).
Dina, Dine (**dee**-na, **dee**-neh) Either a short form of names like Bernardina, or from Hebrew 'judgment' or 'she who judges.' Norwegian writer Herbjørg Wassmo's novel *Dinas bok* (Dina's Book) was filmed in 2002 with Maria Bonnevie as Dina; film title *I Am Dina*.
Dorte, Dorthe, Dort(h)ea (**doar**-teh, doar-**tay**-a) Mainly Danish forms of Greek Dorothea, composed of 'gift' and 'god,' in English Dorothy, short form Dot and pet form Dolly or Dotty. Several variants in Scandinavia: Dora, Dorde, Dordi, Dorit, Durdei, etc.

Ebba (**ehb**-ba) Swedish, most likely a short form of German names starting with *eber* 'wild boar.' Also Danish. Swedish journalist and TV personality Ebba von Sydow (b. 1981).
Edda (**ehd**-da) Icelandic, from Old Norse *edda* 'foremother, clanmother.'
Edit, Edith (**ay**-deet) From Old English Eadgyth, composed of *ead* 'prosperity' and *gyth* 'battle, strife,' the same meaning as Norwegian Audgunn. Especially popular in Denmark up to the 1940s. Very rare today.
Edvarda (ehd-**vaar**-da) Feminine form of Edvard. Rare. Main character in Norwegian author Knut Hamsun's novel *Pan* (1894).

Eivor, Eyvor (**æi**-vor) Norwegian and Swedish, from Old Norse Eyvǫr, a compound of *ey* 'luck, gift' and *vǫr* 'careful' or 'the protected.' Rare.

Eldbjørg (**ehl**-byoerg) Norwegian, a twentieth-century coinage comprising *eld* 'fire' and *bjørg* 'protection,' or in Telemark an adaption of Hallbjørg.

Eldrid, Eldri, Elri (**ehl**-dree, **ehl**-ree) Norwegian, from Old Norse Eldfríðr, composed of *eld* 'fire' and *fríðr* 'beautiful, fair.' Mostly used in western Norway (Vestlandet). Variant form Ildri.

Elen, Elena, Elene (**ay**-lehn, eh-**lay**-na, eh-**lay**-neh) Norwegian forms of Helene.

Eleonora (ay-leh-oo-**noo**-ra) Possibly of Arabic origin. Not common. See Nora.

Eli (**ay**-lee) Mostly Norwegian, a form of Helene. Very common before 1950. The Biblical masculine name Eli has a different origin and is not used in Scandinavia.

Elin (**ay**-leen, **ay**-linn) Norwegian and Swedish, from Helene, known in Norway since the fourteenth century. Popular after 1950, also in combinations like Gunn-Elin. Swedish model Elin Nordegren (b. 1980), former wife of Tiger Woods.

Elina, Eline (ay-**lee**-na, ay-**lee**-neh) Variants of Elin, from Helene. Common before 1900.

Elisa, Elise (ay-**lee**-sa, ay-**lee**-seh) Older short forms of Elisabet, especially in the west of Norway. Also used today.

Elisabet, Elisabeth (ay-**lee**-saa-beht) From Hebrew 'God is my oath.' Spelling variants Elizabet, Elizabeth. Frequently used in the nineteenth century, also in the last generation. The most popular variant is the short form Else. The Old Norse name Ellisif is derived from Elisabet through Russian Elisava. Numerous variants: Elsebet, → Elisa, → Elise, → Elsa, → Else, → Lisa, → Lise, → Lisbet, Lis, Liss, Bet, Betty.

Ellen (**ehl**-lehn [as in English]) Either from Helene or a short form of Eleonora. Very common, especially in Denmark. Often used in combinations, like Ellen Marie.

Ellisiv, Ellisif (**ehl**-lee-seev, **ehl**-lee-seef) See Elisabet.

Elsa, Else (**ehl**-sa, **ehl**-seh) Very popular up to 1950; a short form of Elisabet. Common

as the first part of double names like Else Marie and Else Irene. In the United States spelled Elsie for pronunciation purposes.

Elsie (**ehl**-see) See Elsa.

Elvira (ehl-**vee**-ra) Swedish, originally Spanish of Arabic origin, probably 'the white one.' Danish tightrope walker Elvira Madigan (1867–89) was the subject of a popular film in 1967. Mozart's Piano Concerto number 21 is known as "Theme from Elvira Madigan." Short forms Elvi, Elvy.

Embla (**ehm**-bla) Norwegian and Swedish, from Old Norse. In Norse mythology, Embla was the first woman to be created, corresponding to the Biblical Eve; the parallel to the Biblical Adam is Ask in Norse mythology. See page 146.

Emma (**ehm**-ma) From German, most likely a short form of German names with first elements like Erm- and Irm-, meaning 'whole, entire.' Popular around 1900, also among second generation immigrants. Again fashionable in Scandinavia in recent years.

Engla (**ehng**-la) Swedish, from German. See first element in Engelbrekt in boys section.

Erica, Erika (**eh**-ree-ka) Feminine form of Erik, also influenced by Latin *erica* 'heather.'

Erna (**ehr**-na) Feminine form of Ernest. See Ernst in boys section.

Estrid (**ehs**-treed) Swedish and Danish form of Astrid; more recent form Ester.

Eva (**ay**-va) According to the Bible, the first woman. Derived from a word for 'living.' Comparable to Embla in Norse mythology. Popular in the mid-twentieth century.

Fredrikke, Frederikke, Fredrika (D: freh-theh-**ree**-keh; N:frehd-**rik**-keh, freh-deh-**rik**-keh; S: frehd-**ree**-ka) A feminine form of German Fredrik (Friedrich). Popular in middle-class families in the nineteenth century.

Frid, Frida (**freed**, **free**-da) Most likely from Old Norse *fríðr* 'beautiful, fair,' but also possibly from German elements like *frid*- and *frida* meaning 'peace.'

Frigg, Frigga (**frigg**) From the Norse goddess Frigg, derived from a word for 'love.' Frigg is Odin's wife.

Frøy, Frey (**froey, fray**) Norwegian, from
the Old Norse fertility god Freyr, meaning
'lord, master.' Freyr is Freyja's twin brother
and husband at the same time! Frøy as a
woman's name is probably a short form of
Frøya. See page 146.

Frøya, Freya, Fröja, Freja (**froey**-a, **fray**-ya,
froe-ya, **fray**-ya) From Old Norse Freyja,
the goddess of love in Norse mythology,
derived from a word meaning 'lady, mistress.' Scandinavian *frue* and German *Frau*
are derived from the same word. See popularity today on page 148.

Frøydis, Freydis, Frejdis (**froey**-dees, **fray**-
dees, **fray**-dees) Norwegian (Frøydis),
from Old Norse Freydís, a compound of
the name of the god Freyr and *dís* 'goddess.'
Popular around 1950. The only Freydís in
Old Norse literature is the daughter of Erik
the Red (Eirik Raude), who discovered
Greenland around 985. Freydís was the
first Norse woman to travel to Vinland in
America.

Gerd (**gærd**; S: **yærd**) Mainly Norwegian,
from Old Norse *gerðr* 'protection.' One of
the top names around 1950, rare since 2000.
See page 146.

Gerda (D/N: **gær**-da; S: **yær**-da) A form of
Gerd. One of the most common names in
Denmark in the decades after 1900.

Gertrud (D: **gær**-trooth; N: **gehr**-trew[d]; S:
yær-trewd) From German, already known
in Old Norse as Geirþrúðr, a compound
of *geirr* 'spear' and *þrúðr* 'strength.' Popular
through Saint Gertrud of Nivelles (d. 664),
protector of travelers.

Gitte (D: **gid**-deh; N/S: **git**-teh) Mainly Danish, a short form of Birgitte. Popular in the
1960s and 1970s. Considered by other Scandinavians to be the prototype of Danish
girls names. The Danish singer Gitte Hæn-
ning (b. 1946).

Gjertine (**yær**-**tee**-neh) Norwegian, feminine
form of Gjert. Mostly in use during the
decades of emigration.

Gjertrud (**yær**-trew[d]) Norwegian form of
Gertrud.

Goro (**goo**-ro) Norwegian form of Guro.

Greta, Grete (D: **gray**-deh; N/S: **gray**-ta,
gray-teh) From German, a short form of
Margareta. Fashionable in the first half of
the twentieth century. Famous Swedish
actress Greta Garbo (1905–90). The Norwegian marathon runner Grete Waitz won
nine New York City Marathons between
1978 and 1988. Grimm's well-known fairy
tale *Hansel and Gretel* is called *Hans og
Grete* in Norwegian.

Gro (**groo**) Mainly Norwegian, from Old
Norse Gróa, derived from the verb *gróa*
'grow.' Gro Harlem Brundtland (b. 1939),
was prime minister of Norway for two
terms in the 1980s and 1990s.

Gud- First element in several names from
Old Norse, *goð* 'god,' like Gudbjørg, Gud-
borg, Gudfrid, Gudlaug, Gudny, Gudri,
→ Gudrun, Gudveig. All names are rare and
mainly occur in Norwegian.

Gudrun (D: **gooth**-roon; N/S: **gewd**-rewn)
From Old Norse Guðrún, a compound of
goð 'god' and *rún* 'rune, secret lore.' Mostly
Norwegian, very common in the years
around 1905. Gudrun was the name of the
heroine of *The Saga of the Volsungs*, wife of
Sigurd Dragonslayer (Drakedrepar).

Gull- First element in several names, like
Gullaug, Gullbjørg, Gullborg, Gullveig.
Most often a variant form of Gud-, but
most people associate it with *gull* 'gold.'

Gunda (**gewn**-da) Most likely a short form of
German names ending in *gund* 'battle,' like
Hildegund. Frequent at the end of the nine-
teenth century.

Gunilla (gew-**nil**-la) Swedish, a form
of Gunnhild. A top name in the 1940s.
Gunilla is considered by other Scandinavians to be the prototype of a Swedish girls
name. Comparable to Gitte in Denmark
and Kari in Norway. American actress
Gunilla Hutton was born in Sweden in
1944.

Gun(n) (D: **guhnn**; N/S: **gewn**[n]) From
Old Norse *gunnr* 'battle.' In Norse mythology the name of a Valkyrie, but not used as
a given name until the 1950s. Also a short
form of several names with the same first
element as in Gunnhild.

Gunnel (**gewn**-nehl) A Swedish form of
Gunnhild.

Gunnhild, Gunhild (**gewn**-hill, **gewn**-nill)
From Old Norse Gunnhildr, a compound
of two words that both mean 'battle,' *gunnr*
and *hildr*, which illustrates the fact that even
in the Middle Ages the meaning of names
is not a decisive factor in choosing a name.
Fairly common also today. Queen Gunnhild of Norway (931–33) was married to
Eirik Bloodaxe (Blodøks). She was so powerful that their sons used the matronymic
Gunnhildson instead of Eiriksson!

Gunnvor, Gunvor (D: **guhn**-voar; N/S:
gewnn-voar) From Old Norse Gunnvǫr, a
compound of *gunnr* 'battle' and *vǫr* 'careful'
or 'the protected.' Fairly common especially
in Norway in the first half of the twentieth
century.

Guri (**gew**-ree) Norwegian, from Old Norse
Guðríðr, composed of *guð* 'god' and *fríðr*
'beautiful, fair.' Popular since the fourteenth
century, a typically Norwegian name.

Gurina, Gurine (gew-**ree**-na, gew-**ree**-neh)
Norwegian, a latinized form of Guri. Common among the immigrants in the nineteenth century.

Guro, Goro (**gew**-roo, **goo**-roo) Norwegian,
a more recent dialect form of Gudrun,
popular in the second half of the twentieth
century.

Gusta (**gews**-ta [or as in English]) In North
America a feminine form of Gustav.

Gyda (**gew**-da) From Old Norse Gyða, a
pet form of Gyríðr, composed of *guð* 'god'
and *fríðr* 'beautiful, fair.' According to the
medieval author Snorri Sturluson, Gyda, a
princess, encouraged King Harold Fairhair
(Harald Hårfagre) to unite the whole of
Norway.

Hall- A first element from Old Norse *hallr*
'stone,' in names like → Hallbjørg, → Halldis,
Halldora, Hallfrid, Hallgjerd, Hallgunn,
Hallveig.

Hallbjørg (**haal**-byoerg) Norwegian, from
Old Norse Hallbjǫrg, composed of *hallr*
'stone' and *bjǫrg* 'protection.' See also
Eldbjørg.

Halldis, Haldis (**haal**-dees) Norwegian, from
Old Norse Halldís, composed of *hallr*
'stone' and *dís* 'goddess.' The Norwegian
author and translator Halldis Moren Vesaas
(1907–95).

Hanna, Hanne (D: **hæn**-neh; N/S: **haan**-na,
haan-neh) Especially popular in Denmark,
short form of Johanna, or same origin as
Anna. Less likely derived from Hebrew
from a word meaning 'He [God] has
favored me [with a child].'

Hedda (**hehd**-da) A pet form or short form of
Hedvig. Well known through Norwegian
writer Henrik Ibsen's play *Hedda Gabler*
(1890) and the title character's husband's
famous line, "Fancy that, Hedda!" (Tenk
det, Hedda!).

Hedvig (**hehd**-veeg) From German Hadu-
wig, a compound of *hadu* and *wig*, both
of which mean 'battle.' Comparable to
Gunnhild. In Norwegian writer Henrik
Ibsen's play *The Wild Duck* (*Vildanden*,
1884) one of the main characters is Hedvig
Ekdal.

Hege (**hay**-geh) A Norwegian form of Helga,
originally from Telemark. Known through
Hege, a main character in Norwegian
author Tarjei Vesaas's novel *Fuglane* (*The
Birds*, 1957). Second place in popularity in
the 1970s.

Heidi (**hæi**-dee) From German, a short form
of Adelheid, *adal* 'noble' and *heid* 'gleam,
glitter.' Popular in Norway and Denmark
through the movie *Heidi* (1953), with a peak
in the 1970s.

Helen, Helena, Helene (D: **hay**-lehn, heh-
lay-na, heh-**lay**-neh; N/S: heh-**layn**, heh-
lay-na, heh-**lay**-neh) From Greek of uncertain origin, possibly derived from a word
meaning 'sunbeam' or 'ray.' Popular in the
twentieth century. The source of many variants: Elen, Elena, Elene, Eli, Elin, Elina,
Eline, Ellen, Lena, Lene.

Helga (**hehl**-ga) From Old Norse Helga, a
feminine form of Helge. Popular in the
first half of the twentieth century, most
likely inspired by Helga the Fair in *The Saga
of Gunnlaugur Snake's Tongue* (Soga om
Gunnlaug Ormstunge). See Olga.

Helle (**hehl**-leh) A Danish form of Helga or Helene, one of the most common names in Denmark especially in the 1950s and 1960s.

Henrietta, Henriette (D: hehn-ree-**ehd**-deh; N/S: hehn-ree-**eht**-ta, hehn-ree-**eht**-teh) From French, a feminine form of Henri; see Henrik in boys section. In Sweden Henrietta. Danish vocalist Henriette Sennenvaldt (b. 1977).

Henrikke (hehn-**rik**-keh) From German, a feminine form of Henrik.

Her- A first element from Old Norse *her* 'army,' in names like Herbjørg, Herborg, → Herdis, Herfrid, Hergjerd, Hergunn, Herlaug, Herly, Herny, Hervor.

Herdis (**hær**-dees) From Old Norse Herdís, composed of the elements *her* 'army' and *dís* 'goddess.'

Hild (**hild**) Derived from Old Norse *hildr* 'battle.'

Hild- A first element from old Norse *hildr* 'battle,' in many names: Hildeborg, Hildegard, → Hildegunn, Hildis, Hildrid, Hildrun, Hildvi, Hildvor, etc.

Hilda (**hill**-da) A short form of names with hild as a first or last element. See Hild and Ragnhild. Popular in the first decades of the twentieth century.

Hilde (**hill**-deh) A variant of Hilda. Very common in Norway from the 1950s until the 1970s. Also Danish.

Hildegun(n) (**hill**-deh-gewn) Norwegian and Swedish, from Old Norse Hildigunnr, a compound of *hildr* 'battle' and *gunnr* 'battle'! The reverse form of Gunnhild.

Hildur (**hill**-dewr) Icelandic form of Hild. Some usage in northern Norway.

Hjørdis, Hjördis (**yoer**-dees) From Old Norse Hjǫrdís, a compound of *hjǫrr* 'sword' and *dís* 'goddess.'

Hulda (**hewl**-da) A later variant from Old Norse *huldr* 'the secretive one,' used in Denmark and Norway. More recent usage also from German Hulda, a short form of names beginning with Huld- 'friendly, faithful.' There is also a Biblical name Hulda meaning 'weasel.' Some usage a hundred years ago.

Iben (**ee**-behn) Danish, of uncertain origin, possibly associated with *iben* as in *ibenholt*, English ebony, regarding a person with a dark complexion. Parallel to the English name Ebony. Danish actress Iben Hjejle (b. 1971).

Ida (**ee**-da) Of uncertain origin, possibly from a German word meaning 'work, deed.' Increasing popularity the past fifty years; topped list of girls names in Norway in 1989.

Idun(n) (D: **ee**-duhn; N/S: **ee**-dewn) Mainly Norwegian, in Norse mythology Íðunn was the goddess of eternal youth. The first element is *íð* 'again'; the last element, *unn*, derives from *unna* 'to love.' English Idony. See page 146.

Ina, Ine (**ee**-na, **ee**-neh) A short form of names ending in -ina, like Katarina. Popular in recent decades.

Ing-, Inge- A first element from the Norse fertility god Ing(e) in names like Ingegerd, Ingegjerd, Ingelaug, Ingeleiv, Ingelill, Ingelin, Ingfrid, Ingjerd, Inghild, Inglaug, Ingny, Ingrun, Ingveig, Ingvor, → Ingebjørg, → Ingeborg, → Ingrid, → Ingunn, → Ingvild.

Inga (**ing**-ga) A short form of names with the first element Ing-, like Ingeborg and Ingrid. Most popular in the first decades of the twentieth century.

Inge (**ing**-eh) Danish, a short form of names like Ingeborg; see Inga. Very common in the 1940s, little usage today. Not to be confused with the masculine name Inge used in Norway and Sweden.

Ingebjørg (**ing**-geh-byoerg) Norwegian, from Old Norse Ingibjǫrg, the fertility God Ing(i) and *bjǫrg* 'protection.' Fairly common.

Ingeborg (**ing**-eh-bor[g]) A name parallel to Ingebjørg but more common in Scandinavia. The Danish princess Ingeborg (1175–1237) became queen of France in 1193, and another Ingeborg was queen of Denmark from 1296 to 1319.

Inger (**ing**-ehr) A younger form of Ingegjerd, the god Ing(e) and the last element *gerðr* 'protection.' Common in double names like Inger-Johanne. Popular both in Norway

and Denmark. Film and TV actress Inger
Stevens (b. 1934 in Sweden).

Ingrid, Ingerid, Ingri (D: **ing**-rith; N: **ing**-ree;
S: **ing**-reed) From Old Norse Ingi(f)ríðr,
a compound of the Norse god Ing(e) and
fríðr 'beautiful, fair.' A distinctly Scandinavian name, common since the Middle Ages.
Swedish-born queen Ingrid of Denmark
(1910–2000). Princess Ingrid Alexandra of
Norway (b. 2004). Swedish actress Ingrid
Bergman (1915–82).

Ingunn (**ing**-gewnn) Norwegian, from Old
Norse Ingunnr; first element, see Ing-, last
element derives from *unna* 'to love.'

Ingvild (**ing**-vill) Norwegian, from Old Norse
Yngvildr; first element, see Ing-, last element *hildr* 'struggle.'

Irene, Iren (ee-**ray**-neh, ee-**rayn**) From Greek
'peace.' High up on the name lists in the
1960s in Norway.

Irja (**ir**-ya) Mostly Swedish, a Russian pet
form of Irene.

Iselin (**ee**-seh-leen) A more recent name in
Norway, probably influenced by names like
Sylvelin, Vendelin, and Iselilja, known from
old ballads. Made popular by a character in
Norwegian author Knut Hamsun's novel
Pan (1894).

Jane (D: **yæ**-neh; N: **yaa**-neh; S: **yayn**)
Either a short form (pet form) of names
like Kristiane, or from English Jane, a form
of Johanna.

Janna, Janne (D: **yæn**-na, **yæn**-neh; N:
yan-na, **yan**-neh; S: **yan**-na) A pet form
of Johanna or a short form of names like
Marianne.

Jenny (**yehn**-new, **yehn**-nee) From an English
pet form of Jane. Popular around 1900. The
Norwegian author Sigrid Undset's novel
Jenny (1911). The Swedish soprano Jenny
Lind (1820–87) was christened Johanna.

Jensina, Jensine (yehn-**see**-na, yehn-**see**-neh)
A feminine form of Jens. One of the typical
feminine forms with -ine from the nineteenth century, not common today.

Jette (D: **yehd**-deh; N/S: **yeht**-teh) Pet form
of Henriette, one of the most common girls
names in Denmark 1950–70.

Jofrid (**yoo**-freed) Norwegian, from Old
Norse Jófríðr, a compound of *jór* 'horse'
and *fríðr* 'beautiful, fair.' Variant: Jorid.

Johanna, Johanne (D: yoo-**hæn**-na, yoo-**hæn**-
neh; N: yoo-**haan**-na, yoo-**haan**-neh; S:
yoo-**haan**-na) Originally a Greek name
Ioanna, a feminine form of Johannes; also a
modern derivation from Johan. A top name
in Denmark in the 1990s; also common in
Norway and Sweden.

Jorid (**yoo**-ree[d]) Norwegian, same origin
as Jofrid.

Jorun, Jorunn (**yoor**-ewnn) Norwegian, from
Old Norse Jórunn, a compound of *jór*
'wild boar' and *unn* from *unna* 'to love.'

Josefina, Josefine (D: yoo-seh-**fee**-neh;
N: yoo-seh-**fee**-na, yoo-seh-**fee**-neh; S:
yoo-seh-**fee**-na, yoo-seh-**feen**) A feminine
form of Josef. One of the typical feminine
forms with -ine from the nineteenth century, not common today.

Judit(h) (D: **yoo**-dit; N/S: **yew**-dit) A Biblical
name 'Jewess.' Not common today.

Julia, Julie (D: **yoo**-lee-eh; N: **yew**-lee-a, **yew**-
lee-eh; S: **yew**-lee-a, shew-**lee**) A feminine
form of Julius. Popular around 1900, a top
name again since the 1990s. Also influenced by Shakespeare's play and the movie
versions of *Romeo and Juliet* (Norwegian
Romeo og Julie). The play *Frøken Julie* or
Miss Julie (1888) by the Swedish author
August Strindberg. American actress Julia
Roberts (b. 1967) and British actress Julie
Andrews (b. 1935) have made the names
popular.

Jytte (D: **yewd**-deh; N/S: **yewt**-teh) Danish
pet form of Judit. One of the most common
girls names in Denmark, especially in the
1930s and 1940s.

Jørgina, Jørgine (yoer-**gee**-na, yoer-**gee**-neh)
A feminine form of Jørgen. One of the
typical feminine forms with -ine from
the nineteenth century; not common
today.

Kaia, Kaja (**kI**-ya) Most likely a short form
or pet form of Kajsa, or derived from the
boys name Kai/Kaj.

Kajsa (**kI**-sa) Swedish pet form of Karin.

Karen (**kaarn, kaa**-rehn) Danish form of Katrine. Common in all three countries, but a top name in Denmark since the eighteenth century. Known in Norway since the sixteenth century. Frequent in double names like Karen Marie. Also common in the United States since immigration. Danish author Karen Blixen (Isak Dinesen; 1885–1962). See also Karin.

Kari (**kaa**-ree) Norwegian form of Katrine. Popular all over the country since the seventeenth century, with a peak in the 1940s. The prototype of a Norwegian girls name. Together with the boys name Ola common in the expression "Ola and Kari," or its longer form "Ola nordmann and Kari nordkvinne" (Ola Norseman and Kari Norsewoman), the equivalent of John and Jane Doe. "Ola and Kari" is also a medieval ballad. In the United States with adapted spelling Carrie. In Finland Kari is a boys name, from Greek Makarios.

Karianne (kaa-ree-**aan**-neh) A combination of Kari and Anne; most common in Norway.

Karin (**kaa**-rin) A form of Katarina; most common in Sweden.

Karina, Karine (D: kaa-**ree**-neh; N: kaa-**ree**-na, ka-**ree**-neh; S: kaa-**ree**-na) Either derived from Latin *carus* 'beloved,' or an expanded form of Karin. A top name around the 1960s. Common among Norwegian emigrants, also in the combination Anna Karina.

Karolina, Karoline (D: kæ-ro-**lee**-neh; N/S: kaa-ro-**lee**-na, kaa-ro-**lee**-neh) A feminine form of Latin Carolus; see Karl in boys section. Common around 1900, again in use in recent decades. Top name in Sweden in the nineteenth century. Queen Caroline Mathilde of Denmark (1751–75).

Kat(h)arina, Kat(h)arine (kaa-taa-**ree**-na, kaa-taa-**ree**-neh) From Latin Catarina, originally Greek of unknown etymology, but early associated with *katharos* 'pure.' Numerous forms in several languages.

Katrin (kaa-**treen**) Variant of Katarina.

Katrina, Katrine (D: kaa-**tree**-neh; N: kaa-**tree**-na, kaa-**tree**-neh; S: kaa-**tree**-na) Variants of Katarina.

Kersti (N/S: **khærsh**-tee) Variant of Kjersti.

Kerstin (D: **kehrs**-tin; N/S: **khærsh**-tin, **khærsh**-teen) Variant of Kjerstin.

Kine (**kee**-neh) Short form of Kristine.

Kirsten (D: **kirs**-tehn; N: **khirsh**-tehn; S: **kirsh**-tehn) Norwegian and Danish form of Kristine. The most common name in Denmark 1920–50; also popular in Norway. Norwegian opera singer Kirsten Flagstad (1895–1962) made the name popular in other countries, including the United States. American actress Kirsten Dunst's mother is Swedish.

Kirsti (**khirsh**-tee) Norwegian variant of Kirsten.

Kirstin, Kirstine (D: **kirs**-tin, kirsh-**tee**-neh; N: **khirsh**-tin, khirsh-**tee**-neh) Norwegian and Danish variants of Kirsten. Popular in recent decades in Denmark.

Kjell- First element in names mostly used in Norway, like Kjellaug, Kjellbjørg, Kjellfrid, Kjellrun, Kjellvor, from Old Norse *ketill* 'kettle, cauldron' or 'helmet.' See the masculine Kjell.

Kjersti (**khærsh**-tee) A variant of Kristine. Common in Norway. *Liti Kjersti* (Little Kjersti) is a medieval Norwegian ballad.

Kjerstin, Kjerstine (**khærsh**-tin, khærsh-**tee**-neh) Variants of Kristine.

Klara (**klaa**-ra) From Latin *clarus* 'bright, famous.' Used in the expression "Klara Klok" (Clara the wise).

Kristi (**kris**-tee) Norwegian variant of Kristine.

Kristiana, Kristiane (D: kris-tee-**æn**-eh; N/S: kris-tee-**aan**-na, kris-tee-**aan**-eh) A feminine form of Kristian.

Kristin (**kris**-tin, **kris**-teen) Norwegian form of Kristine, known from the twelfth century, and popular in recent decades. The trilogy *Kristin Lavransdatter* (1920–22) by Norwegian writer Sigrid Undset, filmed in 1995. Norwegian politician Kristin Halvorsen (b. 1960).

Kristina, Kristine (kris-**tee**-na, kris-**tee**-neh) Feminine forms of Latin Christianus 'christian.' Both Kristin and Kristina have been popular since the Middle Ages after the introduction of Christianity ca. 1000. Common in all three countries. Princess Kristina, daughter of King Håkon IV

Håkonsson of Norway, was married to a Spanish prince in 1258. Queen Kristina of Sweden (1626–89). Swedish princess Christina (b. 1940).

Laila, Lajla (**ll**-la) Supposedly a Sámi (Lapp) name, but not documented as such. Most likely coined by J. A. Friis (1821–96), a Norwegian novelist and linguist who specialized in Sámi languages, from Arabic Leila 'night, dark' in his Sámi-themed novel *Lajla* (1881); the novel was made into a movie in 1929. This novel made the name popular throughout Scandinavia in the first half of the twentieth century. Not common today.

Laura (**lou**-ra) Italian short form of Laurentia 'woman from Laurentum.' See also Lars in the boys section. Not common today.

Laurense (lou-**rehn**-seh) Norwegian form of Laurentia; see Laura. Used some by immigrants.

Lena, Lene (**lay**-na, **lay**-neh) Short form of names like Helena, Helene. Popular in the decades after 1950, especially in Denmark. Considered the most typical girls name in many Norwegian American communities, like in the comic strip *Ole and Lena*. Swedish actress Lena Olin (b. 1955).

Lina, Line (**lee**-na, **lee**-neh) Short form of names like Carolina, Caroline. Line in particular has been among the top names for several decades.

Linda (**lin**-da [as in English]) In nineteenth-century Norway derived from surnames like Lindorf and Lindahl. In the twentieth century popular as a short form of German and English Belinda, last element *lind* probably 'weak, soft.' Fairly common from the 1960s until 1980s. American actress Linda Carlson (b. 1945) is of Swedish descent. New Zealand author Linda Olsson (b. 1948), originally from Sweden, wrote the bestselling novel *Let Me Sing You Gentle Songs* (2005), which appeared in the United States and Great Britain with the title *Astrid and Veronika* (2007).

Linn (**linn** [as English Lynn]) Norwegian, associated with the word *linn* 'mild, soft,' but also influenced by the English name Lynn, pronounced in the same way. Famous through author and journalist Linn Ullmann (b. 1966), daughter of Norwegian actress Liv Ullmann and Swedish director Ingmar Bergman. A top name from the 1960s to the 1980s.

Linnea (lin-**nay**-a) Swedish, from Latin *linnea*, a flower name, named for the Swedish botanist Carl von Linné (1707–78).

Lisa, Lise (**lee**-sa, **lee**-seh) Short form of Elisabet, popular in the decades after World War II, not common today. Danish novelist and screenwriter Lise Nørgaard (b. 1917).

Lisbet(h) (**lis**-beht, **lees**-beht) Short form of Elisabet.

Liv (**leev**) Norwegian, from Old Norse *líf* 'protection, shelter,' but associated with *liv* 'life.' Common in double names like Liv Anne. Most popular in the 1940s and 1950s. Norwegian actress and author Liv Ullmann (b. 1938). American actress Liv Tyler (b. 1977).

Liva, Live (**lee**-va, **lee**-veh) Variants of Liv. Liva in western and Live in eastern Norway.

Lone (**loo**-neh) Danish short form of names like Magdelone. Top name in Denmark 1940–70. Danish film director Lone Scherfig (b. 1959).

Lotta, Lotte (D: **lod**-deh; N: **lot**-teh; S: **lot**-ta) Swedish and Danish short form of Charlotte from French. Popular in the 1970s.

Louise (loo-**ee**-seh [or as in English]) French feminine form of Louis; see Ludvig in boys section. Popular in Denmark the decades before 2000. Norwegian princess Märtha Louise (b. 1971). Queen Louise of Sweden (1889–1965).

Lovise, Lovisa (N: **loo**-vee-seh, loo-**vee**-seh, **loo**-vee-sa, loo-**vee**-sa; S: loo-**vee**-seh, loo-**vee**-sa) Norwegian and Swedish form of Louise. Popular early in the twentieth century.

Lykke (D: **loe**-geh) Danish, from *lykke* 'happiness.'

Lærke (**lær**-keh) Danish, from the bird name 'lark.'

Madli (**maad**-lee) Western Norwegian form of Magdalena.

Magda (D: **mow**-da; N/S: **maag**-da) Short form of Magdalena.

Magdalena, Magdalene (D: mow-da-**lay**-neh; N: maag-da-**lay**-na, maag-da-**lay**-neh; S: also maag-da-**layn**) From Greek 'woman from Magdala,' popular from the Biblical Mary Magdalene. The full form is rare, but many variants in Scandinavia as in other countries. Danish form Magdelone.

Magla (**maag**-la) Norwegian form of Magnhild.

Magli (**maag**-lee) Norwegian form of Magdalena. Norwegian author Magli Elster (1912–93).

Magn- First element in several names, including Magna, Magnfrid, Magni, Magny, Magnlaug, Magnvor, Magny, → Magnhild.

Magnhild (**maag**-nill; S: **maang**-hild) From Old Norse Magnhildr, a compound of *magn* 'power, strength' and *hildr* 'battle.' Norwegian and Swedish, most common the first decades of the twentieth century.

Magrete, Magrit (maa-**gray**-teh, maa-**gritt**) Norwegian forms of Margrete. *An-Magrit* (1940) is a novel by Norwegian author Johan Falkberget.

Mai, Maj (**mI**) Either a short form of Maja or from English May. Mostly Swedish. Associated with the month of May: Norwegian *mai*, Swedish *maj*. Popular in double names like Maj-Britt.

Maia, Maja (**mI**-ya) Swedish pet form of Maria or Margit.

Malena, Malene (D: maa-**lay**-neh; N: maa-**lay**-na, maa-**lay**-neh; S: maa-**lay**-na, maa-**layn**) A form of Magdalena.

Mali, Malli, Malin (**maa**-lee, **mal**-lee, **maa**-lin) Forms of Magdalena. Malin most common in Sweden. Canadian film actress and model Malin Maria Akerman was born in Sweden in 1978.

Maren (**maarn, maa**-rehn) A form of Latin Marina, a feminine form of the surname Marinus 'of the sea.' A top name in Denmark for several hundred years; also common in Norway.

Margaret, Margareta, Margarete (**maar**-ga-ret, maar-ga-**ray**-ta, maar-ga-**ray**-teh) From Latin Margarita, related to the word for 'pearl.' A top name in Sweden in the nineteenth century, in Denmark most common

before 1910. In Norway used as early as 1000; Old Norse Margrét(a).

Margit (**maar**-git) Norwegian and Swedish form of Margaret, known in Norway since the fourteenth century. *Margjit Hjukse* is a Norwegian medieval ballad. Fairly common also in Denmark today.

Margreta, Margrete, Margrethe (D: maar-**gray**-teh; N: maar-**gray**-ta, maar-**gray**-teh; S: maar-**gray**-ta) A form of Margareta. One of the most common names in Denmark since the Middle Ages. Queen Margrete of Norway, Denmark, and Sweden (1353–1412). Queen Margrethe II of Denmark (b. 1940).

Mari (**maa**-ree) Norwegian and Swedish form of Maria. Popular in recent decades.

Maria (maa-**ree**-a) From Hebrew Miriam, of uncertain origin. Known since Christianity was introduced in Scandinavia; Old Norse María. In the nineteenth century the most common name in Sweden besides Anna. To some extent replaced during recent decades by the alternative form Marie.

Marian(n) (maa-ree-**aan**) Either from English Marion, or perceived as a combination of English Mary and Anne, or Norwegian Mari and Anne.

Marianne (D: maa-ree-**æn**-neh; N: maa-ree-**aan**-neh; S: maa-ree-**aan**) Extended spelling of Marian, or an assimilated form of French Mariamne, also from Maria.

Marie (maa-**ree**-eh; S: maa-**ree**) An alternative form of Maria, popular in the twentieth century. Often used as a second element in double names like Anne-Marie, Karen-Marie. Princess Anne-Marie of Denmark (b. 1946) was queen of Greece 1964–74.

Marika (maa-**ree**-ka) Mainly Swedish, a diminutive form of Maria.

Marit (**maa**-rit) A form of Margit. Most common in Norway; popular in the twentieth century. Norwegian singer and songwriter Marit Larsen (b. 1983).

Marta, Martha (**maar**-ta) Either from Hebrew 'lady,' or from Margareta. Especially popular around 1900. See also Märta.

Marte (**maar**-teh) A variant of Marta. Increasing popularity in Norway in recent decades, replacing Marta.

Martina, Martine (D: maar-**tee**-neh; N: maar-**tee**-na, mar-**tee**-neh) A feminine form of Martinus; see Martin in boys section. Mostly used around 1900.

Matilda, Matilde (D: maa-**til**-deh; N: maa-**til**-da, maa-**til**-deh) From German Mechthild, a compound of *mecht* 'power, might' and *hild* 'struggle.' Mostly used a hundred years ago, not common today. Also spelled with *th*. Same meaning as Magnhild.

Maud (**moud** [or as in English]) From English, originally a French form of Matilda. Rare. Queen Maud of Norway was born in England in 1869.

Merete (meh-**ray**-teh) A Danish form of Margareta. Popular ca. 1950–70.

Mette (D: **mehd**-deh; N/S: **meht**-teh) Either a German pet form of Mechthild (see Matilda), or a Danish form of Margareta. Fairly common in Norway the first decades after World War II. The top name in Denmark in the 1970s, far ahead of no. 2, Rikke. Crown Princess Mette-Marit of Norway (b. 1973).

Mildred, Mildrid, Milred (D: **mill**-rehth; N: **mill**-rehd, **mill**-ree[d], **mill**-rehd) Possibly from English Mildred, a compound of *mild* 'mild' and *red* 'strength,' associated with similar Old Norse names with the element *fríð* 'beautiful, fair.'

Mina, Mine (**mee**-na, **mee**-neh) Short form of names like Vilhelmina. Mostly Danish, popular in the 1980s and 1990s.

Moa (**moa**-a) Swedish, most likely a pet form of *mor* 'mother.' The Swedish author Moa Martinsson (1890–1964) was christened Helga Maria.

Modgunn (**mood**-gewnn) Norwegian, from Old Norse Móðgunnr, a compound of *móðr* 'courage' and *gunnr* 'battle.' Rare.

Mona (**moo**-na; S: **moa**-na) A short form of names like Monika. Most common in the 1960s and 1970s.

Monika, Monica (**moo**-nee-ka) Most likely from Monnica, of Phoenician origin, but since then influenced by Greek Monakos 'hermit, monk.' Known all over Scandinavia through Swedish director Ingmar Bergman's erotic film *Sommaren med Monika* (*Monika,* the Story of a Bad Girl*) from 1953. A top name in the 1960s and 1970s.

Märta, Märtha (**mehr**-ta) Swedish, but originally a Danish form of Margareta. Crown Princess Märtha of Norway (1901–54) was born in Sweden. Princess Märtha Louise (b. 1971), daughter of King Harald V of Norway. See also Marta.

Målfrid (**moal**-free[d]) Norwegian, from Old Norse Malmfríðr, a compound of *malmr* '(silver) ore' and *fríðr* 'beautiful, fair,' but the first element was early associated with *mál* 'language' and hence associated with the New Norwegian language movement (*målrørsla*). Common in the 1920s and 1930s.

Nanna, Nanne (**naan**-na, **naan**-neh) Perhaps baby talk for *mama*, or a pet form of names like Anna. In Norse mythology Nanna Nepsdotter was Balder's wife. Not common.

Nilla, Nille (**nil**-la, **nil**-leh) A short form of names like Pernille.

Nilsine (nil-**see**-neh) A feminine form of Nils.

Nina (**nee**-na) Either a pet form of names like Kristina, or from a Russian form of Anna.

Nora (**noo**-ra) A short form of Eleonora. Well known from Nora in Norwegian author Henrik Ibsen's play *A Doll's House* (*Et dukkehjem*, 1879). Interpreted as a name for Mother Norway during the nineteenth century, parallel to Svea (Mother Sweden) in Sweden.

Norunn (**noor**-ewnn) Norwegian, a new combination of *nor* 'north' and *unn* from *unna* 'to love.' Used some in the 1920s and 1930s.

Oda (**oo**-da) From German, a short form of names with a word that means 'prosperity, fortune' as the first element. Some usage the last decades of the twentieth century.

Odd- A first element from Old Norse *oddr* 'spear, arrow head' in names like → Oddbjørg, Oddborg, Oddfrid, Oddgunn, Oddhild, Oddlaug, Oddly, Oddny, → Oddrun, → Oddveig, Oddvor. Mostly Norwegian, none of them common.

Oddbjørg (**od**-byoerg) Norwegian, from Old Norse Oddbjǫrg; first element, see Odd-, second element *bjǫrg* 'protection.'

Oddrun (**od**-rewn) Norwegian, from Old Norse Oddrún; first element, see Odd-, second element *rún* 'rune, secret lore.'

Oddveig (**od**-væig) Norwegian, a new combination of *oddr* 'spear, arrow head' (see Odd-) and *veig*, of uncertain origin.

Olaug (**oo**-loug) Norwegian, from Old Norse Ólǫf, a compound of 'ancestor' and 'heir, descendant.' Due to the spelling, it is usually associated with the element *laug*, as in Aslaug. Common in the 1930s and 1940s. See also Olav.

Olava, Olave (oo-**laa**-va, oo-**laa**-veh) Feminine form of Olav.

Olea (oo-**lay**-a) Feminine form of Ole.

Oleanna (oo-lay-**aan**-na) Norwegian, a combination of Ole and Anna. Used some in the decades before 1900. Known from the name of Ole Bull's colony New Norway in Pennsylvania, and a popular song mocking Ole Bull's ambitions of creating a utopian community in the United States. Ole Bull (1810–80) was a famous violinist, often called Norway's first international star.

Olena, Olene (oo-**lay**-na, oo-**lay**-neh) A variant of Olina. Norwegian and Swedish.

Oletta, Olette (oo-**leht**-ta, oo-**leht**-teh) A combination of Ole and the French feminine suffix -ette. Norwegian, used some around 1900.

Olga (**ol**-ga) A Russian form of Helga. Very popular around 1900.

Olina, Oline (oo-**lee**-na, oo-**lee**-neh) Norwegian, a feminine form of Ole and the common suffix -ina, as in Karolina. Popular around 1900.

Olivia (oo-**lee**-vee-a) From Latin 'olive, olive tree.'

Olufine, Oluffa (oo-lew-**fee**-neh, oo-**lewf**-fa) Norwegian, feminine forms of Oluf.

Osa. See Åsa.

Osie. See Åse.

Ot(t)ilia, Ot(t)elie, Otelie (oo-**tee**-lee-a, oo-**tee**-lee-eh, oo-**tay**-lee-eh) From German Odilia, Latin form of Oda.

Paula, Pauline (**pou**-la, pou-**lee**-neh; S: also pou-**leen**) Feminine forms of Paul.

Pernilla, Pernille (pehr-**nil**-la, pehr-**nil**-leh; N/S: also pær-**nil**-la, pær-**nil**-leh) From

Petronella, a Latin diminutive form of the family name Petronius. A top name in Denmark 1970–2000, but also used in Norway and Sweden. Known from Ludvig Holberg's plays from the 1720s. Swedish alpine skier Pernilla Wiberg (b. 1970).

Petra (**pay**-tra) A feminine form of Peter. Mainly Danish.

Pia (**pee**-a) Feminine form of Latin Pius 'pious.' A top name in Denmark from the 1950s until the 1970s. Made popular through Swedish actress Ingrid Bergman's daughter Pia Lindström (b. 1938).

Ragn- First element from Old Norse *ragn-* 'advice, decision,' in names like → Ragna, Ragnborg, Ragndi, → Ragne, → Ragnfrid, Ragnheid, → Ragnhild, Ragni, Ragnilla, Ragnvi, → Ragnveig, Ragnvor, Ragny.

Ragna (**raag**-na) Short form of names like Ragnhild. Common especially in Norway.

Ragne (**raag**-neh) Variant form of Ragna.

Ragnfrid (**raang**-free[d]) From Old Norse Ragnfríðr; first element, see Ragn-, last element *fríðr* 'beautiful, fair.' Mostly Norwegian.

Ragnhild (**raag**-nill, **raang**-nill; S: **raang**-hild) From Old Norse Ragnhildr; first element, see Ragn-, last element *hildr* 'battle.' Mostly Norwegian; common since the Middle Ages. Norwegian queen Ragnhild, wife of Halvdan Svarte, in the ninth century. Norwegian princess Ragnhild (b. 1930), daughter of King Olav V.

Ragnveig (**raang**-væi[g]) From Old Norse Ragnveig; first element, see Ragn-, last element, *veig*, of uncertain origin. Mostly Norwegian. Rannveig is a more common form.

Randi (**raan**-dee) Norwegian, a younger form of Ragnfrid, but known since the fourteenth century. Especially popular around 1950.

Randine (raan-**dee**-neh) Norwegian, an extended form of Randi. Rare after 1920, but fairly common in the nineteenth century.

Rannveig (**raan**-væi[g]) Norwegian. May be from Old Norse Rannveig, a compound of *rann* 'house' or 'advice, decision,' and *veig*, of uncertain origin; or more likely a form of Ragnveig.

Reidun (**ræi**-dewn) Norwegian, from Old
Norse Reiðunn, a compound of *reiðr*
'house, home' and *unn*, from *unna* 'to
love.'

Rie (**ree**-eh) Danish, a short form of Marie.
Swedish form Ria. Danish model, actress,
and filmmaker Rie Rasmussen (b. 1978).

Rigmor (**reeg**-moor) Mainly Danish, probably
from German Ricmut, *ric* 'rich, powerful'
and *mut* 'courage.' Known since the Middle
Ages, most common 1910–30.

Rikke (D: **rig**-geh; N: **rik**-keh) A short form
of names like Henrikke and Frederikke.
Common in recent decades.

Rita (**ree**-ta [as in English]) Italian short form
of Margareta. Popular after World War II
through British and American media.

Ronja (**ron**-ya) Swedish, derived from a Sámi
place name. From the children's book *Ronja
rövardotter* (*Ronia, the Robber's Daughter*,
1981) by Astrid Lindgren.

Runa (D: **roo**-na; N/S: **rew**-na) From Old
Norse Rúna, short form of names with
Run-, from Old Norse *rún* 'rune, secret lore.'
Norwegian and Swedish. See the masculine
form Rune, which is more common.

Runi (**rew**-nee) Norwegian, a newer form of
Runa.

Rut, Ruth, Rutt (D: **root**; N/S: **rewtt**) A Biblical name of uncertain derivation. Common in Denmark, especially 1920–40.

Rønnaug (**roen**-nou[g]) Norwegian, a more
recent variant form of Rannveig.

Saga (**saa**-ga) Swedish, from the Norse goddess Sága, a name for Freya, but gradually
influenced by *folksaga* 'fairy tale.' Popular in
recent decades.

Sandra (**saan**-dra) Short form of Alexandra,
a feminine form of Alexander, from Greek
Alexandros, a compound of *alex* 'defend'
and *andros* 'man, warrior.'

Sanna, Sanne (**saan**-naa, **saan**-neh) Swedish
and Danish short form of Susanna.

Sara (**saa**-ra) From Hebrew Sarah 'princess.'
Popular in recent decades influenced by
British and American media. Swedish
actress and singer Zarah Leander (1907–81).

Selma (**sehl**-ma [as in English]) From English,
originally a Celtic place name from the

Ossian songs. Well known due to Swedish
author Selma Lagerlöf (1858–1940).

Serina, Serine, Serena (seh-**ree**-na, seh-**ree**-
neh, seh-**ray**-na) A contracted form of
Severine. In Norway fairly common at the
end of the nineteenth century. The form
Serena is fairly common in North America.

Severine (seh-veh-**ree**-neh) Feminine form
of Severin. Norwegian, mostly in use in the
late nineteenth century.

Sidsel (**sis**-sehl) Danish spelling of Sissel.

Sig- First element from Old Norse *sigr* 'vic-
tory,' in names like Sigbjørg, Sigborg, Sigdis,
→ Sigfrid, → Signe, Signhild, Signi, → Signy,
→ Sigrid, Sigridur, → Sigrun, Sigtrud, Sigunn,
Sigveig, → Sigvor, Sigyn.

Sigfrid, Sigfrida (**sig**-free[d], sig-**free**-da) Norwegian, from Old Norse Sigfríðr, a com-
pound of *sigr* 'victory' and *fríðr* 'beautiful,
fair.' A more common form is Sigrid.

Signe (**sig**-neh) A variant of Signy. Fairly common ca. 1900, also after World War II. Also
used in Denmark, known from the ballad
"Hagbarth and Signe" by Adam Oehlenschläger. Actress and movie star Signe
Hasso (1910–2002) was born in Sweden.
American Signe Wilkinson (b. 1959) was
the first woman editorial cartoonist to win
the Pulitzer Prize.

Signy (**sig**-new) From Old Norse Signý, a
compound of *sigr* 'victory' and *ný* 'new.'
Less common than the variant Signe. Legendary figure in *The Saga of the Volsungs*.

Sigrid, Sigri (**sig**-ree; S: **sig**-reed) From Old
Norse Sigríðr, a compound of *sigr* 'victory'
and *fríðr* 'beautiful, fair.' Mostly Norwegian and Swedish, very common from
the Middle Ages. See Siri and Sigfrid. The
Norwegian author and Nobel Prize winner
Sigrid Undset (1882–1949).

Sigrun (**sig**-rewn) From Old Norse Sigrún, a
compound of *sigr* 'victory' and *rún* 'rune,
secret lore.' Mostly Norwegian, fairly common from the 1920s till the 1940s.

Sigvor (**sig**-voar) From Old Norse Sigvǫr, a
compound of *sigr* 'victory' and *vǫr* 'careful,
cautious' or 'protector.'

Silje (**sill**-yeh) Short form of Cecilie, mainly
Norwegian. Very common in the 1970s and
1980s.

Silla, Sille (**sil**-la, **sil**-leh) Variants of Silje. Not common.

Sina, Sine (**see**-na, **see**-neh) Short forms of names like Jensina.

Siri (**see**-ree) Developed from Sigrid as early as the Middle Ages. Common especially in Norway. American author Siri Hustvedt (b. 1955 in Minnesota) is of Norwegian descent.

Sissel (**sis**-sehl) Norwegian form of Cecilie. Popular after World War II. Norwegian soprano Sissel Kyrkjebø (b. 1969) has held many concerts in the United States.

Sissil, Sissela (**sis**-sill, **sis**-seh-la) Variants of Sissel.

Siv, Siw (**seev**) From Old Norse Sif, a name of a Norse goddess, from a word meaning 'relationship, kinship,' Thor's beautiful wife. Popular in Norway and Sweden, common in the 1960s and 1970s. Frequently used in double names like Siv-Marie. Swedish actress Siw Malmquist (b. 1936). See page 146.

Snefrid, Snøfrid (**snay**-free[d], **snoe**-free[d]) From Old Norse Snæfríðr, a compound of snær 'snow' and fríðr 'beautiful, fair.' Not common, sporadic occurrence in the twentieth century.

Sofia, Sofie (D: so-**fee**-eh; N: so-**fee**-a, so-**fee**-eh; S: so-**fee**-a, so-**fee**) From Greek 'wisdom.' Mostly used in recent decades. Swedish queen Sofia, married to King Valdemar in 1260. American TV personality Sofia Lidskog Dickens was born in Sweden in 1979. Also written Sophie.

Sol (**sool**) Norwegian and Swedish from sol 'sun.' Associated with the first element in Solveig and used as a short form of this name. Not common.

Sol- A first element from sol 'sun,' in names like Solbritt, Solfrid, Solgull, Solgunn, Solhild, Solunn, all of them fairly recent compounds.

Solveig (**sool**-væi) Mostly Norwegian, from Old Norse Sǫlveig, a compound of sǫl or salr 'house, large room' and veig, of uncertain origin. The first element was early associated with sol 'sun,' which contributed to its popularity. Compare expressions like Norwegian "blid som ei sol" (happy as a

sunny day). In widespread use in Norway around 1930. Next to Kari considered the most typical Norwegian girls name. Known from the character Solveig and "Solveig's Song" in Norwegian writer Henrik Ibsen's play Peer Gynt (1867).

Solvor, Solvår (**sool**-voar) Norwegian, from Old Norse Solvǫr, a compound of sǫl or salr 'house, large room' and vǫr 'careful' or 'the protected.' The spelling -vår is probably associated with the word vår 'spring.'

Sonja, Sonia, Sonya (**son**-ya [as in English]) From Russian, a pet form of Sofia. Popular in the first half of the twentieth century. Sonja Henie (1912–69), a Norwegian figure skater and actress. Queen Sonja of Norway (b. 1937).

Stina, Stine (**stee**-na, **stee**-neh) Short form of names like Kristina. Popular in the 1970s and 1980s. Archeologist Anne Stine Ingstad (1918–97) led the excavation of the Viking Age houses at L'Anse aux Meadows in Newfoundland, Canada.

Sunniva (**sewn**-nee-va) Norwegian, from Old Norse Sunnifa, an early loan from English Sunngifu, a compound of 'sun' and 'gift.' Saint Sunniva is supposed to have been an Irish princess who fled to the monastry of Selja in western Norway (Vestlandet) in the tenth century. More common today is the variant Synnøve.

Susanna, Susanne (D: soos-**æn**-neh; N/S: sews-**aan**-na, sews-**aan**-neh; S: sews-**aan**-na, sews-**aann**) Biblical, from Hebrew 'lily.' Very common in Denmark, a top name from 1950–80. Danish author Susanne Brøgger (b. 1944) and Danish director Susanne Bier (b. 1960).

Svanhild (**svaan**-nill; S: **svaan**-hild) From Old Norse Svanhildr, a compound of svanr 'swan' and hildr 'battle.' Common especially in Norway 1900–1950; also used in Sweden.

Svea (**svay**-a) Swedish, originally derived from the name Svea-rike, 'the kingdom of the Swedes.' Popular through Esaias Tegnér's epic poem Svea (1811).

Sylvi, Sølvi (**sewl**-vee, **soel**-vee) Norwegian, most often a short form of Sylvia, but also possibly from Solveig.

Sylvia (**sewl**-vee-aa) From Latin, a feminine form of *silvius* 'belonging to the wood, forest.'

Synne (**sewn**-neh) Norwegian, a short form of Synnøve.

Synnøve (sewn-**noe**-veh) A Norwegian form of Sunniva. Common, most popular in the 1920s. Norwegian author Bjørnstjerne Bjørnson's novel *Synnøve Solbakken* (1857) made the name known all over Scandinavia.

Syster, Søster (**sews**-tehr, **soes**-ter) Swedish and Danish 'sister,' not common. In Danish also short forms Sys, Søs. See Bror in boys section.

Søs (**soess**) Danish, see Syster.

Tea, Thea (**tay**-a) Short form of names like Dortea. Thea Foss (1857–1927), founder of Foss Maritime in Tacoma, Washington, and the inspiration for the character Tugboat Annie in the *Saturday Evening Post* and the film from 1933. She was born in Eidsberg, Norway.

Tekla, Thekla (**tehk**-la) Swedish, from Greek Theokleia, feminine of Theoklés, 'God' and 'reputation.' Name of the first female martyr.

Teresa, Terese, Teresia, Teresie (D: teh-**ray**-seh; N: teh-**ray**-sa, teh-**ray**-seh, teh-**ray**-see-a, teh-**ray**-see-eh; S: teh-**rays**) First known in Spain, of uncertain origin. Also begins Th-. The variant Therese is most popular, especially in recent decades.

Thelma, Telma (**tehl**-ma, **thehl**-ma) Known in English from the Norwegian heroine in the novel *Thelma* (1887) by the British author Marie Corelli. Although it was first recorded in Norway in 1872, the name is not made from a Norwegian element. Most likely inspired by the name Selma.

Tina, Tine (**tee**-na, **tee**-neh) Short form of names like Kristina. Popular since the 1960s. Danish singer and songwriter Tina Dico (b. 1977).

Tindra (**tin**-dra) Swedish, corresponds to the verb *tindra* 'glitter, sparkle.'

Tiril, Tirill (**tee**-rill) Norwegian, probably a variant of Toril.

Tomasine, Thomasine (toa-maa-**see**-na, toa-maa-**see**-neh) Feminine form of Tomas.

Tone (**too**-neh) Norwegian, a form of Old Norse Þorný, a compound of the god Thor and *ný* 'new,' developed in the late Middle Ages. Popular from the 1950s.

Tonje (**ton**-yeh) Perhaps a dialect form of Torny; see Tone.

Tor- A first element from Old Norse Þórr 'Thor,' in names like → Torbjørg, → Torborg, → Tordis, → Torfrid, → Torgerd, → Torgunn, → Torhild, → Torill, Torlaug, Torny, → Torunn, Torveig, Torø, Torøy.

Tora (**too**-ra) From Old Norse Þóra, a short form of names with Tor-, Old Norse Þórr 'Thor.'

Torbjørg (**toor**-byoerg) Norwegian, from Old Norse Þorbjǫrg, a compound of the god Thor and *bjǫrg* 'protection.'

Torborg (**toor**-borg) A variant of Torbjørg. Norwegian author Torborg Nedreaas (1906–87).

Tordis (**toor**-dees) Mostly Norwegian, from Old Norse Þordís, a compound of the god Thor and *dís* 'goddess.'

Torfrid (**toor**-free[d]) From Old Norse Þorfríðr, younger form Þorríðr, a compound of the god Thor and *fríðr* 'beautiful, fair.' See Turid.

Torgerd, Torgjerd (**toor**-gærd, **toor**-yærd) From Old Norse Þorgerðr, a compound of the god Thor and *gerðr* 'protection.'

Torgunn (**toor**-gewnn) From Old Norse Þorgunnr, a compound of the god Thor and *gunnr* 'battle.'

Torhild (**toor**-hild) From Old Norse Þórhildr, a compound of the god Thor and *hildr* 'battle.' One of the four names of Queen Margrethe II of Denmark is Þórhildur, the Icelandic form of the name.

Toril, Torill, Torild (**toor**-ill, **toor**-ild) Variants of Torhild. Film director, animator, and author Toril Kove was born in Norway in 1958, but has lived in Quebec, Canada, since 1982.

Torun, Torunn (**toor**-ewnn) From Old Norse Þórunnr, a compound of the god Thor and *unnr* from *unna* 'to love.'

Tove, Tova (D: **toa**-veh; N: **toa**-veh, **toa**-va) From Old Norse Tófa, short form of names with Þór-, like Torfrid. Popular in Norway in the 1950s and 1960s. See Tuva.

Trine, Trina (D: **tree**-neh; N: **tree**-neh, **tree**-na) Short form of Katrine. A top name from the 1960s.

Trude (D: **troo**-theh; N/S: **trew**-deh) German short form of Gertrud.

Turid (D: **too**-ree; N: **tew**-ree[d]) From Old Norse Þuríðr, a variant of Þorríðr; see Torfrid, which is the etymological form. Common in Norway from the 1940s.

Tuva (**tew**-va) A Norwegian and Swedish variant of Tove.

Tyra, Thyra (**tew**-ra) Latin form of Danish Thyre, a compound with Thor as the first element and a second element of unknown origin. Traditional in the Danish royal family: Queen Tyra, wife of King Olav Tryggvason of Norway (ca. 1000), and Queen Thyra (b. ca. 900), wife of King Gorm and mother of Harald Blåtand. According to legend, Queen Thyra built the Danish fortress Dannevirke. African American actress and model Tyra Banks (b. 1973).

Ulla (D: **uhl**-la; S: **ewl**-la) Pet form of Ulrikke. Top name in Sweden in the twentieth century, popular in double names like Ulla-Britt.

Ulrikke, Ulrika (D: uhl-**rig**-geh; N: ewl-**rik**-keh, ewl-**rik**-ka; S: ewl-**rik**-ka) Feminine forms of Ulrik.

Unn (**ewnn**) From Old Norse Unnr, derived from *unna* 'to love.' In Norse mythology Unnr is the daughter of Æge (Aegir), god of the sea.

Unndis, Undis (**ewnn**-dis) Norwegian, a new combination of Unn and *dis* 'goddess.'

Unni (**ewn**-nee) Norwegian, a new combination of Unn and *ny* 'new,' or a form of Unn.

Ursula (D: **oor**-soo-la; N/S: **ewr**-sew-la) A diminutive of Latin *ursus* 'bear.' Rare in Scandinavia; most common in German and English.

Valborg (D: **væl**-bor; N/S: **vaal**-bor[g]) From German Walburg, a compound of *wal* 'rule' and *burg* 'protection.' Popular in the decades up to the 1920s.

Vanja (**vaan**-ya) Actually a pet form of Russian Ivan, which is a form of Johannes, but in Sweden Vanja is considered a girls name. Also used in Norway in recent decades.

Venke (**vehng**-keh) See Wenke.

Vera (**veh**-ra [as in English]) From Russian *vera* 'faith,' or possibly a short form of Veronika.

Veronika (veh-**roo**-nee-ka) From Greek 'victory bringer.'

Veslemøy (**vehs**-leh-moey) Norwegian, literally 'little girl.' Most likely taken from Arne Garborg's narrative verse work *Haugtussa* (1895) where Veslemøy is the main character. Norwegian singer Veslemøy Solberg (b. 1964).

Vibeke (D: **vee**-beh-geh; N: **vee**-beh-keh) German short form of names with *wig*- 'battle.' Popular from the 1950s until the 1970s.

Victoria, Viktoria (D: vik-**toa**-ree-a; N/S: vik-**too**-ree-a) From Latin 'victory.' Known also in Scandinavia through British queen Victoria (reigned 1837–1901). Crown Princess Victoria of Sweden (b. 1977).

Vigdis (**vig**-dis) Norwegian, from Old Norse Vígdís, a compound of *víg* 'battle' and *dís* 'goddess.' Popular in the decades after World War II. Former president of Iceland Vigdís Finnbogadóttir (b. 1930).

Vilde (**vill**-deh) Mainly Norwegian, a short form of Alvilde. Common in recent years.

Vilma (**vill**-ma) See Wilma.

Vivan (**vee**-vaan) Swedish pet form of Vibeke and Vivianne.

Vivi (**vee**-vee) Short form of Vivian.

Vivian(n), Vivianne (D: vee-vee-**aan**; N: vee-vee-**aan**, vee-vee-**aan**-neh; S: vee-vee-**aan**) Derived from Latin *vivus* 'living.'

Vår (**voar**) A new name from *vår* 'spring.'

Wenche, Wenke, Wencke (**vehng**-keh) From German, a diminutive form of names with *win*- 'friend.' Popular in Norway 1945–70. Norwegian singer-entertainer Wenche Myhre (b. 1947).

Wilma (**vill**-ma) Short form of names like Vilhelmina. See Vilhelm in the boys section.

Ylva (**ewl**-va) Swedish, derived from *ulv* 'wolf.'

Yngvild (**ewng**-vill) Mostly Norwegian. See Ingvild.

Yrsa (**ewr**-sa) Swedish, of uncertain origin. Known from the Viking Age as a queen's name, possibly related to Latin *ursus* 'bear'. See Ursula.

Ärna (**ær**-na) Swedish short form of names beginning with *Ern*- as Erna or *Arn*- 'eagle'.

Øydis (**oey**-dees) Norwegian, from Old Norse Eydís, a compound of *ey*, possibly 'luck, gift,' and *dís* 'goddess'.

Øyunn (**oey**-ewnn) Norwegian, a new combination of *ey*, possibly 'luck, gift,' and *unn* from *unna* 'to love'.

Ågot (**oa**-goat) Norwegian form of Agate.

Ås- A first element from Old Norse *áss* 'god,' in names like Åsfrid, Åsgjerd, → Åshild, Åslaug, Åsny, Åsrun, Åsveig, Åsvor.

Åsa (**oa**-sa) From Old Norse Ása, short form of names with *áss* 'god'. Queen Åsa was married to the Norwegian king Harold Fairhair (Harald Hårfagre) in the eighth century. Also spelled Osa by immigrants.

Åse (**oa**-seh) A more common variant of Åsa. Mother Åse (Mor Åse) in Norwegian playwright Henrik Ibsen's *Peer Gynt* (1867). Also spelled Osie by immigrants.

Åshild (**oas**-hil[d]) Norwegian, from Old Norse Áshildr, a compound of *áss* 'god' and *hildr* 'battle'.

Åsne (**oas**-neh) Norwegian, from Old Norse Ásný, a compound of *áss* 'god' and *ný* 'new'.

Åsta (**oas**-ta) From Old Norse Ásta, a short form of Astrid. Åsta (ca. 1000) was the mother of Saint Olav. Fairly common in the first decades of the twentieth century.

Åste (**oas**-teh) A variant of Åsta.

Boys Names

Following the practice of Scandinavian languages, note that names beginning with Æ-, Ä-, Ø-, Ö-, and Å- (which are all separate letters rather than accented vowels) are to be found at the end of the alphabet.

Aade. See Odd.

Adolf, Adolph (D: æ-dolf; N/S: aa-dolf) From German Adalwolf, a compound of *adal* 'noble' and *wolf* 'wolf.' Almost no usage since World War II, but fairly common among immigrants in the nineteenth century.

Agnar, Agner (**aag**-nar, **aag**-nehr) From Old Norse, a compound of *agn* 'sword point' or 'respect' and *ar* 'warrior.' The name is known from the legends in the medieval work *Ynglingesaga*, but was not used again until the Names Renaissance in the nineteenth century. Norwegian author Agnar Mykle (1915–94).

Ahlef (**aa**-lehf) Used some by Scandinavian immigrants. Most likely a German form of Adolf, but associated with Olaf.

Aksel, Axel (**aak**-sehl) Danish and Norwegian, a form of Hebrew Absalon 'father of peace.' Especially popular around 1900. Royal name in Denmark: Prince Axel (1888–1964).

Albert (D: æl-bæhrt; N: **aal**-behrt, **aal**-bært; S: **aal**-bært) From German Adalberacht, newer form Adalbert, a compound of *adal* 'noble' and *bert* 'bright, shining.'

Albin (**aal**-been) Swedish, short form of Albinus from Latin Albus 'white.' Major League Baseball shortstop Albin Oscar Carlstrom (1886–1935), of Swedish descent.

Albrekt, Albrikt, Albregt, Albrigt, Albrecht (**aal**-brehkt, **aal**-brikt, **aal**-brehkt, **aal**-brikt, **aal**-brehkt) Forms of Albert, the last one mostly in families of German origin. Albrekt of Mecklenburg was king of Sweden (1364–89).

Alf, Alv (D: ælf; N/S: **aalf**, **aalv**) From Old Norse Alfr 'elf, fairy,' also possibly short form of German names like Alfred. Common both in men's names like Toralv and women's names like Alfhild. The form Alf is most popular. Alf Erling Porsild (1901–77) was a Danish Canadian botanist.

Alfred (D: æl-frehth; N/S: **aal**-frehd) From English, a compound of *alf* 'elf' and *red* 'counsel.' Popular around 1900, inspired by the name of the defendant in the famous court case against the Jewish French officer Alfred Dreyfus, who was wrongfully convicted of treason in 1894. Swedish inventor of dynamite Alfred Nobel (1833–96) willed his fortune to institute the Nobel Prizes.

Algot(t), Allgot(t) (**aal**-gott) Swedish, forms of Old Norse Algautr, a compound of *al* 'elf' or 'all' and *gautr* 'man from Götaland.' Not common.

Allvar, Alvar (**aal**-vaar) From Old Norse Alfarr, a compound of 'elf' and *arr* 'warrior'; in Swedish also associated with *allvar* 'seriousness.' The Swede Allvar Gullstrand (1862–1930) received the Nobel Prize in medicine in 1911.

Almar, Almer (**aal**-maar; N/S: **aal**-maar, **aal**-mehr) From Old Norse Almarr, either *almr* 'elm' and *arr* 'warrior' or 'spear'; or *al* 'elf' and *mar* 'famous.'

Alvin (D: æl-vinn; N/S: **aal**-vinn) From
Old Danish Alfwin, a compound of 'elf'
and *win* 'friend.' Possibly also of German
origin. Also known from Old English.
Popular in the United States.

Ambjørn, An(n)bjørn (**aam**-byoern, **aan**-
byoern) Forms of Arnbjørn.

Amund (**aa**-mewnn) Norwegian, either from
Old Norse Qgmundr (see Ogmund) or
ámundi a compound of *á* 'very' and *mundi*
'protector.' See also Ommund, Åmund.

Anders, Andres (D: **aan**-dehrs; N/S: **aan**-
dehrs, **aan**-drehs) Scandinavian forms of
Andreas, known from the Middle Ages. Very
popular after World War II. In the United
States often replaced by Albert or Andrew.
Swedish inventor Anders Celsius (1701–
44) established the thermometer standard.
In Denmark Donald Duck is called Anders
And. The patronymic Andersson is the sec-
ond most frequent surname in Sweden.

Andreas (D: æn-**dray**-aas; N/S: an-**dray**-aas)
From Greek, a short form of several names
with *andro* 'man, warrior.' Popular in all
three countries; in the United States often
replaced by Albert or Andrew.

Andres (**aan**-drehs) See Anders.

Anfinn (aan-**finn**) A form of Arnfinn.

Anker (D: **aang**-kehr) Danish, most likely
from *annkarl* 'harvester, farm worker.'
Anker Jørgensen (b. 1922), former prime
minister of Denmark.

An(n)- First element from Old Norse *ǫrn*
'eagle' in names like → Anbjørn, Andor,
→ Anfinn, Angrim, Ankjell, Anstein.

Annar (**aan**-naar) Norwegian, from Old
Norse Annarr, a compound of *anu* 'descendant' and *arr* 'warrior.' Variant Onar.

Anund (**aa**-newnn) See Ånund.

Are, Ari (**aa**-reh, **aa**-ree) Mostly Norwegian,
from Old Norse *ari* 'eagle.' Fairly common
in the 1960s and 1970s. The Icelandic historian Are frode (Are the Wise; 1067–1148).
Norwegian author Ari Behn (b. 1972), husband of Princess Märtha Louise.

Arent (**aa**-rehnt) See Arnt.

Arild (**aa**-rill) Either from Harald or a Danish form of German Arnold. Popular in the
1940s and 1950s.

Arn- A first element identical with An(n)-,
in names like → Arnbjørn, → Arnfinn, Arn-
fred, Arngeir, Arngrim, Arnkjell, Arnleiv,
→ Arnljot, → Arnstein, Arntor, → Arnulv,
Arnvid.

Arnbjørn (**aarn**-byoern) From Old Norse
Arnbjǫrn, a compound of *ǫrn* 'eagle' and
bjǫrn 'bear.'

Arne (**aar**-neh) From Old Norse Arni 'eagle.'
A top name for several centuries, common
in double names like Kjell-Arne. Known
through Bjørnstjerne Bjørnson's novel *Arne*
(1859). Norwegian dialect form Ådne. Former Minnesota governor Arne Carlson
(b. 1934) is of Swedish descent. Arne Dun-
can (b. 1965), Secretary of Education under
President Barack Obama, is of Norwegian
descent.

Arnfinn (**aarn**-finn) Mostly Norwegian, from
Old Norse Arnfinnr, a compound of *arn*
'eagle' and *finnr* 'Lapp, Finn.' Variant form
Anfinn.

Arnljot (**aarn**-lee-oat) Norwegian, from Old
Norse Arnljótr, a compound of *arn* 'eagle'
and *ljótr* probably 'shining.' Not common,
known from Bjørnstjerne Bjørnson's epic
poem *Arnljot Gelline* (1870).

Arnold (**aar**-nol[d] [as in English]) Borrowed
early from German, a compound of *arn*
'eagle' and *old* 'ruler.' One of the world's
largest shipping companies is Danish
A(rnold). P. Møller.

Arnstein (**aarn**-stæin) Norwegian, from Old
Norse Arnsteinn, a compound of *arn* 'eagle'
and *steinn* 'stone.' Used some in the 1940s
and 1950s. Norwegian architect Arnstein
Arneberg (1882–1961) designed Oslo City
Hall and the interior of the United Nations
Security Council Chamber in New York.

Arnt, Arndt (**aarnt**) A form of Arnold, or
short form of names with *arn* 'eagle.'

Arnulv, Arnulf (**aar**-newlv, **aar**-newlf) See
Ørnulv. Norwegian author Arnulf Øverland
(1889–1968).

Arve (**aar**-veh) Norwegian, a form of Arvid.
Popular in the 1930s and 1940s.

Arvid (**aar**-vid) A more recent form of Arnvid,
from Old Norse Arnviðr, a compound of
arn 'eagle' and *viðr* 'wood, forest.'

As- First element from Old Norse *áss* 'god,' in names like → Asbjørn, Asgaut, → Asgeir, → Askjell, → Askill, → Aslak, → Asmund.

Asbjørn (**aas**-byoern) Norwegian, from Old Norse Ásbjǫrn, a compound of *áss* 'god' and *bjǫrn* 'bear.' See Åsbjørn, Esbjørn.

Asgeir, Asger, Asgar (D: **æs**-gehr; N: **aas**-gæir, **aas**-gehr, **aas**-gaar) From Old Norse Ásgeirr, a compound of *áss* 'god' and *geirr* 'spear.' The Norwegian form is Asgeir, Danish Asger and Asgar. Danish painter Asger Jorn (1914–73).

Ask (D: **æsk**; N/S: **aask**) From Old Norse *askr* 'ash (tree).' The Norse mythological figures Ask and Embla correspond to Adam and Eve. More common in recent years. See page 146.

Askjell, Askill, Askild, Askell (**aas**-khyehl, **aas**-kill, **aas**-kill, **aas**-kehl) Forms of Old Norse Áskell, older Ásketill, a compound of *áss* 'god' and *ketill* 'kettle, helmet.' See Eskil.

Aslak (**aas**-lakk) Mostly Norwegian, from Old Norse Áslákr, a compound of *áss* 'god' and *lákr* 'battle, giant.'

Asle (**aas**-leh) A variant of Atle.

Asmund (**aas**-mewnn) From Old Norse Ásmundr, a compound of *áss* 'god' and *mund* 'protector.' See Osmund, Åsmund.

Assar, Asser (**aas**-saar, **aas**-sehr) Mostly Swedish, a form of Old Norse Qssur, derived from *andsvar* 'he who gives advice (in legal matters).' The first archbishop of Denmark (and Lund in Sweden) was Asser (d. 1137). Swedish skier Assar Rönnlund (b. 1935).

Atle (**aat**-leh) Mostly Norwegian, from Old Norse Atli 'little father.' The same origin as Attila the Hun (d. 453). *Atlakvida* is a heroic poem about King Atli's plot to get his hands on a treasure. Common the first decades after 1950. Variant Asle.

Audun (**ou**-dewn) Norwegian, from Old Norse Auðunn, derived from Auðvin, a compound of *auðr* 'wealth' and *vin* 'friend.'

Auen, Augun (**ou**-ehn, **ou**-gewn) Norwegian variants of Audun.

Axel (**aak**-sehl) See Aksel.

Baard (**boar**) See Bård.

Balder (**baal**-dehr) From the name of the Norse god Baldr 'chieftain,' a handsome,

wise, and mild god, son of Odin. Growing popularity for mythological names like Balder, → Ask, → Odin, → Tor, → Trym, → Frøya. See page 146.

Bastian, Baste (**baas**-tee-an, **baas**-teh) Short forms of Greek Sebastian 'man from the town Sebastia.'

Bendik, Bendiks, Bendix, Bendikt (**behn**-dikk, **behn**-diks, **behn**-diks, **behn**-dikt) Mostly Danish and Norwegian forms of Latin Benedictus 'blessed.' Not common today.

Bengt, Benkt, Bent, Beint (**bengt**, **bengt**, **behnt**, **bæint**) Short forms of Bendik. Bent is very common in Denmark, Benkt and Bengt mostly Swedish.

Berge, Berger (**bær**-geh, **bær**-gehr; S: **bær**-yehr) Variants of Birger. In Sweden Berger is also a family name of a different origin: 'mountain, hill.'

Bernhard, Bernard (**behrn**-haard or **bærn**-haart, **behr**-naard or **bær**-naard) From German, a compound of 'bear' and *hard* 'hard.'

Bernt, Berndt, Berent (**behrnt**, **bærnt**, **behrehnt**) Forms of Bernhard. Used by the Swedish nobility.

Bersvend, Bergsvein (**bær**-svehn, **bærg**-svæin) Norwegian, from Old Norse Bergsveinn, a compound of *berg* 'protection' and *sveinn* 'young man.'

Bertel, Bertil (**behr**-tehl or **bær**-tehl, **behr**-till or **bær**-till) Forms of the first element in German names like Berthold, from *bert* 'bright, shining.' Prince Bertil of Sweden (1912–97). Danish Icelandic sculptor Bertel Thorvaldsen (1770–1844), known especially for his figure of Christ at Church of Our Lady in Copenhagen. Copies of this statue are in Salt Lake City and Baltimore.

Bertin(i)us (**bær**-**teen**-[ee-]ews) Norwegian derivation of German *bert*-; see Bertrand. Variant Berdines.

Bertrand (**bær**-trann) From German, a compound of *bert* 'bright, shining' and *rand* 'shield.'

Birger (**bir**-yehr, **bir**-gehr) Swedish, from Old Norse Birgir 'helpful' or 'helper, ally.' Used by the Swedish nobility, e.g., Birger Jarl in the thirteenth century. Fairly common in all countries.

Birk (**birk**) German short form of names like Berkhard; first element *berk* 'protection,' last element *hard* 'hard,' but associated with *birk* 'birch tree.' Parallel to the girls name Björk. The character Birk Borkason in the children's book *Ronia the Robber's Daughter* (*Ronja Rövardotter*, 1981) by Swedish author Astrid Lindgren.

Bjarke (**byaar**-keh) Danish pet form of Bjare 'bear.' Known from old Danish legends about Rolf Krake.

Bjarne, Bjerne (**byaar**-neh, **byær**-neh) Danish and Norwegian, short form of names with the element 'bear.' Fairly common, especially before World War II. Danish cyclist Bjarne Riis (b. 1964).

Bjarte (**byaar**-teh) Norwegian short form of names with *bjart* 'bright, shining.'

Bjorn. See Bjørn, Björn.

Bjug (**byewg**) Norwegian, from Old Norse Bjúlfr, a contracted form of an unclear first element and last element *ulfr* 'wolf.' Very rare. Norwegian immigrant Bjug Harstad founded Pacific Lutheran University in Tacoma, Washington, in 1890.

Bjørge, Bjøro (**byoer**-geh, **byoer**-oo) Norwegian short forms of Bjørgulv, Old Norse Bjǫrgulfr, a compound of *bjǫrg* 'protection' and *ulfr* 'wolf.' Norwegian singer Bjøro Håland (b. 1943) has performed many times at Norsk Høstfest in Minot, North Dakota.

Bjørn, Björn (**byoern**) From Old Norse *bjǫrn* 'bear,' also a frequent element in many names like Asbjørn and Torbjørn. Popular in all countries. Swedish tennis champion Björn Borg (b. 1956). Norwegian cross-country ski champion Bjørn Dæhlie (b. 1967). In English written Bjorn.

Bjørnar, Bjørner, Bjørne (**byoer**-naar, **byoer**-nehr, **byoer**-neh) Extended forms of Bjørn.

Bo, Boe (**boo**) Danish and Swedish 'settler, farmer,' i.e., the person who settles permanently instead of wandering around to survive. Pet form Bosse. Swedish author Bo Bergman (1869–1967). Danish guitarist Bo Madsen (b. 1976).

Bodvar (**boad**-vaar) From Old Norse Boðvarr, a compound of *boð* 'battle' and *arr* 'warrior.' Icelander Egil Skallagrims-son (ca. 910–992) wrote the famous poem

"Sonetapet" (Loss of a Son) about his son Bodvar, who was drowned at sea.

Boie, Boje, Boye, Bøje, Bøye (**boy**-yeh, **boy**-yeh, **boy**-yeh, **boey**-yeh, **boey**-yeh) Mainly Danish variants of a Frisian name of uncertain origin. Some forms may possibly be derived from Old Norse Bogi 'bow, arch.'

Borger, Borgar (**bor**-gehr, **bor**-gaar) From Old Norse Borgarr, a compound of *borg* 'protection, rescue' and *arr* 'warrior.'

Botolv, Botolf, Botulf (**boo**-tolv, **boo**-tolf, **boo**-tewlf) Mainly Norwegian, from Old Norse Bótólfr, a compound of *bót* 'support, help' and *ólfr* 'wolf.'

Brage (D: **brow**-eh; N/S: **braa**-geh) Mainly Norwegian, from Old Norse Bragi 'the foremost' or 'art of poetry,' the Norse god of poetry. Brage is one of the names of Norse gods that has become increasingly popular. See page 146.

Brede (D: **bray**-theh; N: **bray**-deh) Possibly from Danish *brejde* 'battle-ax.'

Brigt, Brikt (**brikt**) Short forms of Ingebrigt.

Bror, Broder (**broo**-ehr, **broo**-dehr) From Old Norse *bróðir* 'brother.' Bror has been a marker name for the Swedish nobility. Swedish Baron Bror von Blixen-Finecke (1886–1946) was married to Danish author Karen Blixen (Isak Dinesen).

Brynjulv, Brynjulf, Bryn(j)olf (**brewn**-yewlv, **brewn**-yewlf, **brewn**-yolf) Norwegian and Swedish, from Old Norse Brynjulfr, a compound of *brynja* 'coat of mail' and *ulfr* 'wolf.' Swedish bishop Brynulf av Skara (ca. 1300). Pet form Brynte.

Bue (**bew**-eh) Same origin as Bo. The Dane Bue Digre is known from Norse sagas.

Børge, Børre, Börje, Byrge (D: **boer**-weh; N/S: **boer**-geh, **boer**-reh, **boer**-yeh, **bewr**-geh) Younger forms of Birger.

Bøye (**boy**-yeh) See Boie.

Bård (**boar**) Norwegian, from Old Norse Bárðr, derived from a compound of 'battle' and 'peace, protection.'

Carl (**kaarl** [as in English]) See Karl. Swedish king Carl XVI Gustaf (b. 1946). Also used in the Danish royal family. Carlsberg brewery was founded by the Dane Carl Jacobsen (1842–1914). Swedish botanist Carl von

Linné (1707–78). American author Carl Sandburg (1878–1967) was the son of Swedish immigrants.

Carsten (**kaar**-stehn) German form of Kristian, mostly Danish. Popular in the 1950s. See Karsten. Danish author and political columnist Carsten Jensen (b. 1952).

Christen (**kris**-tehn, **krehs**-tehn) See Kristen.

Christer (**kris**-tehr) See Krister.

Christian (**kris**-tee-aan, **krehs**-tyaan) See Kristian. The name of ten Danish kings. The spelling with Ch for K is influenced by German and English. Danish American portraitist Christian Gullager (1759–1826).

Christoffer, Christopher (kris-**tof**-fehr, krehs-**tof**-fehr) See Kristoffer.

Clas, Claes (D: **klæ**-ehs; N/S: **klaas**) See Klas.

Claus (**klous**) See Klaus.

Clement, Clemens (**klay**-mehnt, **klay**-mehns) See Klement.

Colben (**koal**-behn) See Kolbein.

Conrad (D: **kon**-ræth; N/S: **kon**-raad) See Konrad.

Cornelius (kor-**nay**-lee-ews) See Kornelius.

Dag (**daag**) Norwegian and Swedish, from Old Norse dagr 'day.' Also used in compounds, e.g., → Dagfinn, Dagbjørn, Dagmund; and women's names → Dagny, Dagrun. The Swede Dag Hammarskjöld was secretary-general of the United Nations from 1953 to 1961.

Dagfinn (**daag**-finn) Norwegian, from Old Norse Dagfinnr, a compound of dagr 'day' and finnr 'Lapp, Finn.'

Dan (D: **dænn**; N/S: **daan**) Either from the first element in Danmark—i.e., dan 'dane'—or short form or pet form of Daniel. A legend says that Dan was the first king of Denmark. Swedish author Dan Turèll (1946–93).

Dane (D: **dæ**-neh; N/S: **daa**-neh [or as in English]) Either an ethnic name to mark Danish ancestry (see Dan) or a transferred use of the English surname Dean.

Daniel (D: **dæ**-nee-ehl; N/S: **daa**-nee-ehl) From Hebrew 'God is my judge.'

Detlef, Detlev, Ditlef, Ditlev, Detlof, Detlov (D: **deet**-lehv; N/S: **deht**-lehf, **deht**-lehv,

dit-lehf, dit-lehv, **deht**-loff, **deht**-lov) Variants of a German name with elements 'people' and 'heir, descendant.'

Didrik (D: **deeth**-rehk; N/S: **dee**-drik) From German Theodarich, a compound of 'people' and rich 'powerful, ruler.' Also in Old Norse Þjóðrekr. Known through the saga Didrik av Bern (about Theoderic the Great, d. 525).

Dines (**dee**-nehs) Danish, a form of Greek Dionysios.

Dreng (**drehng**) Norwegian, from Old Norse Drengr, originally 'young, daring man,' later 'farm hand.'

Dyre (**dew**-reh) Norwegian, from Old Norse Dýri 'deer.' Norwegian sculptor Dyre Vaa (1903–80).

Ebbe (**ehb**-beh) Danish, either short form of Esbjørn or German Eberhard. Danish author Ebbe Kløvedal Reich (1940–2005). Danish medieval ballad "Ebbe Skammelsen."

Eberhard, Ebert (**ay**-behr-hard, **ay**-behrt or **ay**-bært) From German Eburhart, a compound of eber 'wild boar' and hard 'hard.' Short forms Ebbe and Evert.

Edgar (**ehd**-gaar) From English Eadgar, a compound of ead 'prosperity, riches' and gar 'spear.' Variants Audgeir, Edgeir.

Edmund, Edmond (D: **ehth**-monn; N/S: **ehd**-mewnn, **ehd**-mon; S: **ehd**-mewnd, **ehd**-mond) From English Eadmund, a compound of ead 'prosperity, riches' and mund 'protector.' Norwegian forms Jetmund and Audmund.

Edvard (D: **ehth**-vaart; N/S: **ehd**-vaard) From English ead 'prosperity, riches' and weard 'guard.' In Old Norse transformed to Játvarðr, then Jetvard. Norwegian artist Edvard Munch (1863–1944). Norwegian composer Edvard Grieg (1843–1907).

Edvin (**ehd**-vinn) From English Eadvin, composed of ead 'wealth, riches' and vin 'friend.' Corresponds to Audun.

Egil, Eigil (**ay**-geel, **æi**-geel) From Old Norse Egill, probably derived from agi 'sword point' or 'respect.' Very common in Norway, even today. Eigil is mostly Danish. Norse

author and skald (poet) Egil Skallagrims-
son (ca. 910–92), also hero of *The Saga of
Egil Skallagrimsson.* Patronymic form Eielsen; see Elling.

Eiler, Ejler, Eilert (æi-lehr, æi-lehr, æi-lehrt)
From German, an alternative form of
Eilhard, 'sword point' or 'respect' and last
element *hard* 'hard.' Danish form Ejler.

Eiliv, Eilif, Ejlif, Eilev, Eilef, Eilov, Eilof, Ellev,
Ellef (æi-leev, æi-leef, æi-leef, æi-lehv,
æi-lehf, æi-loav, æi-loaf, ehl-lehv, ehl-lehf)
From Old Norse Eilífr, a compound of *ei*
'alone, exceptional' and *lífr* 'heir, descendant.' Mostly Norwegian, but Ejlif is
Danish.

Einar, Ejnar, Ejner, Ener (æi-naar, æi-naar,
æi-nehr, eh-nehr) From Old Norse Einarr,
a compound of *ei* 'alone, exceptional' and
arr 'warrior,' the same meaning as *einheri*
'the lonely warrior.' Especially popular from
ca. 1900 to the 1940s. The Norwegian warrior and chieftain Einar Tambarskjelve
(d. ca. 1050). Norwegian prime minister
Einar Gerhardsen (1897–1987). American
linguist Einar Haugen (1906–94), professor
at Harvard, of Norwegian descent.

Einvald, Enevald, Enevold (æin-vaald, ay-
neh-vaald, ay-neh-vold) From Old Norse,
a compound of *ein* 'alone, exceptional' and
vald 'ruler.' Norwegian nobleman Enevold
de Falsen (1755–1808).

Eiolv, Eiolf, Ejolf, Eiulf (æi-olv, æi-olf, æi-olf,
æi-ewlf) Norwegian, variant of Øyolv. Also
Eyolf. Norwegian author Henrik Ibsen's
play *Little Eyolf* (1894).

Eirik (æi-reek) From Old Norse Eiríkr, a
compound of *ei* 'alone, exceptional' and
ríkr 'powerful, ruler.' Eirik Raude (Erik the
Red) discovered Greenland ca. 985. Common variant Erik. In Norway most often
Erik, but in recent decades Eirik is equally
frequent.

Eivind (æi-vinn) Norwegian, alternative form
of Øyvind. More recent Norwegian variant
Even.

Ejvind (æi-vinn) Danish spelling of Eivind.

Eldar, Eldor, Eljar (ehl-daar, ehl-door, ehl-
yaar) Norwegian, more recent compounds.

Ellev, Ellef (ehl-lehv, ehl-lef) See Eiliv.

Elling (ehl-ling) Norwegian variant of Erling,
known since the fourteenth century. Elling
Eielsen (1804–83) was the first Norwegian
Lutheran pastor in the United States. The
Norwegian film *Elling,* based on the novel
by Yngvar Ambjørnsen, was nominated for
an Academy Award in 2002.

Elo (ay-loo) Danish, most likely a form of Elov.

Elov, Elof, Eluf (ay-loav, ay-loaf, ay-lewf)
Swedish, a compound of 'always' or 'lonely'
and 'heir.' Rare. Swedish linguist Elof
Hellquist (1864–1933).

Embret, Embrik (ehm-breht, ehm-brikk)
Norwegian dialect forms of Engelbrekt.

Emil (ay-meel) From French Émile, originally
a Latin surname Aemilius, perhaps from
aemulus 'rival.' Made very popular from the
main character in Astrid Lindgren's series
Emil i Lönneberga (*Emil of Lönneberga,*
1963–97).

Endre (ehn-dreh) Norwegian, from Old
Norse Eindriði, a compound of *ein* 'lonely,
alone' and most likely a derivation of *ríða*
'to ride,' i.e., 'the lone rider,' one of the
many names for the god Thor. Fairly common, including in recent decades. Endre
Johannes Cleven (1874–1916), prominent
in Norwegian Canadian Manitoba, was in
charge of Canada's Scandinavian settlement
program.

Ener (ay-nehr) See Einar.

Enevald, Enevold (ay-neh-vaald, ay-neh-vold)
See Einvald.

Engebret (ehng-eh-breht) See Engelbrekt.

Engelbrekt, Engelbregt, Engelbrecht, Engel-
bert (ehng-ehl-brehkt, ehng-ehl-brehkt,
ehng-ehl-brehkt, ehng-ehl-bært) From
German Engelbrecht; first element same as
angles (as in *Anglo*-Saxon), later associated
with *engel* 'angel,' last element *bert* 'bright,
shining.' Variants Ingebret, Ingebrigt, Engebret, Embret, Embrik. Swedish freedom
fighter Engelbrekt Engelbrektsson (d. 1436).

Engelhardt, Engelhart (ehng-ehl-haart) From
German, a compound of *engel* 'angel' and
hard 'hard.' Mostly Danish.

Enok (ay-nok) From Hebrew Chanōk 'conse-
crated, sacred.' Rare today, fairly common
among immigrants.

Erhardt, Erhard (**ehr**-haart) From German, a compound of 'honor' and *hard* 'hard.' Mostly Danish.

Erik (**eh**-reek [or as in English]) See Eirik. Used by Danish and Swedish royalty in the Middle Ages. German Erich, French and English Eric. Common in double names like Jan-Erik. Erik Ramstad was one of the founders of Minot, North Dakota, in 1886. In the United States also Eric, Erick, Erich. Eric Sevareid (1912–92), pioneering broadcast journalist for CBS, was of Norwegian descent. Swedish-born Eric Wickman (1887–1954) founded the Greyhound Bus Lines. American speed skater Eric Heiden (b. 1958) won five gold medals at the Lake Placid Winter Olympics in 1980.

Erland, Erlend (**ær**-laand, **ær**-lehnd; D/S: **ær**-laan[d]) From Old Norse Erlandr or Erlendr, probably originally a nickname meaning 'foreign' or 'from a foreign country.' Erlend Nikolaussøn in Norwegian author Sigrid Undset's trilogy *Kristin Lavransdatter* (1920–22).

Erling (**ehr**-ling, **ær**-ling) From Old Norse Erlingr, probably 'son of an earl.' Most popular before World War II. Norse chieftain Erling Skjalgsson (ca. 1000). Danish politician Erling Olsen (b. 1927).

Ernst (**ehrnst**, **ærnst**) From German Ernust 'earnestness, seriousness.' Swedish entertainer Ernst Rolf (1891–1932).

Esben (**ehs**-behn) Danish form of Esbjørn; in Norwegian mostly written Espen.

Esbjørn (**ehs**-byoern) Derived from Åsbjørn. See Espen.

Eskil, Eskild (**ehs**-kill) Variants of Askjell.

Espen (**ehs**-pehn) Norwegian form of Esben. Popular the last decades of the twentieth century. Espen Oskeladd (Cinderlad) is the main character in many folk tales collected in the nineteenth century by Norwegians Peter Christian Asbjørnsen and Jørgen Engebretsen Moe.

Esten (**ehs**-tehn) Variant of Øystein.

Evald (D: **ay**-væl; N/S: **ay**-vaald) From German Ewald, a compound of 'law, order' and *vald* 'ruler.' Danish and Swedish.

Even (**ay**-vehn) Norwegian form of Eivind. Fairly common. Even Heg, leader and lay preacher in nineteenth-century Wisconsin, born in Norway in 1790.

Eyolf (**ay**-yolf) Variant of Eiolf.

Eystein (**ay**-stæin) A more historic form of Øystein.

Eyvind (**ay**-vinn; S: **ay**-vind) A more historic form of Øyvind.

Finn (**finn**) From Old Norse Finnr 'Lapp, Finn.' Popular until the 1950s.

Fleming, Flemming (**flehm**-ming) Originally a Dutch nickname, Vleminc, 'man from Flanders.' Also known from Old Norse as Flæmingr. Mostly Danish.

Folke (**foal**-keh) From Old Norse *folki* 'people,' short form of names with *folk-* as Folkmar, → Folkvard. Especially Swedish. Swedish diplomat Folke Bernadotte (1895–1948).

Folkvard (**foalk**-vaard) Norwegian, from Old Norse Folkvarðr (see Folke); last element *varðr* 'protector.' Rare today.

Folmer (**foal**-mehr) Danish, from German Volkmar, a compound of *folk* 'people' and *mar* 'famous.' Also written Volmer. See Folke.

Fredrik, Frederik (D: **frehth**-rik; N: **frehd**-reek, **freh**-deh-reek) From German Frithuric, a compound of *fred* 'peace' and *ric* 'powerful, ruler.' Known in Old Norse since 1000 as Friðrekr. The name of nine Danish kings, e.g., Frederik IX (d. 1972). Crown Prince Frederik (b. 1968) is heir apparent to the Danish throne.

Fridtjov, Fridtjof, Fritjof, Fritjov (**fritt**-yoff) From Old Norse Friðþjófr, a compound of *friðr* 'peace, protection' and *þjófr* 'thief.' Swedish author Esaias Tegnér wrote "Frithiofs saga" (1825), based on the Norse saga about Fridtjov the Brave. Norwegian diplomat, scientist, and polar explorer Fridtjof Nansen (1861–1930).

Frode (D: **froo**-theh; N: **froo**-deh) From Old Norse Fróði 'wise.' Icelandic historian Are frode (Are the Wise; 1067–1148). Popular in Norway in the 1970s, and in Denmark before World War II.

Frøystein, Freystein (**froey**-stæin, **fray**-stæin)
From Old Norse Freysteinn, the god Frey
(see Frøydis in girls section) and *steinn*
'stone.' Rare.

Gabriel (D: **gæ**-bree-ehl; N/S: **gaa**-bree-ehl)
Biblical, from Hebrew 'man of God.'

Gard (**gaar**[d]) Norwegian, from Old Norse
Garðr 'fence, protection.'

Gardar (**gaar**-daar) From Old Norse Garðarr;
first element see Gard, last element a suffix. Rare.

Gaute (**gou**-teh) Norwegian, from Old Norse
Gauti, a form of *gautr* 'gaut, man from Götaland (in Sweden).' Fairly common.

Geir- First element, see Geir; in names like
Geirbjørn, Geirbrand, Geirfinn, Geirleiv,
→ Geirmund, Geirodd, Geirstein, Geirvald.
All of them rare.

Geir, Geirr, Ger (**gæir**, **gæir**, **gehr**) From Old
Norse *geirr* 'spear.' Geir is most popular
in Norway, with a peak in the 1960s. Norwegian composer Geirr Tveitt (1908–81).
Norwegian guitarist and singer Geir Zahl
(b. 1975). Frequent in double names like
Geir-Arne.

Geirmund, Germund (**gæir**-mewnn, **gehr**-
mewnn or **gær**-mewnn) From Old Norse
Geirmundr, a compound of *geirr* 'spear' and
mundr 'protector.' A younger form, Gjermund, is more common.

Georg (**gay**-oarg; S: **yay**-oarg) From Greek
Géorgios 'farmer.' Many derived forms in
Scandinavia: Gøran, Jørgen, Jøran, Jørn,
Ørjan. Danish silversmith Georg Jensen
(1866–1935).

Gerhard, Gerhardt (**gehr**-haard or **gær**-
haard, **gehr**-haart or **gær**-haart; S: **yehr**-
haard) From German, a compound of *ger*
'spear' and *hard* 'hard.' Contracted forms
Gjert, Gert.

Gisle (**gis**-leh) Short form of names like Torgils. Main character in *The Saga of Gisli
Sursson*. Norwegian actor Gisle Straume
(1917–89).

Gjermund (**yær**-mewnn) A younger form of
Geirmund. Popularized by Norwegian skier
Gjermund Eggen (b. 1941).

Gjert, Gert (D: **gehrt**; N: **yært**, **gært**) Contracted forms of Gerhard. Norwegian
author Gert Nygårdshaug (b. 1946). Danish
politician Gert Petersen (b. 1927).

Gjest (**yehst**) Norwegian, from Old Norse
Gestr 'guest.' Known through the legendary
Gjest Baardsen (1791–1849), a Norwegian
Robin Hood.

Gjurd, Gjord, Gyrd (**yewrd**, **yoard**, **gewrd**)
From Old Norse Gyrðr, of uncertain origin.
Most common in the forms Jul and Juel.

Gorm (**gorm**) Danish, a contracted form of
Old Norse Guðþormr; see Guttorm. Danish king Gorm den Gamle (Gorm the Old;
d. ca. 960), husband of Queen Thyra and
father of Harald Blåtand (Bluetooth). Infre-
quently used.

Gott- First element 'god' in German names,
like → Gottfred, Gotthard, Gottlieb, Gott-
mar, Gottskalk, Gottvald.

Got(t)fred, Godtfred, Gottfried (D: **gott**-
frehth; N/S: **gott**-frehd, **gott**-freed)
From German *gott* 'god' and *fred* 'peace,
protection.'

Greger, Gregers, Gregor, Gregert, Gregus,
Greis, Grels, Gres, Gravers (**gray**-gehr,
gray-gehrs, **gray**-gor, **gray**-gært, **gray**-
gews, **græis**, **grehls**, **grehs**, **graa**-vehrs)
Rare variants of Latin Gregorius 'watchful.'
Gregers Werle in Norwegian author Henrik Ibsen's play *Vildanden* (*The Wild Duck*,
1884).

Grim (**grim**) From Old Norse Grímr 'man
with a helmet or a mask.' Rare. Grim Kam-
ban was supposedly the first settler in the
Faroe Islands.

Grunde (**grewn**-deh) Norwegian, derived
from Old Norse *grunda* 'think, meditate,
ponder.' Norwegian diver Jon Grunde
Vegard (b. 1957). Some usage throughout
the country.

Gud- First element from Old Norse *goð* 'god'
in names like → Gudbrand, Gudfast, Gudlaug, Gudleik (Gullak, Gullik, Gulleik),
Gudleiv, Gudmar, → Gudmund, → Guttorm.

Gudbrand, Gul(d)brand (**gewd**-braan, **gewl**-
braan) From Old Norse Guðbrandr, a compound of *goð* 'god' and *brandr* 'sword.' Also

first element in the place name Gudbrands-dalen (Gudbrand's Valley) in Norway.

Gudmund (D: **guhth**-moonn; N: **gewd**-mewnn; S: **gewd**-mewnd) Mostly Norwegian and Swedish, from Old Norse Guðmundr, a compound of *goð* 'god' and *mundr* 'protector.'

Gunder, Gunner (**guhn**-nehr) Danish forms of Gunnar.

Gunn- First element from Old Norse *gunnr* 'battle' in names like Gunne, Gunni, Gunnbjørn, Gunnleik, → Gunnleiv, Gunnmar, → Gunnstein, Gunnulv, → Gunnvald, Gunnvard.

Gunnar (D: **guhn**-naar; N/S: **gewn**-naar) From Old Norse Gunnarr, a compound of *gunnr* 'battle' and *arr* 'warrior.' Popular in all countries. Latin form Gunnerius, German Günter, Danish spelling Gunder. Swedish economist and Nobel laureate Gunnar Myrdal (1898–1987). Norse chieftain Gunnar på Lidarende.

Gunnerius (gewn-**nehr**-ee-ews) Latin form of Gunnar; scattered usage among Norwegian immigrants.

Gunnleiv (**gewnn**-læiv) Norwegian, from Old Norse Gunnleifr, a compound of *gunnr* 'battle' and *leifr* 'heir, descendant.'

Gunnstein, Gunnsten (**gewnn**-stæin, **gewnn**-stehn) Norwegian, from Old Norse Gunnsteinn, a compound of *gunnr* 'battle' and *steinn* 'stone.'

Gunnvald (D: **guhn**-væl; N: **gewnn**-vaald) Norwegian, from Old Norse Gunnvaldr, a compound of *gunnr* 'battle' and *valdr* 'ruler.'

Gustav, Gustaf (D: **guhs**-tow; N/S: **gews**-taav, **gews**-taaf) Swedish, of uncertain origin, perhaps a byname 'the stick or staff [*stav*] of the gauts [man from Götaland],' i.e., the protector of the Gauts. Latin Gustavus. Since Gustav Vasa was elected king of Sweden in 1523, Gustav has been a royal name. The present king Carl XVI Gustaf (b. 1946). Gustavus Adolphus College was founded by Swedish immigrants in 1862 in Minnesota. Illustrator Gustaf Tenggren (1896–1970) was born in Sweden. Gustaf Unonius, pioneer pastor in Wisconsin, born in Hel-

sinki in 1810. Norwegian sculptor Gustav Vigeland (1869–1943).

Guttorm (**gewt**-toarm) Norwegian, from Old Norse Guðþormr, *goð* 'god' and last element derived from *þyrma* 'to honor, be careful of,' i.e., the one who honors the gods. Norwegian politician Guttorm Hansen (1920–2009).

Gyrd (**gewrd**) Norwegian, an historic form of Gjurd.

Göran (**yoer**-aan) Swedish form of Ørjan. Also Jøran. Former Swedish prime minister Göran Persson (b. 1949).

Gösta (**yoes**-ta) Dialect form of Gustav. Main character in the Swedish novel *Gösta Berlings saga* (*The Story of Gösta Berling*, 1891) by Selma Lagerlöf.

Haakon, Haagen (**hoa**-koon, **hoa**-gehn) See Håkon.

Hadle (**haad**-leh) Norwegian dialect form of Halle.

Haftor (**haaf**-toor) See Havtor.

Hakon (**haa**-koon) See Håkon.

Halfdan (**haalf**-daan) See Halvdan.

Hall- First element from Old Norse *hallr* 'stone' in names like Hallbjørn, → Halldor, Hallfred, → Hallgeir, Hallgrim, Hallkjell, → Hallstein, → Hallvard, → Hallvor, → Halvdan, and the girls name → Halldis.

Halldor, Haldor (**haal**-door) Norwegian, from Old Norse Halldórr, a compound of *hallr* 'stone' and a form of the name of the god Þórr 'Thor.'

Halle (**haal**-leh) Short form of names with Hall-, e.g., Hallgeir. Halle Steensland, born in Norway 1832, Wisconsin businessman and philanthropist.

Hallgeir, Halgeir (**haal**-gæir) Norwegian, from Old Norse Hallgeirr, *hallr* 'stone' and *geirr* 'spear.' Skier Hallgeir Brenden (1929–2007).

Hallstein, Halstein, Halsten (**haal**-stæin, **haal**-stæin, **haal**-stehn) From Old Norse Hallsteinn, 'stone' and 'stone'! Both elements (*hallr* and *steinn*) mean 'stone,' evidence that compounds in the Viking age were mostly arbitrary without a significant meaning.

Hallvard, Halvard, Halvar (**haal**-vaar[d])
From Old Norse Hallvarðr, *hallr* 'stone' and
varðr 'protector, guardian.' Common variant
Hallvor. Former Norwegian foreign minister Halvard Lange (1902–70). Oslo's patron
saint, Hallvard, from the eleventh century.
Hallvor, Halvor (**haal**-voor) A more recent
form of Hallvard, known since the fourteenth century. Common in eastern
Norway.

Halvdan, Halfdan (**haalf**-daan) From Old
Norse Halfdan 'half Danish'! King Halvdan
Svarte (the Black) in the ninth century. For-
mer Norwegian foreign minister Halvdan
Koht (1873–1965).

Hampe, Hampus (**haam**-peh, **haam**-pews)
Swedish pet forms of Hans.

Hannes (**haan**-nehs) Older form of Hans, and
short form of Johannes.

Hans (**haans**) Short form of Johannes, known
already in the fourteenth century. Swedish
pet forms Hasse, Hampe, Hampus. Danish king Hans (d. 1513). Danish fairy tale
author Hans Christian Andersen (1805–75).
Hans Heg, born in Norway 1829, colonel
of the 15th Wisconsin Volunteer Regiment
during the Civil War, composed mainly
of Norwegian immigrants. Common in
double names like Hans-Petter. One of
the most popular names in Denmark. The
patronymic Hansen is number 1 in Norway and number 3 in Denmark in surname
frequency.

Harald (**haa**-raald) From Old Norse Haraldr,
a compound of *har* 'army' and *valdr* 'ruler.'
King Harald Hårfagre (Fairhair) unified
Norway into one kingdom in 872. King
Harald V of Norway (b. 1937). English form
Harold. Alternative form Arild. Danish
king Harald Blåtann (Harald Bluetooth; ca.
935–85).

Harding (**haar**-ding) Danish form of Frisian
Herding, of uncertain origin.

Hardy (**haar**-dew) Danish short form of German names like Hartwig, Bernhard.

Harold (**haa**-rold [or as in English]) English
form of Harald.

Hartvig (**haart**-vig, **haart**-vee) Mostly Dan-

ish, from a German name with elements
hart 'hard' and *vig* 'battle.' Danish politician
Hartvig Frisch (1893–1950).

Hasse (**haas**-seh) Swedish pet form of Hans.
Swedish comic team Hasse and Tage.

Hauk (**houk**) Norwegian, from Old Norse
haukr 'hawk.' Norwegian musician Hauk
Buen (b. 1933).

Havtor, Haftor (**haav**-toor, **haaf**-toor) From
Old Norse Hafþórir, *haf* 'ocean' and last
element derived from the name of the god
Þórr 'Thor.'

Hein (**hæin**) Either from Old Norse Heðinn,
of uncertain origin, or a variant of Heine.

Heine, Hejne, Heini (**hæi**-neh, **hæi**-neh,
hæi-nee) Most likely a pet form of German
Heinrich; see Henrik. Latin form Heino.

Helge (D: **hehl**-yeh; N: **hehl**-geh) From
Old Norse Helgi, derived from *heilagr*
'holy, devoted to the gods.' Especially
popular around the mid-twentieth century.
Woman's name Helga. Russian Oleg is
derived from Helge. Danish Helle has gradually been replaced by Helge. Dialect form
Helje. Several men named Helge are mentioned in Norse literature, e.g., Helge Hun-
dingsbane. Norwegian lawyer, adventurer,
and explorer Helge Ingstad (1899–2001)
discovered the Norse settlement at L'Anse
aux Meadows in Newfoundland, Canada.

Hellik, Hellek, Helleik (**hehl**-leek, **hehl**-lehk,
hehl-læik) Variants of Herleik.

Helmer (**hehl**-mehr) From German, a
compound of *heil* 'healthy, well' and *mer*
'famous'; or *helm* 'helmet' and *her* 'warrior.'

Helmuth, Helmut (D: **hehl**-moot; N/S: **hehl**-
mewt) Mostly Danish, from a German
compound; first element *hel* 'healthy, well'
or 'battle,' last element *mut* 'courage, fury.'

Hemming, Heming (**hehm**-ming, **hay**-
ming) From Old Norse Hemingr, meaning
unclear. In Norwegian folklore Heming
unge (Heming the Young) is an excellent
skier. Swedish bishop Hemming Gadd
(d. 1520).

Henning (**hehn**-ning) Mostly Danish, derived
from Johannes and Henrik, often confused
with Hemming. Variant Hennig. Danish

politician Henning Christophersen
(b. 1939). Swedish crime writer Henning
Mankell (b. 1948).

Henrik (**hehn**-rik) From German Heinrich,
composed of *hein* 'home' and *ric* 'ruler,
powerful.' Known by the Middle Ages as
Heinrikr. The most popular German name
in Scandinavia. Used over most of Europe:
French Henri, English Henry and Harry,
Finnish Heikki. Norwegian playwright
Henrik Ibsen (1828–1906). Prince Henrik
of Denmark (b. 1934).

Her- First element from Old Norse *herr* 'army,'
in names like → Herbjørn, → Herbrand,
Herfinn, → Hergeir, Herjulv, Herleik, → Her-
leiv, → Herlof (Herluf, Herløv), → Hermod,
→ Hermund, Herulv, Herstein, Hervald,
Hervard.

Herbert (**hehr**-behrt, **hær**-bært; S: **hær**-bært)
From German, composed of *herr* 'army' and
bert 'bright, shining.'

Herbjørn (**hehr**-byoern, **hær**-byoern) Norwegian, from Old Norse Herbjǫrn, *herr* 'army'
and *bjǫrn* 'bear.' Rare.

Herbrand (**hehr**-braan[d], **hær**-braan[d])
Norwegian, from Old Norse Herbrandr,
herr 'army' and *brandr* 'sword.' Rare.

Hergeir (**hehr**-gæir, **hær**-gæir) From Old
Norse Hergeirr, *herr* 'army' and *geirr* 'spear.'
Rare.

Herleiv, Herleif (**hehr**-læiv or **hær**-læiv, **hehr**-
læif or **hær**-læif) From Old Norse Herleifr,
herr 'army' and *leifr* 'heir, descendant.'
Rare.

Herlof, Herlov, Herluf, Herløv (**hehr**-loff,
hehr-loov, **hehr**-lewf, **hehr**-loev [also pronounced **hær**-]) Variants of Herleiv. Danish
naval hero Herluf Trolle (d. 1565).

Herman, Hermann (D: **hær**-mænn; N/S:
hehr-maan, **hær**-maan) From German Hermann, *herr* 'army' and *mann* 'man.' French
form Armand. Frequent in Danish, e.g.,
author Herman Bang (1857–1912).

Hermod (**hehr**-mood, **hær**-mood) From Old
Norse Hermóðr, probably originally German, a compound of *herr* 'army' and *móðr*
'courage, excitement.' In Norse mythology
Hermod is the son of Odin.

Hermund (**hehr**-mewnn, **hær**-mewnn) Nor-

wegian, from Old Norse Hermundr, *herr*
'army' and *mundr* 'protector.' Often confused with Herman.

Hilbert (**hil**-behrt, **hil**-bært) From German, a
compound of *hild* 'battle' and *bert* 'bright,
shining.'

Hildemar (**hil**-deh-maar) From German, a
compound of *hild* 'battle' and *mar* 'famous.'

Hilmar, Hilmer (**hil**-maar, **hil**-mehr) Short
forms of Hildemar. Danish prime minister
Hilmar Baunsgaard (1920–89).

Hjalmar (D: **yæl**-maar; N/S: **yaal**-maar)
From Old Norse Hjalmarr, a compound of
hjalmr 'helmet' and *arr* 'warrior.' Swedish
politician Hjalmar Branting (1860–1925).
Hjalmar Ekdal in Norwegian author Henrik Ibsen's play *Vildanden* (*The Wild Duck*,
1884). Norwegian speed skater Hjalmar
Andersen (b. 1923).

Hjarrand, Hjarand (**yaar**-raan[d]) From
Old Norse Hjarrandr, a compound of *herr*
'army' and *rand* 'shield.' Norwegian variants Kjeran(d) and Tjeran(d), all forms
borne by immigrants from western
Norway.

Hogne (**hogg**-neh) Norwegian, from Old
Norse Hogni, probably 'protector.' Used
occasionally after World War II.

Holger (**hol**-gehr) Danish and Swedish, older
form Holmger, a compound of *holmr* 'islet,
small island' and *ger* 'spear.' Holger Danske
(Ogier the Dane, French Ogier de Dane-
marche) is a legendary character who first
appears in an Old French *chanson de geste*.
He is said to sleep in Kronborg Castle until
Denmark is in danger, when he will awake
and save the nation. During World War II
the largest Danish resistence group was
named Holger Danske.

Hroar (**roo**-aar) A more historic spelling of
Roar, from Old Norse Hróarr.

Hugo (D: **hoo**-goa; N/S: **hew**-goa) From a
German short form of names like Hugbert;
first element *hug* 'mind.'

Högne, Høgne (**hoeg**-neh) See Hogne.

Hågen, Håkan (D: **hoa**-wehn; S: **hoa**-kaan)
Danish form and Swedish form of Håkon.

Håkon (**hoa**-koan) From Old Norse Hákon,
of uncertain origin; perhaps *hár* 'tall, high'

and last element 'son, descendant.' Danish forms Hågen, Haagen; Swedish Håkan. Common especially in Norway since the Middle Ages: King Håkon IV Håkonsson (1204–63), King Haakon VII (1872–1957), and Crown Prince Haakon Magnus (b. 1973). Also King Håkan Magnusson of Sweden (1340–80).

Hårek (**hoa**-rehk) Norwegian, from Old Norse Hárekr; uncertain first element, last element *rekr* 'powerful.' Hårek den hardbalne (Hagar the Horrible), main character in the popular comic strip.

Håvar (**hoa**-vaar) See Håvard.

Håvard (**hoa**-vaar[d]) Norwegian, from Old Norse Hávarðr; first element *há*- 'battle' or 'tall, high,' last element *varðr* 'protector.' Frequently confused with Håvar, a compound of *hár* 'tall, high' and *ar* 'warrior' or 'spear.'

Ib (**ib**) From Jep, Danish form of Jakob.

Idar, Idolf (**ee**-daar, **ee**-dolf) More recent compounds with first element from woman's name Ida.

Ingar, Ingard, Inggard (**ing**-gaar) Norwegian, newer compounds with Ing-; see Inge.

Inge (**ing**-geh; S: **ing**-eh) From Old Norse Ingi, the Norse fertility god Ing or Yngvi, other names for Frey. Frequent in double names like Knut-Inge. Swedish king Inge (d. 1122). Norwegian king Inge Krokrygg (d. 1161). Not to be confused with the Danish girls name Inge.

Ing(e)björn (**ing**-byoern, **ing**-eh-byoern) Newer Swedish compound of Ing- (see Inge) and *björn* 'bear.'

Ingebjørn (**ing**-eh-byoern) Norwegian, from Old Norse Ingibjǫrn, a compound of Ingi (see Inge) and *bjǫrn* 'bear.' Rare.

Ingebret (**ing**-eh-breht) Norwegian form of Engelbrekt.

Ingebrigt (**ing**-eh-brikt) Norwegian form of Engelbrekt. Short forms Brigt, Brikt.

Ingeir, Inggeir, Ingegeir (**ing**-gæir, **ing**-gæir, **ing**-eh-gæir) Newer Norwegian compounds with the elements Ing (see Inge) and *geir* 'spear.'

Ingemann, Ingeman (D: **ing**-eh-mæn; N/S: **ing**-eh-maan) Danish form of Ingemund.

Ingemar (**ing**-eh-maar) Swedish, from Old Norse Ingimarr, a compound of Ingi (see Inge) and *marr* 'famous.' International boxing champion Ingemar Johansson (1932–2009), also called Ingo.

Ingemund (**ing**-eh-mewnn) From Old Norse Ingimundr, a compound of Ingi (see Inge) and *mundr* 'protector.'

Ingjald (**ing**-yaald) Most likely a variant of Ingvald.

Ingmar (**ing**-maar) Swedish variant of Ingemar. Swedish film, stage, and opera director Ingmar Bergman (1918–2007).

Ingo (**ing**-goo) Danish; Latin form of Inge.

Ingolv, Ingolf (**ing**-golv, **ing**-golf) From Old Norse Ingolfr, a compound of Ing (see Inge) and *ulfr* 'wolf.' The Norwegian Ingolv Arnason settled Iceland in 874. Prince Ingolf of Denmark (b. 1940).

Ingvald, Ingevald (D: **ing**-væl; N/S: **ing**-vaald, **ing**-eh-vaald) From Old Norse Ingivaldr, a compound of Ingi (see Inge) and *valdr* 'ruler.'

Ingvar, Ingvard (**ing**-vaar[d]) Variant of Yngvar. The Swede Ingvar Kamprad (b. 1926) founded the furniture chain store IKEA. Ingvar Carlsson was prime minister of Sweden in the 1980s and 1990s. Russian Igor is derived from Ingvar.

Ingve (**ing**-veh) Norwegian variant of Yngve.

Ivar, Iver (D: **ee**-vaa; N: **ee**-vaar, **ee**-vehr; S: **ee**-vaar) From Old Norse Ívarr, probably a compound of *iv* 'yew, bow' and last element *arr* 'warrior.' Popular. Danish form Iver. Norwegian linguist Ivar Aasen (1813–96) changed his name from Iver. Folk singer and founder of Ivar's Fish Restaurants in Seattle, Ivar Haglund (1905–85), of Norwegian and Swedish ancestry.

Jakob, Jakop, Jacob (D: **yaa**-koab; N/S: **yaa**-koap) From Hebrew of uncertain origin, perhaps 'may God protect.' Danish American photographer, journalist, and social reformer Jacob Riis (1849–1914). Danish pet form Jeppe. See Ib.

Jan (D: **yænn**; N/S: **yaan**) Short form of German Jahan, a form of Johan. A top name for many years, especially after World

War II. Common in double names like Jan-Erik.

Jardar (**yaar**-daar) Norwegian, from Old Norse Jarðarr; first element *jarð* 'earth' and the suffix *arr*.

Jarl (**yaarl**) From Old Norse Jarl 'earl.' Swedish actor Jarl Kulle (1927–97).

Jarle (**yaar**-leh) Norwegian, extended form of Jarl. Popular in the 1960s and 1970s.

Jasper (D: **yæs**-behr; N: **yaas**-pehr) Mostly Danish; see Jesper.

Jehans (**yay**-haans) See Johannes.

Jens (**yehns**) Danish form of Johannes, but common in all countries. Swedish form Jöns. Popular in double names like Jens-Erik. The prototype of a Danish name. Danish Jens soldat (soldier) corresponds to Norwegian Ola soldat and English GI Joe. Danish prime minister Jens Otto Krag (1914–78). Norwegian prime minister Jens Stoltenberg (b. 1959). American landscape architect Jens Jensen was born in Denmark in 1860. The patronymic Jensen is the most common surname in Denmark.

Jeppe (D: **yehb**-beh; N/S: **yehp**-peh) Danish pet form of Jep, from Jakob. Danish author Jeppe Aakjær (1866–1930). Norwegian Danish author Ludvig Holberg's play *Jeppe paa Bierget* (*Jeppe of the Hill*, 1772).

Jerker (**yær**-kehr) Swedish form of Eirik.

Jesper (**yehs**-behr) Danish form of Jasper, from Kaspar. A top name in Denmark in the 1960s and 1970s. Jesper Kyd (b. 1972), composer of music for video games and film scores.

Jo (**yoo**) Norwegian form of Jon. Politician Jo Benkow (b. 1924) and author Jo Nesbø (b. 1960), both Norwegian.

Jo- First element from Old Norse *jór* 'horse' in Norwegian names like Jobjørn, Jofred, Jogeir, Jogrim, Joleik, Joleiv, Jomar, Jomund, most of which are recent compounds.

Joakim, Joachim (**yoa**-aa-keem) From Hebrew 'established by God.' Popular from the 1990s. Danish form Jokum. Danish prince Joachim (b. 1969).

Joar (**joo**-aar) From Old Norse Jóarr, a compound of *jó*- 'horse' and *ar* 'warrior' or 'spear.' Norwegian and Swedish.

Johan, Johann (D: yoo-**hænn**; N/S: yoo-**haan**, yoo-aan) German short form of Johannes. Very common. King Carl XIV Johan of Sweden (1763–1844). The Swede Johan (John in the United States) Nordström (1871–1936) cofounded the Nordstrom department store chain. The patronymic Johansen is number 2 in Norway, and Johansson is number 1 in Sweden.

Johannes (D: yoo-**hæn**-nehs; N/S: yoo-**haan**-nehs) From German, originally Hebrew 'God is gracious.' Common, especially before World War II. Danish author Johannes V. Jensen (1873–1950). Norwegian author Johannes Heggland (1919–2008). Origin of the many variants of this name in use, the name with the most variants in Scandinavia: Jan, Jon, Jón, Jo, Hans, Jens, Johan, Jehans, Jöns, etc. A number of international forms: Italian Giovanni, Scottish Ian, Hungarian Janos, French Jean, Spanish Juan, Finnish Juhani and Jukka, English John.

John. See Jon.

Jokum (**yoa**-koom) Danish form of Joakim.

Jon (**yoon**) Short form of Johan or Johannes. Very common for hundreds of years, known since 1000. In Sweden most often spelled John. In Denmark usually spelled John and pronounced as in English. Frequent in double names like Jon-Erik. Jon Blund is the Norwegian variant of Wee Willie Winkie or the Sandman. Norwegian dramatist Jon Fosse (b. 1959). Norwegian software engineer and cofounder of doubleTwist corporation Jon Lech Johansen (b. 1983), known as DVD Jon for making it possible to bypass the encryptions on commercial DVDs. Jon Torsteinson Rue (1827–76), known as Snowshoe Thompson, the father of skiing in California. Icelandic-born journalist Jón Ólafsson (b. 1850) petitioned President Ulysses S. Grant for land in Alaska for an Icelandic settlement. Former mayor of Dallas and philanthropist John Erik Jonsson (1901–95) was born in Sweden.

Jon- First element from Jon, in newer Norwegian names like Jonar, Jonfinn, Jonfred, Jongeir. All names are rare.

Jonas (**yoo**-naas) From Hebrew 'dove,' or short form of Johannes. Popular in recent decades. Norwegian foreign minister Jonas Gahr Støre (b. 1960). The Bronx in New York is supposedly named for the Swede Jonas Bronk (1600–1643). Icelandic poet and nationalist Jónas Hallgrímsson (1807–45).

Jone (**yoo**-neh) Norwegian, an extended form of Jon, mainly in southwestern Norway.

Jor- First element from a word meaning 'wild boar,' in names like Joralv, Jorleiv, Jorodd, Jorstein, Jorulv. Rare. Corresponds to German Eber-, as in Eberhard.

Jostein (**yoo**-stæin) Norwegian, from Old Norse Jósteinn, a compound of *jór* 'horse' and *steinn* 'stone.' Norwegian soccer star Jostein Flo (b. 1964).

Jul, Juel (**yewl**) Forms of Gjurd.

Julius (D: **yoo**-lee-ews; N/S: **yew**-lee-ews) From Latin of uncertain derivation. Growing popularity in recent decades.

Jöns (**yoens**) Swedish form of Johannes. Scientist Jöns Jacob Berzelius (1779–1848).

Jöran (**yoer**-aan) Swedish form of Göran. Swedish linguist specializing in place names Jöran Sahlgren (1884–1971).

Jørgen (D: **yoe**-ehrn; N: **yoer**-gehn) From German Jürgen, a form of George. Known since the fourteenth century, popular especially before World War II. Norwegian author and folklorist Jørgen Moe (1813–82).

Jørn (**yoern**) A form of Jørgen. Danish architect Jørn Utzon (1918–2008) designed the Sydney Opera House.

Jørund (**yoer**-ewnn) Norwegian, from Old Norse Jǫrundr, a compound of *jǫr* 'battle' and *undr* of uncertain origin.

Kaare (D: **koa**-eh; N: **koa**-reh) See Kåre.

Kai, Kaj, Kay (**kI**) Mostly Danish, of uncertain origin. Danish author and pastor Kaj Munk (1898–1944).

Kalle (D: **kæl**-leh; N/S: **kaal**-leh) Pet form of Karl.

Karl (**kaarl** [as in English]) From Old Norse Karl 'free man,' also spelled Carl. Royal name in Sweden: King Karl XII (1682–1718). Karl Rove (b. 1950), political advisor to President George W. Bush, is of Norwe-

gian descent. Governor of Minnesota Karl F. Rolvaag (1913–90), son of Ole Rolvaag (see Ole). The patronymic Karlsson is number 3 in Sweden. *Karlsson on the Roof* (*Lillebror og Karlsson på taket*, 1955) by Astrid Lindgren.

Karsten, Karstein (**kaar**-stehn, **kaar**-stæin) From German, a form of Kristian, rare after World War II. See also Carsten.

Kasper, Kaspar (D: **kaas**-behr; N/S: **kaas**-pehr, **kaas**-paar) Most likely from Persian 'treasurer.' Variants Jesper and Jasper. Most common in Denmark. Also spelled with C. Known from the Norwegian author Thorbjørn Egner's children's book *People and Robbers of Cardamon Town* (*Folk og røvere i Kardemomme by*, 1955) about the three thieves Kasper, Jesper, and Jonatan. Danish singer and guitarist Kasper Elstrup (b. 1973).

Keld (**kehll**) A form of Kjell.

Ketil (D: **kay**-till; N: **keh**-till) Historic form of Kjetil. Norwegian author and composer Ketil Bjørnstad (b. 1952).

Kittel, Kittil (**khit**-tehl, **khit**-til) Norwegian dialect forms of Kjetil. Around 1900 Kittel was replaced by Kjetil and Kjell. Often changed by immigrants to Charlie. Kittel Halvorson, Minnesota congressman, was born in Norway in 1846. The patronymic Kittelsen was Americanized to Kittleson.

Kjartan (**khaar**-taan) Norwegian, from Irish, possibly 'sea warrior.' Norwegian author Kjartan Fløgstad (b. 1944). Danish author Adam Oehlenschläger's play *Kjartan og Gudrun* (1848).

Kjell, Kjeld (D: **kehll**; N/S: **khell**) Short form of Kjetil. Popular most decades of the twentieth century. Danish form Kjeld. Common in double names like Kjell-Arne. Norwegian prime minister Kjell Magne Bondevik (b. 1947). Danish author and playwright Kjeld Abell (1901–61).

Kjeran(d) (**khær**-aan[d]) See Tjeran(d).

Kjetil (**kheh**-til) From Old Norse Ketill, same word as *kettle*. In Norse religion kettles were used in sacrificial ceremonies. Most common in Norway. Norwegian champion alpine racer Kjetil André Aamodt (b. 1971).

Kjølv (**khoelv**) Norwegian, a more recent form of Tjodolv. See also Tjølv.

Klas, Klaus (D: **klæs, klous**; N/S: **klaas, klous**) German short forms of Nikolaus. Swedish naval hero Klas Uggla (1614–76). Pop art sculptor Claes Oldenburg was born in Stockholm in 1929.

Klement, Klemet, Klemens (**klay**-mehnt, **klay**-meht, **klay**-mehns) German, from Latin Clemens 'mild.' Not common.

Kleng (**klehng**) Norwegian, from Old Norse Klæingr, related to the English word *claw*. Cleng Peerson (originally Kleng Pedersen, 1783–1865), father of Norwegian immigration to America, sailed the ship *Restaurationen* to New York in 1825 with fifty-two emigrants. The name is very rare today.

Knud, Knut (D: **knooth**; N/S: **knewt**) From Old Norse Knútr 'knot,' most likely a byname given to a squat man. Danish spelling Knud, English Canute, Latin Canutus, among immigrants often Knute or Knudt. Common in all three countries. The Danish king Knud den store (ca. 995–1035), English Canute the Great, Viking king of England. Politician Knute Nelson (1843–1923), governor of Minnesota, was born in Norway. Football player Knute Rockne (1888–1931) was born in Voss, Norway.

Kol- First element from Old Norse *kol* 'coal (black),' as in names like → Kolbein, → Kolbjørn, Kolfinn, Kolfred, Kolgrim, Kolstein, Kolsvein. Not common.

Kolbein (**koll**-bæin) Norwegian, from Old Norse Kolbeinn; first element, see Kol-, last element *beinn* 'bone, leg.' Among immigrants often spelled Colben, Kolben. Norwegian poet Kolbein Falkeid (b. 1933).

Kolbjørn (**koll**-byoern) Norwegian, from Old Norse Kolbjǫrn; first element, see Kol-, last element *bjǫrn* 'bear.' Author Kolbjørn Hauge (1926–2007).

Konrad (D: **kon**-ræth; N/S: **koon**-raad) From German, a compound of *kon* 'brave, bold' and *rat* 'councillor.' Also spelled Conrad. Conrad Hilton (1919–79), founder of the Hilton Hotel chain, was of Norwegian descent.

Kornelius (D: kor-**nay**-lee-oos; N/S: kor-**nay**-lee-ews) From Latin, originally a sur-name possibly derived from *cornu* 'horn.' Also spelled Cornelius. Rare.

Kristen (**kris**-tehn, **krehs**-tehn) A form of Kristian. Fairly common in the early twentieth century. Also spelled Christen. Danish painter Christen Købke (1810–48).

Krister (**kris**-tehr) Swedish form of Kristian. Also spelled Christer. Astronaut Arne Christer Fuglesang (b. 1957) is of Norwegian and Swedish descent.

Kristian (D: **krehs**-tyaan; N/S: **kris**-tee-aan) From Latin Christianus 'christian, follower of Christ.' Popular in recent decades; often spelled Christian. Ten kings by the name of Christian in Denmark, e.g., King Christian IV (1577–1648). Danish author of fairy tales Hans Christian Andersen (1805–75). Norwegian painter Christian Krohg (1852–1925). Kristian Prestgard (1866–1946), born in Norway, was editor of the Norwegian-language newspaper *Decorah-Posten* in Decorah, Iowa, for many years.

Kristoffer (kris-**tof**-fehr, krehs-**tof**-fehr) From Greek, a compound of 'Christ' and 'carry, bear,' i.e., 'the one who bears Christ.' Often spelled Christoffer, more rarely Christopher. Kristofer of Bayern (1416–48), King of Denmark, Norway, and Sweden. Father of Danish painting Christoffer Wilhelm Eckersberg (1783–1853).

Kurt (D: **koort**; N/S: **kewrt**) Short form of Konrad. Danish author Kurt Aust (b. 1955). Danish cartoonist Kurt Westergaard (b. 1935) drew perhaps the most controversial of the Mohammed cartoons that sparked conflict and protests around the world in 2005.

Kyrre (**khewr**-reh, **kewr**-reh) Norwegian, from an Old Norse byname *kyrr* 'quiet, peaceful.' Norwegian king Olav Kyrre (1067–93).

Kåre (D: **koa**-eh; N: **koa**-reh) Derived from an Old Norse word *kári* 'curly,' referring to a person with curly hair. Also spelled Kaare. Norwegian prime minister Kåre Willoch (b. 1928).

Lage (D: **læ**-eh; N/S: **laa**-geh) Danish, same origin as last element in Old Norse *félagi* 'friend.'

Lars (**laars**) A form of Lavrans, from Latin Laurentius 'man from Laurentum.' Frequent in all three countries. Common in double names like Lars-Erik. Pet form Lasse. Swedish author Lars Gyllensten (1921–2006). Danish film director Lars von Trier (b. 1956). Lars Lindstrom is the main character in the movie *Lars and the Real Girl* (2007), set in Wisconsin.

Lasse (D: **læs**-seh; N/S: **laas**-seh) Pet form of Lars. Swedish film director Lasse Hallström (b. 1946). Norwegian alpine racer Lasse Kjus (b. 1971).

Laurits, Laurids, Lauritz, Laurens, Lauris (**lou**-rits, **lou**-rits, **lou**-rits, **lou**-rehns, **lou**-ris) From Latin Laurentius; see Lars. General Lauris Norstad (1907–88), from Minnesota, former NATO Supreme Allied Commander for Europe, was of Norwegian descent.

Laust (**lowst**) Danish, a form of Laurits. Danish musician Laust Sonne (b. 1974).

Lavrans, Lavrants (**laav**-raans) A form of Latin Laurentius; see Lars. Not common. Lavrans is the name of Kristin's father in Norwegian author Sigrid Undset's trilogy *Kristin Lavransdatter* (1920–22).

Leidulv, Leidulf (**læid**-ewlv, **læid**-ewlf) Norwegian, from Old Norse Leiðulfr, a compound of *leið* 'path, direction' and *ulfr* 'wolf.' Rare.

Leiv, Leif (**læiv**, **læif**) Short form of names with Old Norse *leifr* 'heir, descendant.' Danish spelling mostly Leif; in Norwegian also Leiv. The Viking Leif Erikson (Leifr Eiríksson) discovered America ca. 1000; October 9 is Leif Erikson Day in the United States. Norwegian pianist Leif Ove Andsnes (b. 1970). Swedish ice hockey player Leif Holmqvist (b. 1942). Danish author Leif Panduro (1923–77).

Lennart (**lehn**-naart) Mostly Swedish, a form of Leonhard. Swedish entertainer Lennart Hyland (1919–93). Common.

Leo, Leon (**lay**-oo, **lay**-oon) Short forms of Leonhard.

Leonhard, Leonard (**lay**-oon-haard, **lay**-oon-aard or **lay**-oon-aart) From German, a compound of *leon* 'lion' and *hard* 'hard.' Most common in the derived forms Lennart, Leo, and Leon. Mostly Danish and Swedish.

Levar, Levard, Levor, Livar (**lay**-vaar, **lay**-vaar[d], **lay**-voor, **lee**-vaar) Norwegian, from Old Norse Liðvarðr, *lið* 'people' or 'generation' and *varðr* 'protector.' Rare.

Lief (**leef** [as in English, actually incorrect]) Occasional (incorrect) American spelling of Leif.

Loke (**loa**-keh) A mythological name recently adopted from Old Norse Loki, of uncertain origin, possibly related to *logi* 'flame, fire.' Loki was a half-god in the Norse cosmos, known for his ability to change into a woman and as a troublemaker for the other gods. See page 148.

Lorents, Lorentz, Lorns, Lorenz, Lorens (**loo**-rehnts, **loo**-rehnts, **lorns**, **loo**-rehnts, **loo**-rehns) Forms of Latin Laurentius; see Lars.

Ludvig, Ludvik (D: **looth**-vee; N/S: **lewd**-veeg, **lewd**-veek) From German, a compound of *lud* 'famous' and *vig* 'battle.' Rare after World War II. Norwegian Danish author Ludvig Holberg (1684–1754). Author Johan Ludvig Runeberg (1804–77), from Finland, wrote in Swedish.

Mads (D: **mæss**; N/S: **maats**) From Mattias. Common. See Mats. Danish actor Mads Mikkelsen (b. 1965).

Magnar (**maag**-naar) Norwegian, a more recent compound of *magn* 'strength, power' and *ar* 'warrior.' Common from the 1920s to the 1940s.

Magne (**maag**-neh) Norwegian, derived from Old Norse *magni* 'strength, power.' Popular before World War II. In Norse mythology Magne is the god Thor's son.

Magnus (D: **mow**-noos; N/S: **maag**-news) From Latin Magnus 'great,' already known in the Viking Age. First known in Norway when King Magnus den gode (the good) was given his name in 1024, named after the Frankish king Charlemagne (Karl den store, 747–814), in Latin Carolus Magnus. The Norse history writer Snorri Sturluson comments on this in his work *History of the Norwegian Kings*. The king said, "Why did you give the boy the name Magnus? We don't use that name in our family." Sigvat replied, "I named him after King Charlemagne;

he is the most worthy man I could think of in the whole world" (see also page 126). Dialect form Mons, Danish Mogens, Swedish Måns. Common in all three countries. Crown Prince Haakon Magnus of Norway (b. 1973). King Magnus (Ladulås) of Sweden (1240–90). Norwegian international chess champion Magnus Carlsen (b. 1990). United States Senator from Minnesota Magnus Johanson (1871–1936) was of Swedish descent.

Malenius (maa-**leh**-nee-ews) Norwegian, extended form with Latin suffix -ius from the woman's name Malena. In America replaced by Martin or Matt.

Malte, Malthe (D: **mæl**-deh; N/S: **maal**-teh) Danish, short form of German Helmold, a compound of *helm* 'helmet' and *old* 'power.' Danish World War II resistance hero Kim Malthe-Bruun (1923–45) was born in Canada.

Manfred (D: **mæn**-frehth; N/S: **maan**-frehd) Danish, a variant of German Manfried, a compound of *mann* 'man' and *fried* 'peace.' Swedish bishop Manfred Björkquist (1884–1985).

Marius (**maa**-ree-ews) From Latin, derived from *mare* 'ocean, sea,' or woman's name Maria. A top name in the 1970s and 1980s. Norwegian film producer Marius Holst (b. 1965).

Markus, Marcus (D: **maar**-koos; N/S: **maar**-kews) Possibly derived from the name of the Latin war god Mars. Popular in recent decades.

Martin (**maar**-tin [as in English]) Short form of Latin Martīnus, derived from the name of the god Mars. Variants Morten, Mårten. Danish author Martin A. Hansen (1909–55).

Martinus, Martinius (D: maar-**teen**-oos, maar-**tee**-nee-oos; N/S: maar-**teen**-ews, maar-**tee**-nee-ews) From Latin Martīnus, derived from the name of the god Mars. Very rare today, but used some by immigrants.

Mats, Matts, Mads, Mattis, Matias, Mattias, Mathias (D: **mæss**, mæ-**tee**-ews; N/S: **maats**, **maat**-tees, maa-**tee**-aas) From Greek 'gift of God.' Popular in recent decades, especially Mathias. Swedish tennis cham-

pion Mats Wilander (b. 1964). Swedish photographer Matias Klum (b. 1967).

Maurits, Mauritz (**mow**-rits) Short form of Latin Mauritius 'man from Mauritania,' i.e., with a dark complexion. Norwegian author Maurits Hansen (1794–1842).

Ments, Mentz (**mehnts**) German, short form of names like Meinhard; a compound of *mein* 'strength, power' and *hard* 'hard.'

Mikal, Mikael, Michael (D: **mee**-kæl; N: mi-**kaal**; S: **mee**-kehl) From Hebrew 'who is like God?' Swedish actor Mikael Persbrandt (b. 1963).

Mikkel, Mikkjel, Mickel (D: **mik**-kehl; N: mik-kehl, **mi**-khell, **mik**-kehl) Dialect forms of Mikal. Norwegian author Mikkjel Fønhus (1894–1973).

Mogens (D: **mow**-ehns) Danish form of Magnus. Politician Mogens Glistrup (1926–2008).

Mons, Måns (**moans**) Norwegian and Swedish form of Magnus.

Morten, Mortein, Mårten (**moar**-tehn, **moar**-tæin, **moar**-tehn) Forms of Martin. Swedish form Mårten. Popular in the 1960s and 1970s. Swedes celebrate Mårtensgås November 11 (St. Martin's Day or Martinmas).

Mourits (**mow**-rits) See Maurits.

Narve (**naar**-veh) Norwegian, from Old Norse Narfi, possibly derived from a word for 'narrow.' In Norse mythology Narfi is the son of the half-god Loki. See page 148.

Nels (**nehls** [as in English]) English form of Nils. Next to Olson, the surname Nelson is the most common Scandinavian surname in the United States.

Neri, Nerid, Nere, Niri (**neh**-ree, **neh**-ree, **neh**-reh, **nee**-ree) Norwegian, from Old Norse Neriðr of complicated origin. Rare.

Niels (**nils**) Danish form of Nils. The patronymic Nielsen is the number 2 surname in Denmark.

Nikolaus, Nikolai, Nikolaj, Niklas, Nikolas (nik-ko-**lous**, nik-ko-**ll**, nik-ko-**ll**, **nik**-laas, nik-ko-**laas**) All are forms of Greek Nikólaos, a compound of *nikó* 'victory' and *laos* 'people.' Common variants begin

with Nic-. Swedish: Niklas. See Nils, Niels, Klas, Klaus. Swedish entrepreneur Niklas Zennström, cofounder of Skype (b. 1966). Danish pastor, poet, and philosopher Nikolai F. S. Grundtvig (1783–1872).
Nils, Niels (**nils**) A form of Nikolaus, known since 1000. Very common for hundreds of years, but not popular in recent decades. Nils is Norwegian and Swedish; Niels is Danish. The word *nisse* 'santa' or 'elf, sprite' is most likely derived from Nils. Common in double names like Nils-Erik. The patronymic Nielsen ranks number 2 as a surname in Denmark, which illustrates the popularity of the given name; Swedish Nilsson is number 4, and Norwegian Nilsen is number 6. Selma Lagerlöf's novel *Nils Holgerssons underbara resa genom Sverige* (*The Wonderful Adventures of Nils*, 1906–7). The Nielsen rating bureau was founded by a Dane in 1950. The Danish nuclear physicist Niels Bohr (1885–1962). Musician Nils Lofgren, born in 1951 in Chicago, is of Swedish descent. Both Nils and Niels were Americanized to Nels by immigrants; see Nels.
Njeld (**nyell**) See Njål.
Njord (**nyoard**) From a Norse god Njǫrðr, corresponding to Latin Nerthus. A god of sea voyages, hunting, and fishing. See page 146.
Njål (**nyoal**) Norwegian, originally from Irish, possibly 'hero, champion.' English Niall, Neal, Neill. The Norse saga *Njála* or *Njål's Saga*. Some usage today. In the nineteenth century often written Njeld.
Nor- First element of varied origin in Norwegian names like Noralv, Norleiv, → Normann, Norvald.
Normann, Norman (**noor**-maan [or as in English]) Same as Old Norse *norðmaðr* 'Norwegian, man from the north, Scandinavian.' Popular in the United States especially among Norwegian immigrants, e.g., Nobel Peace Prize winner Norman Borlaug, born in Iowa in 1914.

Odd (**od**) Norwegian, from Old Norse *oddr* 'spear, point.' Fairly common. Sometimes written Aade.

Odd- First element in names like → Oddbjørn, Oddfinn, → Oddgeir, Oddleiv, → Oddmar, → Oddmund, → Oddvar, Oddvin; see Odd. Most of them Norwegian.
Oddbjørn (**od**-byoern) Norwegian, from Old Norse Oddbjǫrn, a compound of *oddr* 'spear, point' and *bjǫrn* 'bear.'
Oddgeir (**od**-gæir) Norwegian, from Old Norse Oddgeirr, a compound of *oddr* 'spear, point' and *geirr* 'spear.'
Oddmar (**od**-maar) Norwegian, from Old Norse Oddmarr, a compound of *oddr* 'spear, point' and *marr* 'famous.'
Oddmund (**od**-mewnn) Norwegian, either a variant of Ommund, or a new compound of Odd-. First element *oddr* 'spear, point'; second element *mund* 'protector.' Variant Udmund.
Oddvar (**od**-vaar) Norwegian, a new compound of Odd- (see Odd), and *var* 'warrior.' Norwegian ski champion Oddvar Brå (b. 1951).
Odin (**oo**-dinn) Mainly Norwegian, from Old Norse Óðinn, possibly derived from a word that meant 'wild, furious.' Odin is god of war in Norse mythology. Growing popularity in recent decades along with other mythological names like Ask, Balder, and Brage for boys; Embla and Frøya for girls (see page 146).
Ogmund (**og**-mewnn) Norwegian, from Old Norse Ǫgmundr, a compound of *agi* 'awe, fear' or 'spear, point' and *mund* 'protector.' Very rare, known from Old Norse literature.
Ola (**oo**-laa) Mostly Norwegian, the most common variant of Olav. A top name in Norway from the fifteenth to nineteenth centuries; in some rural communities every fourth man was called Ola. Also used some in Sweden. Danish form Ole. In the United States often changed to Ole. The patronymic Olsen is number 3 in Norway and Olsson number 7 in Sweden. Olsen was most often changed to Olson in the United States, which is considered the prototype of a Scandinavian surname. In the nineteenth century Ole gradually became more common in Norway, influenced by church records, which always used the Danish

spelling Ole, despite the fact that the parents gave the child the name Ola. Ola is definitely the prototype of a Norwegian name, used in expressions like Ola nordmann (which corresponds to John Doe), Ola soldat (GI Joe), and *ola-bukse* (blue jeans).

Olaf (**oo**-laaf) From Old Norse Ólafr; see Olav. Olaf is both a spelling variant and a more historic form. Men named Olav are often called Olaf by family and friends. Olaf is also the English form of Olav, as in Saint Olaf College in Minnesota, named after Olav den heilage or Saint Olaf (d. 1030) and founded by Norwegian immigrants in 1874. See Ahlef.

Olafr (**oo**-laaf-ehr) From Old Norse Ólafr, an historic and literary form; rare. See Olav. Norwegian actor Olafr Havrevold (1895–1972).

Olafur (**oa**-laa-fewr) Icelandic form of Olav. Icelandic president Ólafur Ragnar Grímsson (b. 1943).

Olai (oo-**II**) A form of Olaus, or short form of Nikolai.

Olaus (oo-**laa**-ews) Latin form of Olav.

Olav (**oo**-laav) Mostly Norwegian, from Old Norse Ólafr, Proto-Nordic AnulaibaR, a compound of *anu* 'ancestor' and last element *laibaR* 'heir, descendant.' Immigrants preferred the spelling Olaf, which spread from North America to Great Britain, but was known in England already in the tenth century. Crown Prince Alexander Edward Christian Fredrik (b. 1903) was renamed Olav when his father was designated King Haakon of Norway in 1905, which made the name popular in the twentieth century. See variants Ola, Olaf, Olafr, Olafur, Olai, Olaus, Olavus, Ole, Oleiv, Olof, Oluf. Royal name in Norway: King Olav Tryggvason (d. 1000), King Olav Haraldsson (Saint Olaf; d. 1030), King Olav V (1903–91). Saint Olaf's canonization is celebrated on July 29; the last weekend in July is called Olsok (Feast of Saint Olaf) and is still celebrated in Norway and the Faroe Islands. This has also contributed to the popularity of the name Olav. Known in England as Saint Olave; Saint Olave's Grammar School in London founded 1571. The forms Olaf, Ola, and Ole ranked high in the United States during the late nineteenth century (see page 106). Minnesota politician Martin Olav Sabo (b. 1938). There are several patronymics based on Olav and its variants, but Olsen is the most common.

Olavus (oo-**laa**-vews) Latin form of Olav.

Ole (**oo**-leh) Danish and Norwegian form of Olav. In Norway introduced by ministers who wrote Danish Ole instead of Norwegian Ola in the church registers. Also used in North America, since Ole was considered the "correct" form. Common in double names like Ole-Petter. The comic strip *Ole and Lena* made the name well-known among immigrants in the Midwest. Violinist and composer Ole Bull (1810–80) had unrealistic plans of establishing a Norwegian settlement called Oleana in Pennsylvania. Inventor of the outboard motor Ole Evinrude (1877–1934) was born in Norway as Ole Evinrudstuen. Author Ole Rolvaag (Rølvaag), who wrote *Giants in the Earth*, was born in Norway in 1876. Ole Lukøje is the Danish equivalent to Norwegian Jon Blund and English Wee Willie Winkie or the Sandman.

Oleiv (**oo**-læiv) Norwegian, from Old Norse Óleifr, a parallel form of Olav. Danish Olev.

Olof, Olov (**oo**-loaf) Swedish form of Olav. Pet form Olle. Swedish prime minister Olof Palme (1927–86). Royal name in Sweden, e.g., Olof Trätälja (the Tree-feller, seventh century), Olof Skötkonung (d. 1022).

Oluf (D: **oa**-loof; N/S: **oo**-lewf) Danish form of Olav. Also used in Norway, known through the stories about Oluf i Rallkattlia (Oluf in Rallkattlia) by Arthur Arntzen (b. 1937).

Olve (**oal**-veh) Norwegian, from Old Norse Ølvir, a compound of *alu* 'protection, luck' and a last element 'warrior, hero.' Known from the Norse chieftain Olve på Egge (d. 1022).

Ommund, Omund (**om**-mewnn) Norwegian, variants of Åmund, or most likely Ogmund.

Onar (**oo**-naar) Norwegian, from Old Norse Ánarr; see Annar.

Ordin (**oar**-dinn) Norwegian, from German Ortwin, a compound of *ort* '(sword) point' and *win* 'friend.' Rare, but used some by immigrants from western Norway.

Orla (**oar**-laa) Danish, from an Irish name in Scottish poet James Macpherson's Ossian songs from the 1760s, a compound of *ór* 'gold' and *flaith* 'woman, princess.' Danish politician Orla Lehmann (1810–70). Rare today.

Orm (**oarm**) Norwegian, from Old Norse Ormr 'snake.' Rare today, in some families replaced by Ordin, but in use among immigrants.

Orvar (**oar**-vaar) Norwegian and Swedish, from Old Norse *ǫr* 'arrow.' Known through the saga hero Orvar-Odd (Arrow-Odd).

Oskar, Oscar (**os**-kaar [as in English]) From Irish, a compound of *os* 'deer, hart' and *cara* 'friend.' Popular through *The Poems of Ossian* from the 1760s by Scottish poet James Macpherson; see Orla. A top name in the nineteenth century. Royal name in Sweden: King Oskar I (b. 1799; reigned 1844–59) and King Oskar II (b. 1829; reigned 1872–1907), whose name and likeness grace the famous King Oscar Sardines.

Osmund (**os**-mewnn; S: **os**-mewnd) Norwegian, a variant of Åsmund.

Osvald (D: **os**-væl; N/S: **os**-vaald) From Old Norse Osvaldr, a compound of *áss* 'god' and *valdr* 'ruler,' but most likely an early loan from English. Rare after World War II. Osvald is a character in Norwegian writer Henrik Ibsen's play *Gengangere* (*Ghosts*, 1881). Mathematician Oswald Veblen (1880–1960) was of Norwegian descent.

Ottar (**ot**-taar) From Old Norse Óttarr, a compound of *ótti* 'fear, anxiety' and *arr* 'warrior' or 'spear.' Some usage before World War II. Norwegian Chieftain Ottar in Hålogaland in the ninth century.

Otto, Otte (**ot**-to, **ot**-teh) From German, short form of names with the element *ot-* 'property, wealth,' e.g., Otmar. Danish actor Otto Brandenburg (1934–2007). Swedish polar explorer Otto Nordenskjöld (1869–1928).

Ove (**oo**-veh) Danish, derived from a word meaning 'spear.' Fairly popular before and after 1940. Common in double names like Geir-Ove.

Paal (**poal**) See Pål.

Palle (D: **pæl**-leh; S: **paal**-leh) Danish, from Old Norse Pálni of uncertain origin; also pet form of Paul. Falling popularity since the 1970s. Danish author Palle Lauring (1909–96). Swedish actor Palle (Paul) Granditsky (1923–2001).

Paul (**poul**) Short form of Latin Paulus 'small.' Borrowed in the Viking Age into Old Norse as Páll; see Pål. Among immigrants used for Pål and Paal.

Peder (D: **pay**-theh; N: **pay**-dehr) Danish form of Latin Petrus 'stone, rock.' Danish ministers in Norway most often wrote Peder in church registers instead of Per. Common among immigrants. Danish statesman Peder Griffenfeld (1635–99). Norwegian painter Peder Balke (1804–87). Norwegian Danish painter P. S. (Peder Severin) Krøyer (1851–1909) painted many of the most famous paintings from Skagen in Denmark. See Per, Peter, Petter, Pär.

Peer (**pehr**) Spelling variant of Per, as in the play *Peer Gynt* (1867) by Norwegian writer Henrik Ibsen.

Pelle (**pehl**-leh) Danish and Swedish pet form of Per or Peter. Popular from the title character in the novel *Pelle Erobreren* (*Pelle the Conqueror*, 1910) by the Dane Martin Andersen Nexø.

Per (**pehr**; S: **pær**) Contracted form of Peter, frequent in all countries; in Sweden also spelled Pär. Common in double names like Per-Anders. Per and Pål are the names of the older brothers of Cinderlad, the hero of many Norwegian folktales. Also used in common expressions like "nysgjerrig-per" (Nosy Nancy, Miss Nosy-Parker) and "viktig-per" (a conceited fellow). The Norwegian Per Petterson (b. 1952), author of *Out Stealing Horses*. Swedish author Per Olof Sundman (1922–92). Written form in the immigrant years mostly Peder, hence common patronymic Pedersen and not Persen as one should expect. See Kleng.

Peter (**pay**-tehr) From Latin Petrus 'stone,
rock,' also in Old Norse Pétr. The most
common Danish first name in 1985, also
frequently used as a middle name, such as
Hans Peter. Swedish actor Peter Stormare
(b. 1953). Norwegian naval hero Peter Wes-
sel Tordenskjold (1690–1720). Danish car-
toon artist Peter Madsen (b. 1958).

Petter (**peht**-tehr) Variant of Peter. Most common in Norway. Norwegian hymn writer
Petter Dass (1647–1707).

Poul (**poal**) Danish form of Paul. Former
Danish prime minister Poul Nyrup Rasmussen (b. 1943).

Povel (**poa**-vehl) Swedish form of Paul. Swedish entertainer Povel Ramel (1922–2007).

Preben (**pray**-behn) Danish, from Old Danish Pridbor, a compound of *prid* 'foremost,
leading' and *bor* 'battle.' Falling popularity.
Danish soccer player Preben Elkjær
(b. 1957).

Pär (**pær**) Swedish spelling of Per. Swedish
author Pär Lagerkvist (1891–1974).

Pål, Paal (**poal**) Mostly Norwegian, from Old
Norse Páll; see Paul. In church registers
written Paul, hence no patronymic Pålsen,
but the form Pål as a first name is far more
frequent than Paul. See also Per. "Per og
Pål" is a common Norwegian expression for
everyman.

Påvel (**poa**-vehl) Swedish variant of Povel.

Ragnar (**raag**-naar) Mostly Norwegian, common also in Sweden, from Old Norse Rag-
narr, a compound of *ragn* 'advice, decision'
and *arr* possibly 'warrior,' corresponding to
German and French Rainer. Ragnar Lodbrok was a legendary Danish Viking chieftain in the ninth century. In the computer
game *Civilization*, Ragnar Lodbrok repre-
sents the Viking civilization. President of
Iceland Ólafur Ragnar Grímsson (b. 1943).

Ragnvald (**raang**-vaald) Mainly Norwegian,
from Old Norse Rǫgnvaldr, a compound
of *ragn* 'advice, decision' and *valdr* 'ruler,'
corresponding to English Ronald. Ragnvald
Mørejarl, Earl of Møre in Norway in the
ninth century. Ragnvald Nestos, governor
of North Dakota in the 1920s, was born in
Norway in 1877.

Ralf (**raalf**) Mainly Danish, from English
Ralph.

Ramn (**raam**) See Ravn.

Randolf, Randolv, Randulf, Randulv (**raan**-
dolf, **raan**-dolv, **raan**-dewlf, **raan**-dewlv)
Norwegian and Swedish, an Old Norse
compound of *rǫnd* 'shield' and *ulfr* 'wolf,'
corresponding to English Randolph.

Rasmus (D: **raas**-moos; N/S: **raas**-mews)
Mostly Danish and Norwegian, common
also in Sweden today, from Greek Erasmos,
derived from a word meaning 'to love.'
Popular especially before World War II.
Danish linguist Rasmus Rask (1787–1832).
Main character Rasmus Berg, Latinized
form Erasmus Montanus, in Norwegian
Danish author Ludvig Holberg's play *Erasmus Montanus* (1723). Norwegian American
professor Rasmus B. Anderson (1846–1936)
initiated the observance of Leif Erikson
Day (October 9) in the United States.

Raval, Ravel (**raa**-vaal, **raa**-vehl) Swedish
forms of Ragnvald. Rare.

Ravn (**raavn**) From Old Norse Rafn 'raven,'
originally most likely a byname 'black.'
Rare.

Regin (**ray**-ginn) From Old Norse *reginn*
'advisor.' In Norse mythology Regin was a
name for the supernatural powers. A main
character in the story of Sigurd the Dragonslayer is the blacksmith Regin, who also has
magical powers. Rare. Faroese author
Regin Dahl (1918–2007).

Regner (**ræi**-nehr) Danish form of Ragnar.

Reidar (**ræi**-daar) Mainly Norwegian, from
Old Norse Reiðarr, composed of *reið*
'house, home' and *arr*, of uncertain origin.
Fairly common up to 1950. Among immigrants also Reier.

Reidulf, Reiulf, Reiolv, Reidolv, Reiel (**ræi**-
dewlf, **ræi**-ewlf, **ræi**-olv, **ræi**-dolf, **ræi**-ehl)
Also other spelling variants, from Old
Norse Reiðulfr, a compound of *reið* 'house,
home' and *ulfr* 'wolf.' Norwegian politician
Reiulf Steen (b. 1933).

Reier (**ræi**-ehr) Older form of Reidar.

Reimund (D: **ræi**-moon; N: **ræi**-mewnn; S:
ræi-mewnd) Either a new coinage from *rei-*
and *mund* 'protector,' or from German Rag-
inmund; for first element see Reinhard.

Rein (**ræin**) Either from Old Norse *reinn* 'reindeer,' or first element in German names like Reinhard. Belongs to the group of names derived from the animal kingdom like Bjørn, Orm, Ulf.

Reinert (**ræi**-nehrt) From German Reinhard.

Reinhard, Reinhardt (**ræin**-haart) From German Raginhart, a compound of *ragin* 'advice, decision' and *hart* 'hard.'

Reinhold, Reinholdt (**ræin**-holt) Mainly Danish, from German Raginald, a compound of *ragin* 'advice, decision' and *vald* 'ruler.' Same compound as Ragnvald.

Rejar, Rejer, Rejor (**ræi**-aar, **ræi**-ehr, **ray**-yoar) Forms of Reidar.

Roald (D: **roo**-æl; N: **roo**-aald) Mostly Norwegian, from Old Norse Róaldr, a compound of *ro* 'honor, fame' and *valdr* 'ruler.' See Vrold, Vrål. Popular before 1950. Norwegian polar explorer Roald Amundsen (1872–1928). British author Roald Dahl (1916–90) was of Norwegian descent.

Roar (**roo**-aar) Mostly Norwegian, from Old Norse Róarr, a compound of *ro* 'honor, fame' and *ar* 'spear,' same as Rodgeir, Roger. Popular after World War II. Norwegian ski jumping champion Roar Ljøkelsøy (b. 1976).

Rodgeir, Rogeir (**roo[d]**-gæir) Norwegian, from Old Norse Róðgeirr, a compound of *rod* 'honor, fame' and *geirr* 'spear.' Norse form of Roger.

Roe (**roo**-eh) Norwegian, from Old Norse Rói, either originally Roir of disputed origin or short form of names with *ro* 'honor, fame.' Rói in Faroese. Faroese author and philosopher Rói Reynagarð Patturson (b. 1947).

Roger (**roa**-gehr) See Rodgeir.

Rognald (**rog**-naald) A form of Ragnvald.

Roland (**roo**-laan[d]) From German; first element *ro* 'honor, fame' and second element *land*. Very rare. Norwegian ballad "Roland og Magnus kongjen."

Rolf, Rolv (**rolf**) From Old Norse Rólfr, a contracted form of *ro* 'honor, fame' and *ulfr* 'wolf.' Popular especially before 1950. Danish legendary king Rolf Krake. The Norwegian Viking Gange-Rolv conquered Normandy in 911.

Ronald (D: **roo**-næl; N: **roo**-naald; S: **ron**-aald) From Scottish, same meaning as Ragnvald.

Runar (**rew**-naar) Most likely a new coinage of *run* 'rune, secret lore' and the male suffix *ar*. Popular especially in Norway from the 1950s.

Rune (D: **roo**-neh; N/S: **rew**-neh) Most likely a short form of various names with *run* 'rune, secret lore,' like Runolv. Common after 1950, especially in Norway. Norwegian drummer Rune Solheim (b. 1978).

Saksbjørn (**Saaks**-byoern) From Old Norse Saxbjørn; first element *sax* 'large knife, sword' and last element *bjørn* 'bear.' Rare.

Sakse, Saxe (**saak**-seh) Derived from Old Norse *sax* 'large knife, sword.' Rare. The Danish historian Saxe Grammaticus (ca. 1200).

Salmund (**saal**-mewnn) From Old Norse Salmundr, a compound of *salr* 'house' and *mundr* 'protector.' Variants Samund, Solmund, Somund, Såmund. Rare.

Salve (**saal**-veh) Norwegian, from Old Norse Salvi of complicated origin, perhaps derived from a compound with the elements *salr* 'house' and *ve(r)* 'warrior, giant.' Variants Solve, Sølve, Såvi, and Såve. Rare.

Samson (**saam**-soan) From Hebrew 'sun.' Used some by immigrants in the last decades of the nineteenth century, rare today.

Sandolv, Sandov (**saan**-dolv, **saan**-doav) See Sondov.

Sebjørn (**say**-byoern) See Sigbjørn, Sæbjørn.

Sefast (**say**-faast) Swedish, a compound of *sær* 'sea' and *fast* 'firm, reliable.'

Seger, Segol (**say**-gehr, **say**-gool) Swedish forms of Sigurd.

Sejer, Seier (**sæi**-ehr) Danish, from Siger, a compound of *sigr* 'victory' and *er* 'warrior,' or a variant of Sigurd.

Seming, Semming (**say**-ming, **sehm**-ming) See Sæming.

Semund (**say**-mewnn) See Sæmund.

Serkve (**særk**-veh) See Sverker.

Sevald (**say**-vaald) See Sigvald, Sævald.

Sevard (**say**-vaard) See Sævar(d).

Sevat (**say**-vaat) Norwegian dialect form of Sigvat.

Seved (**say**-vehd) See Sigvid.

Severin, Sevrin (seh-veh-**reen**, sehv-**reen**) From Latin Severinus 'severe, serious.' Used some ca. 1900. Swedish short form Seve. See Søren.

Severt, Sever (**see**-vehr[t]) Americanized forms of Sivert.

Sig- Frequent first element from Old Norse *sigr* 'victory,' in names like Sigbjørn and Sigurd.

Sigbjørn (**sig**-byoern) Norwegian and Swedish, from Old Norse Sigbjǫrn, a compound of *sigr* 'victory' and *bjǫrn* 'bear.' Norwegian variant Sebjørn, Swedish pet form Sibbe. Norwegian fiddler Sigbjørn Bernhoft Osa (1910–90).

Sigfast (**sig**-faast) From Old Norse Sigfastr, a compound of *sigr* 'victory' and *fastr* 'firm, reliable.'

Sigfred (D: **see**-frehth; N: **seeg**-frehd) A newer form of German Sigifrith, a compound of *sigr* 'victory' and *frith* 'peace.' Modern German Siegfried. Danish actor Sigfred Johansen (1908–53).

Sigfrid, Sigfried (**seeg**-freed) Swedish variant of Sigfred. Sweden's apostle Saint Sigfrid in the eleventh century.

Sigfus (D: **sigg**-foos; N/S: **sig**-fews) From Old Norse Sigfúss, a compound of *sigr* 'victory' and *fúss* 'eager, keen.'

Sigge (**sig**-geh) Swedish pet form of names with Sig-. The Swedish author Sigge Eklund's given name is Sigvard (b. 1974).

Siggeir (**sig**-gæir) From Old Norse Siggeirr, a compound of *sigr* 'victory' and *geirr* 'spear.' Rare.

Sigleiv, Sigleif (**sig**-læiv, **sig**-læif) A compound of *sigr* 'victory' and *leiv* 'heir, descendant.' Rare.

Sigmar (**sig**-maar) A compound of *sigr* 'victory' and *mar* 'famous.' Rare.

Sigmund (D: **sig**-moon; N: **sig**-mewnn; S: **sig**-mewnd) From Old Norse Sigmundr, a compound of *sigr* 'victory' and *mundr* 'protector.' Common, but falling popularity in recent decades. Sometimes confused with Simon. German form Sigismund. Norwegian musician and composer Sigmund Groven (b. 1946). Professor Sigmund Skard

(1903–95) taught American literature at the University of Oslo and translated several American works into New Norwegian.

Sigstein (**sig**-stæin) A compound of *sigr* 'victory' and *steinn* 'stone'; corresponds to Swedish Sixten. Rare.

Sigsten (**siks**-tehn) See Sixten.

Sigtor (**sig**-toor) A more recent coinage of *sigr* 'victory' and the god's name Thor. Rare.

Sigtrygg (**sig**-trewgg) A compound of *sigr* 'victory' and *trygg* 'safe, confident.'

Sigurd, Sigur (D: **see**-goord; N/S: **sig**-gewr[d], **see**-gewrd) From Old Norse Sigurðr, a compound of *sigr* 'victory' and a form of *varðr* 'protector,' i.e., same as Sigvard. Popular down through the centuries, the most common man's name until ca. 1350. Common dialect form Sjur. The legendary Germanic hero Sigurd Fåvnesbane (Sigurd Dragonslayer). Norwegian king Sigurd Jorsalfar (1090–1130). The legendary ninth-century Swedish king Sigurd Ring.

Sigvald (**sig**-vaald) From Old Norse Sigvaldr, a compound of *sigr* 'victory' and *valdr* 'ruler.' Variant Sevald.

Sigvard, Sigvart (**sig**-vaard, **sig**-vaart) German form of Sigurd, borrowed through Danish. Fairly common around 1900. Younger forms Siver, Sivert, Sivar, Syver, Syvert. Swedish count Sigvard Bernadotte of Wisborg (1907–2002). Norwegian entertainer Sigvart Dagsland (b. 1963). The Danish ballad figure Sivar Snarensvend corresponds to Sigurd Fåvnesbane (see Sigurd).

Sigvat (**sig**-vaat) From Old Norse Sigvatr, a compound of *sigr* 'victory' and *hvatr*, possibly 'brave, quick.' Norwegian dialect form Sevat. Norse skald (poet) Sigvat Tordsson lived in the eleventh century.

Sigve (**sig**-veh) Norwegian, from Old Norse Sigviðr, a compound of *sigr* 'victory' and *viðr* 'wood, forest.'

Sigvid (**sig**-veed) Swedish, a compound of *sigr* 'victory' and *viðr* 'wood, forest.' Variant Seved.

Simen (**see**-mehn) Mostly Norwegian, a form of Simon. Popular in recent decades.

Simon (**see**-moan) From Hebrew 'hearkening.' Rare today.

Sindre (**sin**-dreh) Norwegian, from Old Norse Sindri, derived from a verb *sindra* 'sparkle, flash.' Popular in recent decades. The son of Icelandic singer Björk is named Sindri.

Sivar, Sivard (**see**-vaar[d]) Swedish forms of Sigvard.

Siver, Sivert (**see**-vehr[t]) Mostly Norwegian, younger forms of Sigvard. Fairly common in the immigration period, also in recent years. In North America written Sever or Severt.

Sixten (**siks**-tehn) Swedish, a compound of *sigr* 'victory' and *steinn* 'stone.' Rarer form: Sigsten. Ski champion Sixten Jernberg (b. 1929).

Sjugur (**shew**-gewr) Norwegian dialect form of Sigurd.

Sjur, Sjurd (**shewr**[d]) Mostly Norwegian, more recent forms of Sigurd. Common before the twentieth century.

Skjalg (**shaalg**) From Old Norse Skjalgr 'cross-eyed, crooked.' A single example is known in the Middle Ages, the Norwegian Viking Erling Skjalgsson (ca. 975–1028), son of Skjalg.

Skjold, Sköld (D: **skyold**; N/S: **shold, shoeld**) From Old Norse *skjǫldr* 'shield.' According to legends the Danish king Skjold is ancestor of the royal lineage Skjoldungerne.

Skule (**skew**-leh) Norwegian, from Old Norse Skúli 'protection, shelter.' The Norwegian Viking Skule jarl (1189–1240). Norwegian sculptor Skule Waksvik (b. 1927).

Snorre (**snor**-reh, **snoor**-reh) Mostly Norwegian, from Old Norse Snorri 'the quick one' or possibly 'the wild one.' Fairly frequent in recent decades. Historian Snorre Sturlason (Snorri Sturluson; 1179–1241).

Solmund (D: **soal**-moon; N: **sool**-mewnn) A form of Salmund.

Solve (**soal**-veh) A variant of Salve.

Sondov, Sondolv (**son**-dov, **son**-dolv) From Old Norse Sandulfr, a compound of *sand* 'sand' and *ulfr* 'wolf.'

Sondre (**son**-dreh) Norwegian, from Old Norse Sundri, a compound possibly of words meaning 'swimming' and 'peace, protection.' Originally a name in the Telemark area of Norway, but common today all over the country. Father of skiing Sondre Norheim (1825–97), from Telemark.

Sone (**soo**-neh) Norwegian, from Old Norse Sóni, of uncertain origin, or Swedish variant of Sune.

Soren (**soar**-ehn) American spelling of Søren.

Staffan (**staaf**-faan) Swedish form of Latin Stephanus 'garland, crown.' Staffan stalledreng in the Swedish Christmas song, known as "Saint Steven and Herod" (child ballad 22) in English.

Steen, Sten (**stayn**) Mostly Danish and Swedish, from Old Norse *steinn* 'stone.' Danish rock singer Steen Jørgensen (b. 1959). Swedish statesman Sten Sture (1440–1503).

Steffen (**stehf**-fehn) Norwegian and Danish form; see Staffan.

Stein (**stæin**) Norwegian, from Old Norse *steinn* 'stone.' Fairly common in the decades around 1950. Norwegian author Stein Mehren (b. 1935). Champion slalom skier Stein Eriksen (b. 1927), who emigrated from Norway to Utah after the 1952 Oslo Olympics.

Steinar (**stæi**-naar) Norwegian, from Old Norse Steinarr, a compound of *steinn* 'stone' and *arr* 'warrior' or 'spear' or 'protector.' Popular in the decades around 1950. Danish Stener; Swedish Stenar.

Steingrim (**stæin**-grim) Norwegian, from Old Norse Steingrímr, a compound of *steinn* 'stone' and *grímr* 'man with a helmet or a mask.'

Steinulv, Steinulf (**stæin**-ewlv, **stæin**-ewlf) From Old Norse Steinulfr, a compound of *steinn* 'stone' and *ulfr* 'wolf.'

Stener, Stenar (**stay**-nehr, **stay**-naar) Danish form and Swedish form of Steinar.

Stian (**stee**-aan) From Old Norse Stígandr 'wanderer,' or maybe today also from the last element in Kristian. Popular in the decades after 1960.

Stig (D: **stee**; N/S: **steeg**) Derived from the verb *stíga* 'wander, step,' originally Danish. Fairly common. Danish singer Stig Rossen (b. 1962). Swedish author Stig Dagerman (1923–54). Swedish author Stieg Larsson (1954–2004), author of *The Girl with the*

Dragon Tattoo (2007), was christened Karl Stig-Erland Larsson.

Stillev, Stillef, Stilluv, Stellef, Stillaug (**stil**-lehv, **stil**-lehf, **stil**-lewv, **stehl**-lehf, **stil**-loug) Variants of Old Norse Styrlaugr, a compound of *styrr* 'commotion, struggle' and *laug* 'devoted to.'

Sture (**stew**-reh) Swedish, originally a byname derived from *stura* 'cross, grumpy, obstinate.' Swedish statesman Sten Sture the Younger (1493–1550).

Sturla, Sturle (**stewr**-la, **stewr**-leh) Norwegian, from Old Norse Sturla, derived from a verb that meant 'disturb, confuse.' Sturla Tordsson (1115–83) is ancestor to the chieftain lineage called Sturlungane. Norwegian actor and director Svein Sturla Hungnes (b. 1946).

Styrbjörn (**stewr**-byoern) Swedish; last element *björn* 'bear.' Construed with *styr* 'commotion' as a compound meaning 'the wild bear.' Swedish warrior Styrbjörn Starke (the Strong) in the tenth century.

Styrk, Størk (**stewrk**, **stoerk**) Norwegian, corresponding to Old Norse *styrkr* 'strength, power.'

Styrkar, Styrkår, Størker (**stewr**-kaar, **stewr**-koar, **stoer**-kehr) Norwegian, from Old Norse Styrkárr, a compound of *styrr* 'commotion, struggle' and *kárr* 'curly.'

Ståle (**stoa**-leh) Norwegian, from Old Norse *stål* 'steel.' Popular in the decades after 1950. Norwegian sculptor Ståle Kyllingstad (1903–87).

Sune (D: **soo**-neh; S: **sew**-neh) Danish and Swedish, from Old Norse *sunr* 'son.' The Danish Sunesønnerne (ca. 1200), seven sons of Sune Ebbesøn.

Svale (**svaa**-leh) From Old Norse Svali, of uncertain origin.

Svante (D: **svæn**-teh; S: **svaan**-teh) Swedish, short form of Wendish Svantopolk; first element *svanto* 'holy.' Mostly assumed to be a nickname for Sven. Considered the prototype of a Swedish name. Svantepolk Knutsson was a Danish Swedish chieftain in the thirteenth century.

Svein (**svæin**) Norwegian, from Old Norse Sveinn; see Svend. Popular around 1950.

The Norwegian chieftain Svein Håkonsson (d. 1016).

Sveinbjørn, Svenbjörn (**svæin**-byoern, **svehn**-byoern) A compound of *sveinn* 'swain, young man' and *bjørn* 'bear.'

Sveinke, Svenke (**svæin**-keh, **svehn**-keh) Norwegian, from Old Norse Sveinki 'small boy'; derived from Svein.

Sveinung (**svæin**-ong) Norwegian, from Old Norse Sveinungr 'descendant or son of Svein.' Variant Svenning.

Svend, Sven (**svehnn**) From Old Norse *sveinn* 'swain, young man.' Svend is most common in Denmark; Sven in Sweden. In Norway also Svein. Several Danish kings in the Middle Ages, e.g., Svend Tveskæg (ca. 960–1014), called Svein Tjugeskjegg in Norwegian and Sweyn Forkbeard in English. Sven Oftedal, born 1844 in Norway, helped found the Lutheran Free Church in America. Canadian politician Svend Robinson (b. 1952) is of Danish descent.

Svenning (**svehn**-ning) Variant of Sveinung.

Sverker, Sverke (**svær**-kehr, **svær**-keh) Probably originally a compound of *svart* 'black' and *geirr* 'spear.' Royal name in Sweden: King Sverker (d. 1156). Swedish diplomat Carl Sverker Åström (b. 1915).

Sverre (**svær**-reh) Mainly Norwegian, from Old Norse Sverrir, most likely a nickname 'wild, undisciplined man,' derived from the verb *sverra* 'swing, circle.' Norwegian king Sverre Sigurdsson (1151–1202). Norwegian architect Sverre Fehn (1924–2009).

Sylfest, Sølfest, Sylvester (**sewl**-fehst, **soel**-fehst, sewl-**vehs**-tehr) From Latin Silvester 'of the woods.' Short form Sylve.

Syver, Syvert (**sew**-vehr[t]) Norwegian, younger forms of Sigvard. Used some by immigrants.

Sæbjørn (**sæ**-byoern) Norwegian, from Old Norse Sæbjørn, a compound of *sær* 'sea' and *bjørn* 'bear.' Also spelled Sebjørn.

Sæming (**sæ**-ming) Norwegian, from Old Norse Sæmingr, derived from *sámr* 'dark.' Mostly spelled Seming, Semming.

Sæmund, Sämund (**sæ**-mewnn; S: **sæ**-mewnd) A compound of *sær* 'sea' and *mund* 'protector.'

Sævald (**sæ**-vaald) Norwegian, a compound of *sær* 'sea' and *vald* 'ruler.'

Sævar(d) (**sæ**-vaar[d]) Norwegian, a compound of *sær* 'sea' and *vard* 'protector' or *ar* of uncertain origin.

Sølve (**soel**-veh) A variant of Salve.

Søren (**soern**) Mostly Danish, a variant of Severin. A top name in the first decades after 1950, but declining in recent years. Considered the prototype of a Danish name. Danish philosopher Søren Kirkegaard (1813–55). American spelling Soren.

Såmund (**soa**-mewnn) A variant of Salmund.

Såve, Såvi (**soa**-veh, **soa**-vee) Variants of Salve.

Tage (D: **tæ**-eh; S: **taa**-geh) From Danish Taki 'guarantor,' derived from the verb *taka* 'take.' Former Swedish prime minister Tage Erlander (1901–85).

Tallak (**taal**-laak) Norwegian form of Tollak.

Talleiv, Tallev (**taal**-læiv, **taal**-lehv) Norwegian variants of Torleiv.

Tarald, Tharald (**taa**-raald) Norwegian, a variant of Old Norse Þóraldr, a combination of Thor (the god) and *aldr* 'ruler.'

Tarje, Tarjei (**taar**-yeh, **taar**-jæi) Norwegian variants of Torgeir. Norwegian author Tarjei Vesaas (1897–1970); see Terje.

Tellev, Tellef (**tehl**-lehv, **tehl**-lehf) Norwegian variants of Torleiv.

Terje (**tær**-yeh) Norwegian, a more recent form of Torgeir. The poem "Terje Vigen" (1862) by Norwegian writer Henrik Ibsen.

Terkel, Therkild (**tær**-kehl, **tær**-kill) Danish forms of Torkild, from Torkjell.

Theis, Teis (**tæis**) Danish, from a Dutch form of Greek Matteus 'gift of God.'

Thor (**toor**) See Tor.

Thure (D: **too**-reh; S: **tew**-reh) See Ture.

Thyge (**tew**-yeh) See Tyge.

Thøger (**toe**-yeh) See Tøger.

Tjalve (**khaal**-veh) From Old Norse Þjalfi, possibly 'one who encompasses, holds together.' In Norse mythology Tjalve was the god Thor's servant. Rare. See page 146.

Tjeran(d) (**khehr**-aan[d]) Norwegian, from Old Norse Hjarrandr; see Hjarrand.

Tjodgeir (**khood**-gæir) Norwegian, from Old Norse Þjóðgeirr, a compound of *þjóð* 'people' and *geirr* 'spear.' See Tøger.

Tjodolv (**khood**-olf) From Old Norse Þjóðolfr, a compound of *þjóð* 'people' and *ulfr* 'wolf.' See Kjølv, Tjølv.

Tjostolv (**khoos**-tolv) Norwegian, from Old Norse Þjóstolfr, a compound of *þjóst* 'recklessness, fury' and *ulfr* 'wolf.'

Tjølv (**khoelv**) A more recent form of Tjodolv. See also Kjølv.

Tjøstel, Tjøstol, Tjøstolv, Tjøstov (**khoes**-tehl, **khoes**-toll, **khoes**-tolv, **khoes**-toav) Norwegian variants of Tjostolv.

Toke (**too**-keh) Danish, either short form of Torkild or a byname 'fool.'

Tole, Tolle (**toa**-leh, **tol**-leh) Variants of Tåle.

Tollak, Tollek (**tol**-laak, **tol**-lehk) Norwegian forms of Old Norse Þorlákr, a compound of Thor (the god) and *lákr* 'battle, giant.'

Tolleiv, Tollev, Tollef (**tol**-læiv, **tol**-lehv, **tol**-lehf) Norwegian forms of Torleiv.

Tolv (**tolv**) Norwegian, from Old Norse Þolfr, most likely a contracted form of Torolv. See Tov.

Tor, Thor (**toor**) The modern form of the name of the god of thunder, Old Norse Þórr 'the thunderer.' The god's name was not used as a given name in the Middle Ages, so the modern form may also be derived from Old Norse Þórðr (see Tord), which is more historically correct. Frequent element in both men's and women's names. Norwegian archeologist and ethnologist Thor Heyerdahl (1914–2002). Norwegian bicycle racer Thor Hushovd (b. 1978). Very common. See page 146.

Toralv, Toralf (**toor**-aalv, **toor**-aalf) From Old Norse Þóralfr, a compound of Tor (the god Thor) and *alfr* 'elf.'

Torben (**toar**-behn) Danish variant of Torbjørn.

Torbjørn, Torbjörn, Thorbjørn, Thorbjörn (**toor**-byoern) From Old Norse Þorbjǫrn, a compound of Tor (the god Thor) and *bjǫrn* 'bear.' Former Swedish prime minister Thorbjörn Fälldin (b. 1926).

Tord, Thord (**toard**) Norwegian and Swedish, from Old Norse Þórðr, a contracted form of the elements Tor (the god Thor) and *frøðr* 'peace.' See Tor.

Tore, Thore (**too**-reh) From Old Norse Þórir, either derived from Tor or originally a compound of Tor (the god Thor) and a last element *vér*, probably 'giant, he-man.' Very common in the Middle Ages and also today.

Torfinn, Thorfinn (**toor**-finn) Mostly Norwegian, from Old Norse Þórfinnr, a compound of Tor (the god Thor) and *finnr* 'Finn, Lapp.'

Torgeir, Thorgeir, Torger, Thorger (**toor**-gæir, **toor**-gehr) Mostly Norwegian, from Old Norse Þorgeirr, a compound of Tor (the god Thor) and *geirr* 'spear.'

Torgils, Thorgils (**toor**-gills) From Old Norse Þorgísl, a compound of Tor (the god Thor) and *gísl*, most likely a weapon.

Torgny (**toarg**-new) Mostly Swedish, from Old Norse Þorgný, a compound of Tor (the god Thor) and *gnýr* 'noise, clamour.' Torgny Segerstedt (1876–1945), editor-in-chief of *Göteborgs Handels- och Sjöfartstidning*, was a sharp critic of Sweden's neutral position toward Nazi Germany during World War II.

Torgrim (**toor**-grim) Norwegian, from Old Norse Þorgrímr, a compound of Tor (the god Thor) and *grímr* 'man with a helmet or a mask.'

Torjus (**toar**-yews) Norwegian, a form of Torgils.

Torkel (**toar**-kehl) Mostly Norwegian, a form of Torkjell.

Torkild, Thorkild (**toar**-kill) Mainly Danish, a form of Torkjell. Danish author Thorkild Hansen (1927–89).

Torkjell, Thorkjell, Torkjeld, Thorkjeld (**toor**-khehl) From Old Norse Þorketill, a compound of Tor (the god Thor) and *ketill* 'kettle, helmet.'

Torleiv, Thorleiv, Torleif, Thorleif (N: **toor**-læiv, **toor**-læif; S: **toor**-læif) Mostly Norwegian, from Old Norse Þorleifr, a compound of Tor (the god Thor) and *leifr* 'heir, descendant.'

Tormod, Thormod (**toor**-mood) Norwegian, from Old Norse Þormóðr, a compound of Tor (the god Thor) and *móðr* 'courageous.' The Icelandic skald (poet) Tormod Kolbrunarskald (ca. 1000).

Torolv, Thorolv, Torolf, Thorolf (**toor**-olv, **toor**-olf) From Old Norse Þórolfr, a compound of Tor (the god Thor) and *ulfr* 'wolf.' See Tolv.

Torstein, Thorstein, Torsten, Thorsten (**toar**-stæin, **toar**-stehn) From Old Norse Þorsteinn, a compound of Tor (the god Thor) and *steinn* 'stone.' In Danish and Swedish Torsten. Former Swedish foreign minister Torsten Nilsson (1905–97). Sociologist and economist Thorstein Veblen (1857–1929) was of Norwegian descent.

Torvald, Thorvald (D: **toar**-væl; N/S: **toar**-vaald) From Old Norse Þorvaldr, a compound of Tor (the god Thor) and *valdr* 'ruler.'

Tov (**toav**) Norwegian dialect form of Tolv.

Troels, Truels (**trools**) Danish variants of Truls. Danish historiographer Troels Frederik Troels-Lund (1840–1921).

Trond, Tron (**troan, troon**) Mostly Norwegian, from Old Norse Þróndr 'man from Trøndelag.' Very popular in the 1970s and 1980s.

Truls (D: **trools**; N/S: **trewls**) Danish form of Torgils.

Trygve, Tryggve (**trewg**-veh) Mostly Norwegian, from Old Norse Tryggvi 'reliable, faithful.' King Olav Tryggvason (d. 1000). The first secretary-general of the United Nations was Norwegian Trygve Lie (1896–1968). Not common among immigrants; widely used in the twentieth century.

Trym (**trewm**) Norwegian, from Old Norse Trymr, the "cover" name of a giant (jotun) in Norse mythology. See page 147.

Tue (**too**-eh) Danish, derived from names like Torfinn and Torfast.

Ture (D: **too**-reh; S: **tew**-reh) Danish and Swedish form of Tore.

Tyge (**tew**-yeh) Danish, from Old Danish Tyki, most likely derived from names with Tor-, such as Torkild.

Tøger, Thøger (**toe**-yeh) Danish form of German Theodgar, a compound of *þjóð* 'people' and *gar* 'spear.'

Tønnes (**toen**-nehs) Norwegian and Danish form of Latin Antonius, of uncertain origin.

Tørres, Tørris (**toer**-rehs, **toer**-ris) Norwegian form of Torgils.

Tåle (**toa**-leh) Most likely from the first element of names beginning with Tor-.

Udmund (**ewd**-mewnn) See Oddmund.

Uffe (**uhf**-feh) Mainly Danish pet form of Ulf. Danish politician Uffe Ellemann-Jensen (b. 1941).

Ulf, Ulv (D: **uhlf**; N/S: **ewlf**) From Old Norse *ulfr* 'wolf.' Ulf is most common.

Ulrik, Ulrich (D: **uhl**-rik; N/S: **ewl**-rik) From German Ulrich, a compound of *ul* 'heirloom, inheritance' and *rich* 'powerful, ruler.' Danish actor Ulrich Thomsen (b. 1963).

Urban (D: **uhr**-bænn; S: **ewr**-baan) Danish and Swedish, from Latin Urbanus 'city dweller.'

Uwe (**oo**-veh) Danish, a short form of names like Ulrik.

Vagn (**vown**) Danish, from Old Norse *vagn* 'wagon.' English Wagne.

Valdemar (D: **væl**-deh-maar; N/S: **vaal**-deh-maar) Danish form of Russian Vladimir. Danish king Valdemar den Store (the Great; 1131–82).

Vebjørn, Vibjörn (**vay**-byoern, **vee**-byoern) Norwegian and Swedish, from Old Norse Vébjǫrn, a compound of *vé-* 'home, sacred place' and *bjǫrn* 'bear.'

Vegard (**vay**-gaard) Norwegian, from Old Norse Végarðr, a compound of *vé-* 'home, sacred place' and *garðr* 'fence, protection.' Popular in recent decades. Norwegian cross country skier Vegard Ulvang (b. 1963).

Vemund, Vimund (**vay**-mewnn, **vee**-mewnn; S: **vee**-mewnd) Norwegian and Swedish, from Old Norse Vémundr, a compound of *vé-* 'home, sacred place' and *mundr* 'protector.'

Vetle (**veht**-leh) Norwegian, from Old Norse Vetrliðr, most likely 'one-year-old bear.'

Vidar (**vee**-daar) Mostly Norwegian, from Old Norse Víðarr, a compound of *víðr* 'forest' and *arr* 'warrior.'

Vidkun, Vidkunn (**vid**-kewnn) Norwegian, from Old Norse Víðkunnr, 'well-known, famous.' Vidkun Quisling (1887–1945)

served as minister-president of Norway during World War II, appointed by the German authorities. After the war he was tried for high treason and subsequently executed by firing squad. Because of Quisling's actions, his first name gained negative associations after the war, and it is rare today.

Viggo (**vee**-go) Mainly Danish, Latin form of Vigge, a short form of names with *vig-* 'battle.' Known from the work by Saxo (Grammaticus), who was the author of the first full history of Denmark, ca. 1200. Danish American actor Viggo Mortensen (b. 1958).

Vigleik (**vig**-læik) Norwegian, from Old Norse Vígleikr, a compound of *víg-* 'battle' and *leikr* 'battle, a giant.'

Viking (**vee**-king) Norwegian and Swedish, from Old Norske Víkingr 'viking.' Rare today.

Vilhelm, Wilhelm (**vill**-helm) From German Wilhelm, a compound of *wil* 'desire' and *helm* 'helmet.' Common in several countries: English William, French Guillaume, Dutch Willem. Danish Saint Vilhelm (ca. 1127–1203).

Volmer (**vol**-mehr) Danish form of Valdemar.

Vrold, Vrål (**vroal**) Norwegian forms of Roald.

Yngvar (**ewng**-vaar) From Old Norse Yngvarr, a compound of the god's name Ing or Yngve (other names for Frey) and the suffix *arr*, possibly 'warrior.' Russian Igor is derived from Yngvar. A more popular form is Ingvar.

Yngve (**ewng**-veh) From Old Norse Yngvi, most likely related to Yngvar. In Norse mythology Yngve is another name of Frøy (Frey), the god of fertility.

Ægir, Ägir (**ay**-geer) In Norse mythology Ægir is the god of the sea. Very rare. See page 148.

Øjvind (**oey**-vinn S: **oey**-vind) Danish form of Øyvind.

Ørjan, Örjan (**oer**-yaan) A Scandinavian form of George, in Sweden often replaced by Göran.

Ørnulv, Ørnulf (D: **oer**-noolv, **oer**-noolf; N: **oer**-newlv, **oer**-newlf) From Old Norse Qrnulfr, a compound of *qrn* 'eagle' and *ulfr* 'wolf.' Variant Arnulv.

Östen, Østen (**oes**-tehn) Mainly Swedish, a form of Øystein.

Øyolv (**oey**-olv) From Old Norse Eyjolfr, a compound of 'luck, gift' and *ulfr* 'wolf.' Rare. See also Eiolv.

Øystein (**oey**-stæin) From Old Norse Eysteinn, a compound of *ey*, possibly 'luck,' and *steinn* 'stone.' Very common in Norway. Norwegian folk and bluegrass singer Øystein Sunde (b. 1947).

Øyvind (**oey**-vinn) Mainly Norwegian, from Old Norse Eyvindr, a compound of *ey*, possibly 'luck' and *vindr* 'conquerer, victor.' Very common.

Åbjörn (**oa**-byoern) Swedish, a compound of a word possibly meaning 'sword point' or 'respect' and *björn* 'bear.' Rare.

Åge (D: **oa**-eh; N: **oa**-geh) Danish form of

Åke. Very common in the first decades of the twentieth century, also used in Norway. Åke (**aa**-keh) From Old Norse Áki, derived from a word meaning 'little father.' The variant Åge is far more common. Swedish detective fiction writer Åke Edwardson (b. 1953).

Åmund (**oa**-mewnn) Mainly Norwegian, from Old Norse Ámundr, same meaning as Amund. Rare.

Ånund, Ånen, Ånond, Anund (**oa**-newn, **oa**-nehn, **oa**-nonn, **aa**-newnn) Variants of Old Norse Anundr, a compound of *anu* 'descendant' and last element 'conqueror, winner.'

Åsbjørn (**oas**-byoern) A variant of Asbjørn.

Åsmund (D: **oas**-moon; N/S: **oas**-mewnn) Mainly Norwegian, from Old Norse Ásmundr; see Asmund, Osmund.

Åsulv (**oas**-ewlv) Norwegian, from Old Norse Ásulfr, a compound of *áss* 'god' and *ulfr* 'wolf.' Rare.

A Guide to Scandinavian Naming

Scandinavian Immigration to North America

Many fans of the Scandinavian countries would certainly expect a history of immigration to America to start with Leif Erikson and the story of the discovery of North America. And indeed, the very first Scandinavian colony was Vinland in present-day Newfoundland, Canada. Thanks to the doggedness of the Norwegian lawyer-adventurer Helge Ingstad and his archeologist wife Anne Stine, it has been established beyond doubt that Norsemen settled in the New World around the year 1000. In 1960 Helge Ingstad set out to explore the eastern seaboard region of the United States and Canada, looking for traces of Leif Erikson's settlement in Vinland, which was known from the Norse Sagas. Ingstad's efforts were rewarded when he found some suspiciously Norse-looking remains at L'Anse aux Meadows in Newfoundland. The subsequent archaeological excavations (1961–68), led by Anne Stine Ingstad and her Swedish colleague Birgitta Wallace, confirmed that this could only be a Norse settlement.

The Norse colony produced the first European child born in the Americas. Among those who settled there for a period were Gudrid Eriksdottir (Old Norse Guðríðr Eiríksdóttir) and her husband, Thorfinn Karlsefni (Þorfinnr Karlsefni). Gudrid was not Leif's sister, but she had been married to his brother Thorstein, who had died. Between 1004 and 1013 (the exact year is uncertain), Gudrid and Thorfinn had a son and named him Snorri Thorfinnsson (Snorri Þorfinnsson). When Snorri was about three years old, the family returned to Iceland. Snorri became a leader in Iceland, and as an adult he was instrumental in the Christianization of Iceland.

The excavations at L'Anse aux Meadows showed, however, that this was no lasting colonization, as all evidence suggests that the houses at L'Anse aux Meadows were only inhabited for about twenty-five years. The colony was abandoned around 1025 for unknown reasons. Despite the many theories as to the fate of these Norse settlers in the New World and persistent myths that they went on to colonize North and South America, no more tangible evidence has turned up on the level with the finds at L'Anse aux Meadows. Neither the Kensington Rune Stone discovered in Minnesota in 1898, the stone tower in Newport, Rhode Island, the Vinland Map at Yale University, nor the odd report of blue-eyed Indians, has changed the scholarly view that the Vikings did not settle permanently in the Americas. We have to wait over six hundred years before real immigration from the Scandinavian countries to America gets underway.

Even so, the history of immigration from Scandinavia does begin long before the Thirteen Colonies fought for their independence and became the United States.

Sweden

Sweden was the first of the Scandinavian countries to start organized immigration to North America. On March 29, 1638, Swedes founded the colony New Sweden along the Delaware River, in what is now Delaware, New Jersey, and Pennsylvania. The first settlement was named Fort Christina in honor of the Swedish monarch Queen Christina (1626–89), who was twelve years old at the time. About six hundred Swedes settled there. At that time Finland was a part of Sweden, and some of the colonists were actually from Finland, including Admiral Klaus Fleming, who organized the colony (see below). Research has shown that a good number of Norwegians and Danes also immigrated to this area during the seventeenth century. In 1655 Sweden lost the colony when it was incorporated into the Dutch colony New Netherland. Descendants of Swedish colonists distinguished themselves in the American Revolution, and one descendant, John Morton of Pennsylvania, was a signer of the Declaration of Independence in 1776. Another Swede, the nobleman Count Axel von Fersen (1755–1810), spent many years in France in service of the French king, and he was sent to America with Colonel Rochambeau to help the American colonists in the War of Independence. Von Fersen served as interpreter between the colonel and George Washington, and distinguished himself at the Battle of Yorktown (Virginia) in 1781.

Immigration from Sweden got off to a new start in the 1840s, and from 1840 to 1930, 1.3 million Swedes left for the United States and Canada, with mass emigration in the years from 1868 to 1871 (about 100,000), during the 1880s (324,285), 1890s (200,524), and 1901 to 1910 (219,249). The peak year was 1887, when 46,000 Swedes emigrated.

During the early period, a good many Swedes settled in farming communities in western Illinois, Iowa, Minnesota, and western Wisconsin, and after the Civil War Swedish settlement spread west to Kansas and Nebraska. In 1870 about 75 percent of the Swedish Americans were living in Illinois, Minnesota, Kansas, Wisconsin, and Nebraska. In contrast to the Norwegians, the Swedes were drawn to the urban centers, and eventually about 60 percent were living in New York City, Chicago, and in the industrial areas of Massachusetts and other New England states. But Minnesota retained the status as the most Swedish state. Chicago became the "capital city" of Swedish America, boasting a population in 1910 of 100,000 Swedes, or 10 percent of the Swedish American population. It was the second largest "Swedish" city after Stockholm.

Swedes in America soon established a long list of religious and cultural institutions and activities. The Lutheran Augustana Synod was founded in 1860, and the same year Swedish immigrants in Chicago founded Augustana College in Rock Island, Illinois. Other colleges followed, among them Bethany College in Lindsborg, Kansas, Gustavus Adolphus College in St. Peter, Minnesota, North Park University in Chicago, and California Lutheran University in Thousand Oaks, California. Mutual-aid societies and clubs sprang up as well, such as the Vasa Order, the Svithiod Order, and the Viking Order. A very large number of Swedish language newspapers were published, and by 1910 the Swedish American press was the second-largest foreign language press in the United States, with a circulation of 650,000. The most important of these publications were *Hemlandet, Svenska Amerikanaren, Svenska Amerikanska Posten, Nordstjernan,* and *Svea.* Swedish Americans kept up with their native literature and also produced several authors of their own. There were theaters in the cities that staged dramas, as well as comedies and Swedish vaudeville or *bondkomik.* Many choirs and choruses were formed in both urban and rural areas.

Finland

As was pointed out in the preface, Finnish language names will not be treated in this book. But emigration from Finland is intertwined with the emigration from the other Scandinavian countries, and for this reason we include it in this survey.

From about 1200 to 1809 Finland was a part of Sweden. During the colonization of New Sweden in the seventeenth century, Finland Swedes were apparently quite active in moving to North America. It is estimated that about half of the one thousand colonists who came to New Sweden during this period were originally from Finland. A good number of Finns had migrated to Sweden and settled in Värmland, and many of them moved on to the New World. John Morton, the signer of the Declaration of Independence mentioned above, was a descendant of the Värmland Finns. In Finland this family went under the name of Marttinen, but they changed it to Mårtenson after migrating to Värmland, and then to Morton in the New World. The Finnish admiral Klaus Fleming was a member of the New Sweden Company Board. Finnish presence along the Delaware River has been preserved in a number of place names, including Finland, Nya Vasa, Lapland, and Finn's Point.

The Swedish Finnish botanist, explorer, and agricultural economist Pehr (or Pietari) Kalm (1716–79) was sent to North America in 1748 to find seeds and plants that could be cultivated and exploited commercially in Sweden. Of great interest was the red mulberry, which the Royal Swedish Academy hoped could be used to start a silk industry in Finland. Kalm explored extensively in the United States and Canada, and he is credited with writing the first description of Niagara Falls by a trained scientist. Kalm's journal was published in Stockholm (1753–61) and soon translated into a number of languages, including English as *Travels into North America* (1770). It became a standard reference work on the flora and fauna of North America, as well as Native American tribes and British and French colonists. Kalm is also credited for describing ninety species, sixty of them new. Among them is mountain laurel (*Kalmia latifolia*), the state flower of Pennsylvania and Connecticut. The genus Kalmia was named for Pehr Kalm.

In 1809 Sweden lost Finland to Russia, and Finland became the Grand Duchy of Finland. Swedish remained the official language until the Language Decree of 1863, after which a long process to introduce Finnish as an official language was undertaken. Even though only one-seventh of the population spoke Swedish as a first language, Swedish continued to dominate until well into the twentieth century. In 1917 Finland declared its independence from Russia, and in 1919 the Republic of Finland was born.

From 1733 until it was sold to the United States in 1867, Alaska was under Russian rule. In 1794 the Finn Aleksanteri Kuparinen went to Kodiak Island in Alaska, leading a group of Russian Orthodox monks. After Finland came under Russian rule, a good number of Finnish sailors and craftspeople went to Alaska. Arvid Adolf Etholén was a chief manager of the Russian-American Company from 1840 to 1845. He lent his name to several place names in present-day Alaska (spelled Etolin). Another Finn, Johan Hampus Furuhjelm, was governor of the Russian-American Company from 1859 to 1864. Alaska's Mount Furuhelm is named after him.

In the early nineteenth century a number of Finnish sailors abandoned ship to settle in the United States. Among them was Carl Sjödahl (1814–82), who took the name Charles Linn. In 1869 Linn led a group of fifty-three emigrants from southern Finland to settle in Alabama, where he built Birmingham's first industry, Linn Iron Works. Many Finns had earlier been attracted to the 1849 Gold Rush in California. Others arrived in the United States via Norway, settling in Minnesota and Michigan. The copper mining industry in Michigan even sent agents to recruit Finns living in northern Norway.

Major immigration to the United States from Finland got underway in the 1870s. Failed crops at home and glowing reports of the United States as the land of freedom and democracy encouraged Finns to emigrate. They settled mainly in Minnesota and Michigan, where men found employment in agriculture, mining, and logging. Single women usually took employment as domestic servants. Duluth, Minnesota, became known as the "Helsinki of America." Between 1870 and 1920, about 340,000 Finns immigrated to the United States. Other Finnish American settlements were founded in Wisconsin, South Dakota, Illinois, and Massachusetts, and in Boston and New

York City. Finns followed the migration to California, Washington, and Oregon in the later nineteenth century, and a good number also settled in Florida.

As did the other Scandinavian ethnic groups, Finnish Americans established a number of cultural institutions and activities. *Amerikan Suomalainen Lehti,* which started appearing in Hancock, Michigan, in 1876, was the first of many Finnish American newspapers. Literacy was highly valued in the Finnish communities, and by 1900 about 98 percent were able to read and write. Religion was also important. *Amerikan Suomalaisen Kirjallisuuden Seura* (The Finnish Literature Society) was founded in 1878 in Calumet, Michigan, to publish religious and educational material. The Lutheran Suomi Synod was founded in 1890, and Suomi College (now known as Finlandia University) was founded in 1896 in Hancock, Michigan, to train ministers and teachers. Another school was founded in 1903 as a folk high school in Minneapolis, also to train clergy and promote Finnish culture. After a few months it moved to Duluth, Minnesota, and in 1907 was renamed Work People's College. It closed in 1941. The Order of Runeberg and Suomi-Seura (Finland Society) were founded in 1920 and 1927, respectively, to promote Finnish American culture.

Denmark

During the same period that Sweden was setting up its colony in the eastern United States, the Kingdom of Denmark and Norway also had visions of establishing colonies in the New World. But the Danes set their eye on the islands in the Caribbean. The Danish West India and Guinea Company set up a base on Saint Thomas Island in 1672, and after a short time expanded its operations to Saint John and Saint Croix. In 1754 the islands were purchased by the Danish king and became royal colonies (they were sold to the United States in the nineteenth century and are now the U.S. Virgin Islands). Some of the Danes who had gone to the Caribbean moved on to the British colonies. In 1735 the religious movement known as the Pietists was outlawed in Denmark, and members fled Denmark to settle in Pennsylvania together with German members of the movement. It is known that some Danes fought in the American Revolution. Some of the "Danes" who ended up in the continental United States in the early period were certainly from Norway. As a result of the Napoleonic Wars ending in 1814, Denmark lost Norway.

The main period of emigration from Denmark is from 1850 to 1930, and during these years 330,675 Danes immigrated to the United States and Canada. Heavy Danish immigration to the United States did not set in until about 1860, with a peak of 88,132 in the decade 1881 to 1890. The Danes dispersed over a wide area in the United States. Many settled near Norwegian farmers in the rural areas of the Midwest, and eventually they established a number of their own Danish communities in Minnesota, Nebraska, Montana, Texas, and California. Even though religious persecution never was a major factor in Danish emigration, Danish Mormons were an important group in the settlement of Utah from 1860 to 1880. By 1920 California established its position as the state with the largest number of Danish Americans, a position it has held ever since, although the Danes make up only a small percentage of the state population.

Danish Americans founded several religious and cultural institutions, but these are not on a scale with the Norwegian and Swedish ones. The Danish pioneer and Lutheran minister Claus L. Clausen was the first president of the Conference of the Norwegian-Danish Evangelical Lutheran Church of America, an institution that existed from 1870 to 1890. In 1874 a group of Danish pastors, followers of N. F. S. Grundtvig (1783–1872, a highly influential teacher, writer, pastor, and politician and founder of the folk high school movement), formed the Danish Evangelical Lutheran Church in America, and the synod was formed in 1878 in Neenah, Wisconsin. In 1898 this group founded Grand View College in Des Moines, Iowa. In 1884 another group of Danes broke out of the Norwegian-Danish Conference and formed the Danish Evangelical Lutheran Association in America. This group also founded a college in 1884, Dana College in Blair, Nebraska. The Danish newspaper *The Danish Pioneer/ Den Danske Pioneer* was founded in 1872 in Nebraska, but was moved to Illinois, where it is still being published. *Bien* (The Bee), founded in San Francisco in 1882, is the only other Danish newspaper still in circulation. Danes also founded a number of societies and clubs to promote Danish culture and sports.

Norway

The first Norwegian to explore America after Christopher Columbus rediscovered it in 1492 was probably Jens Munk, born in Barbu near Arendal in 1579. He was sent by Danish king Christian IV in 1619 to look for a northwest passage to Asia. Munk explored the Hudson Bay area and claimed the area for the Danish crown, naming it Nova Dania. The expedition was locked into the ice during the winter, however, and only Jens and two other men survived.

Norway was a part of Denmark from the fourteenth century to 1814, and from 1814 to 1905 in a looser union with Sweden. But throughout the period of mass immigration to North America, the Norwegian immigrants retained a distinct identity of their own.

In 1825 Cleng Peerson (originally Kleng Pedersen, 1783–1865) organized the first large group of Norwegians to come to the United States. Peerson is considered the father of Norwegian emigration. The group sailed on a sloop called *Restaurationen* and became known as "The Sloopers." Many of the members of this group were Quakers, and they left Norway to seek freedom to practice their religion. The group settled first in New York State, but in the mid-1830s Cleng led them on to settle along the Fox River in what is now La Salle County in Illinois. The Fox River settlement was the first of many Norwegian communities to spring up in the Midwest. Some new immigrants arrived in the period from 1830 to 1860, but it was not until after the Civil War that Norwegians came to the United States in large numbers. By 1865, there were 77,873 Norwegian immigrants in the United States. The next year emigration from Norway to the United States really took off. Eighty-seven percent of the immigrants to the United States, about 780,000 Norwegians, arrived in the years between 1865 and 1930. The peak year was in 1882, when almost 29,000 Norwegians immigrated to the United States. During the decade from 1881 to 1890, 205,913 Norwegians immigrated, and from 1901 to 1910 the number was 189,352.

Up until the Civil War, Wisconsin was the center of Norwegian America, but farmlands filled up and settlers migrated on into Iowa and Minnesota, then on to the Dakotas in the 1870s. By the early twentieth century, Minneapolis had become the Norwegian capital in the United States. In the East, Brooklyn, New York, became the main Norwegian settlement area, and by 1930 it could boast of having 63,000 inhabitants of Norwegian descent. New groups started to settle in Texas and Washington State, where Seattle became the most important center. Eventually, at least 900,000 Norwegians immigrated to the United States and Canada, but the number may have been closer to 1 million. In his research for the book *Farvel Norge: Utvandringen til Amerika 1825–1975,* Sverre Mørkhagen found many Norwegian immigrants who have not been counted. New calculations are also being done by the Norwegian American Genealogical Center in Madison, Wisconsin.

Most of the Norwegians settled together in farming communities; no other immigrant group in the United States has a higher percentage of people who made their livelihood from agriculture. Of the immigrants from Scandinavia, only the Finns had a comparable pattern of settlement in farming communities. There were large areas in the Midwest where the language was Norwegian, and it didn't take long before churches, schools, newspapers, and cultural activities sprang up. In 1845 the first Norwegian American Lutheran Church was established in the Muskego settlement in Wisconsin (southwest of Milwaukee), and in 1846 Elling Eielsen's Synod was organized. In comparison to the Swedes, Norwegian Americans were extremely active in organizing Lutheran synods. By 1900 there were fourteen different Norwegian Lutheran synods.

In 1847 the first Norwegian newspaper, *Nordlyset* (Northern Light), started coming out in Muskego. Other newspapers followed: *Emigranten* (The Emigrant) in 1852, *Skandinaven* in 1860, *Decorah-Posten* in 1874, *Minneapolis Tidende* in 1887, *Western Viking* in 1890, and *Nordisk Tidende* in 1891. Since 1847 more than 280 Norwegian-language newspapers have been published in the United States. Only German Americans can boast of a larger number of immigrant newspapers. As of 2010 there is only one newspaper still coming out with news in Norwegian, *Norwegian-American*

Weekly, which is published in Seattle. Education was a high priority among Norwegian immigrants. Luther College was founded in Decorah, Iowa, in 1861; Saint Olaf College in 1874 in Northfield, Minnesota; and Pacific Lutheran University in 1890 in Tacoma, Washington. The University of Wisconsin–Madison established the first Norwegian Department in the United States in 1869. A great many cultural organizations were formed: chorus and drama groups, folk dance groups, fifty different *bygdelag* (societies for immigrants from different districts in Norway), and Sons of Norway (founded 1895). By 1906 there were 237 Norwegian cultural societies in the United States.

Iceland

Iceland was colonized in the Viking Age by Norsemen who were often fleeing from conflicts with kings and chieftains in Norway. In the mid-thirteenth century Iceland officially became a part of Norway under King Håkon IV Håkonsson. In 1380 it became, together with Norway, a part of a union with Denmark. When Denmark lost Norway in 1814, it retained the old Norwegian colonies: Iceland, the Faroe Islands, and Greenland. But in 1944 Iceland dissolved the union with Denmark and became an independent country.

Emigration from Iceland to the United States got underway much later than in the rest of Scandinavia. Since Iceland was a part of Denmark during the main period of immigration, it is also difficult to track Icelandic immigrants. Up until the 1930 U.S. census, there was no distinction between Danish and Icelandic ethnicity.

The first Icelanders to immigrate to the United States were Mormon converts who arrived in Utah in 1855. By 1857 eleven converts had left Iceland. Icelanders trickled in during the next couple of decades. An Icelandic community was founded on Washington Island in Door County, Wisconsin, around 1870. This is the oldest Icelandic settlement in the United States. Due to famine and overcrowding in Iceland during the 1870s, more Icelanders began immigrating to the Midwest, mainly to Wisconsin, Minnesota, and the Dakota Territory. There is a story that many Icelanders were attracted to emigrate due to the abundance of coffee in America. Coffee was a favorite drink in Iceland, but it was too expensive to enjoy often. A Danish American named William Wickmann, who had worked in Iceland prior to his emigration, wrote letters to friends in Iceland, and the news got around that coffee was plentiful and cheap in America. This may have been a factor, but the main motivations for emigration were certainly poor conditions and prospects at home.

The main emigration from Iceland took place from 1870 to 1900, and by 1900 it all but ceased. Ten to fifteen thousand Icelanders came to Canada and the United States, about one-fifth of the Icelandic population of seventy-five thousand. Following World War II, a good many war brides were brought to the United States by servicemen who had been stationed in Iceland.

The Icelanders were so few that it was impractical to form their own communities, and for the most part they blended with other Scandinavian immigrants. Despite their relatively small numbers, Icelanders did establish a few towns in Minnesota and Wisconsin, and Icelandic schools and cultural activities like choruses and bands sprang up. Milwaukee was the center of Icelandic immigration to the United States. The majority of the Icelanders originally settled in Winnipeg, Manitoba, in Canada, in a colony called New Iceland, but in 1878 due to bad times and disease, over one hundred of them were forced to move down to the Dakota Territory. This became the largest Icelandic community in the United States. Another Icelandic settlement called Markland near the Caribou Gold Mines in Halifax, Canada, was also short lived, in existence from 1875 to 1882.

Icelandic immigrants were usually farmers, but many of them were also skilled workers and tradespeople. Many took jobs as unskilled factory workers and woodcutters after arrival in order to save the money to buy a farm, and others took jobs as dockworkers in Milwaukee. Among second- and third-generation Icelanders, journalism has become an attractive profession, and a good many have gone into politics.

Summary of Immigration from the Scandinavian Countries

Country	Immigrants to North America
Denmark	ca. 330,000
Finland	ca. 340,000
Iceland	ca. 15,000 (estimate)
Norway	ca. 900,000
Sweden	ca. 1,300,000

The Impact at Home

In order to understand the impact of immigration on the Scandinavian countries, we need to look at the percentages of the population who left their native homes. Norway had the largest emigration in relation to its population. About 18 percent of the Norwegian population immigrated to the United States. Sweden followed with about 12 percent, and Denmark with about 5 percent. Only Ireland sent a larger percentage of its population, about 25 percent from 1845 to 1855, to the United States than Norway did. Sweden ranks number 7. As we have seen above, the percentage of Icelanders who immigrated was strictly speaking even higher than that of Norway, but Iceland was not an independent country during the immigration period. It must also be kept in mind that most Icelandic emigrants originally went to Canada, which is not the case for the other groups.

Scandinavian Ancestry in the United States

Today, the United States is a country with a very large population, and the populations of the Scandinavian countries are modest by comparison. The table below shows 2008 populations.

United States	305,838,231
Denmark	5,475,791
Finland	5,273,331
Iceland	313,376
Norway	4,787,000
Sweden	9,242,595

During the main immigration period, from about 1865 to 1915, most of the Scandinavians settled in the Midwest. In 1900 Minnesota was the state with the largest Scandinavian immigrant population: 115,000 Swedes, 105,000 Norwegians, and 16,300 Danes. Illinois, Iowa, Wisconsin, and North Dakota all had large Scandinavian populations as well. The settlement pattern for the Swedes differed somewhat from that of the Norwegians and Danes. The Swedes spread out more, and many settled in industrial cities in the Northeast. In 1900 there were 42,700 Swedes living in New York and 32,200 Swedes in Massachusetts, as well as large numbers in Minnesota and Illinois.

In the 2000 U.S. Census respondents could cross off at least one ancestry or ethnic origin. Eighty percent of the respondents chose to do so. Among the fifteen largest ancestries, we find Norwegian with 1.6 percent and Swedish with 1.4 percent of the total U.S. population. If we look at the numbers of people, we find that 4.5 million Americans report Norwegian ancestry, a number that was roughly equal to the population of Norway in 2000! Four million Americans reported Swedish ancestry, and that was somewhat less than half of the population of Sweden in 2000. The number of Americans reporting Danish ancestry was significantly less: 1.4 million people, or 0.5 percent of the total U.S. population. Americans claiming Finnish ancestry numbered 623,559, or 0.2 percent of the U.S. population.

On the state level, we find several states with large concentrations of people with Norwegian ancestry: North Dakota (30.1 percent of the population), Minnesota (17.3 percent), South Dakota (15.3 percent), and Montana (10.6 percent). If we go to the county level, we find several counties in Iowa, Minnesota, Montana, North Dakota, and Wisconsin where Norwegian ancestry is the dominant ethnic background. The state with the largest percentage of people with Swedish ancestry is Minnesota (9.9 percent). Americans with Danish ancestry are less concentrated, but 6.5 percent of the population of Utah claim Danish ancestry. The greatest concentration of Finnish Americans is in the Upper Peninsula of Michigan, where they make up 16 percent of the population.

The table below compares the numbers of people claiming various Scandinavian ancestries in the U.S. census for 1990 and 2000. As the numbers show, Norwegian ancestry is the only one claimed by *more* people in 2000 than in 1990, while all the others show a decline. The 2000 census also established that there were significant numbers of Americans with Finnish, Icelandic, and general Scandinavian ancestry. People were also registered who hailed from the smallest of the Scandinavian areas, the Faroe Islands and Åland (each under 300 and thus no actual figures are listed). And 945 people listed "Lapp" ancestry. Lapp refers to a Scandinavian minority group (officially called the Sámi) claiming a nation that covers territory in northern Norway, Sweden, Finland, and Russia.

The U.S. Census Bureau does ongoing research to collect data on the American population. In 2006 a survey was made to collect information on ethnic background. Since it is based on a sampling of people, there is a margin of error. But the findings are nevertheless of interest, and they show that the populations with a Scandinavian background have all increased since 2000. The figures for our area of interest are as follows: Danish ancestry 1,516,126; Finnish ancestry 690,322; Icelandic ancestry 52,190; Norwegian ancestry 4,669,516; Swedish ancestry 4,417,115; Scandinavian ancestry 615,506.

The maps on the following pages are based on the statistics in the 2000 U.S. Census for Americans with Danish, Norwegian, and Swedish ancestry. Here we can see that Norwegian Americans have had a tendency to stick together and stay in the Midwest. Due to hard times during the Depression, a good many Norwegians did migrate on to the Northwest, where they also had a tendency to settle in Norwegian

Americans of Scandinavian Ancestry by Country, Compared to Home Country

Country	1990 Census	2000 Census	% of Home Country (2000)
Denmark	1,634,648	1,430,897	26.8% of 5,336,394
Finland	658,854	623,559	12% of 5,167,486
Iceland	—	42,716	15.4% of 276,365
Norway	3,869,395	4,477,725	99.9% of 4,481,162
Sweden	4,680,863	3,998,310	45% of 8,873,052
Unspecified Scandinavian	678,880	425,099	—
Total	11,522,640	10,998,306	45.5% of 24,134,459

Source: CIA, *The World Factbook 2000*, www.umsl.edu/services/govdocs/wofact2000/index.html (accessed December 14, 2008).

enclaves. But the Swedes and Danes have spread out and settled in a much wider area. We also note that the concentrations of Norwegians are much heavier than is the case for Swedes and Danes. We see that 30.1 percent of the population claim Norwegian ethnicity in the most heavily Norwegian state (North Dakota), while the percentages of people with Danish and Swedish ethnic background are much lower. In the most heavily Danish state (Utah), 6.5 percent claim a Danish background, and in the most heavily Swedish state (Minnesota), 9.9 percent claim Swedish ethnicity.

There is no map for Finland, but a similar map was made by the University of

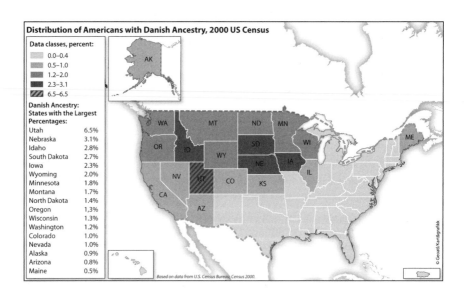

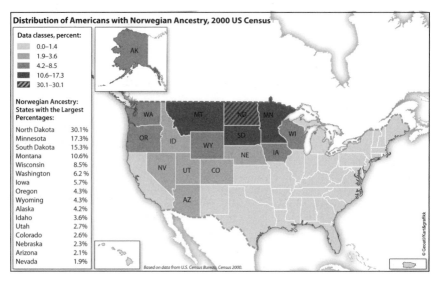

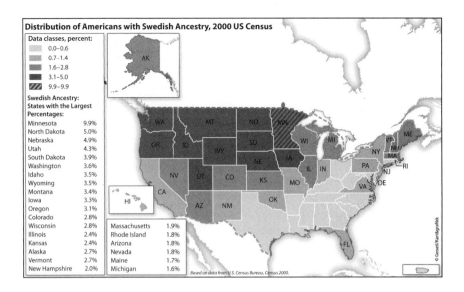

Distribution of Americans with Swedish Ancestry, 2000 US Census

Data classes, percent:
- 0.0–0.6
- 0.7–1.4
- 1.6–2.8
- 3.1–5.0
- 9.9–9.9

Swedish Ancestry:
States with the Largest
Percentages:

Minnesota	9.9%		
North Dakota	5.0%		
Nebraska	4.9%		
Utah	4.3%		
South Dakota	3.9%		
Washington	3.6%		
Idaho	3.5%		
Wyoming	3.5%		
Montana	3.4%		
Iowa	3.3%		
Oregon	3.1%		
Colorado	2.8%		
Wisconsin	2.8%	Massachusetts	1.9%
Illinois	2.4%	Rhode Island	1.8%
Kansas	2.4%	Arizona	1.8%
Alaska	2.7%	Nevada	1.8%
Vermont	2.7%	Maine	1.7%
New Hampshire	2.0%	Michigan	1.6%

Based on data from U.S. Census Bureau, Census 2000.

© Geoati/Kart&grafikk

Minnesota following the 1990 Census. Comparable to the Norwegian settlement pattern, the Finns were concentrated in the Midwest, but there were also significant enclaves in the Northeast, including "Finntown" in Brooklyn, New York, as well as other concentrations in California, Florida, and Alaska. The largest Finnish community was in Lake Worth, Florida, north of Miami. The pattern has certainly not changed significantly since 1990.

There is no map for Iceland, and in any case, the percentages would be very small. But there are statistics for the 1990 census: 19,891 Icelandic Americans were living in the West; 10,904 in the Midwest; 6,000 in the South; and 4,140 in the Northeast. The largest numbers of Icelandic Americans were living in California, Washington, Minnesota, and North Dakota.

Scandinavian Immigration to Canada

Scandinavian immigration to Canada is a part of the general picture of immigration to North America from the Scandinavian countries. Large-scale immigration to Canada got underway in the later nineteenth century, somewhat later than to the United States.

From 1850 on, most immigrant ships from Norway landed at Quebec. Canada was not, however, the final destination for the majority of immigrants. Most were headed for the midwestern states in the United States, and agents arranged further transportation by train and steamer for about nine dollars. It is estimated that only 400 of the 28,460 Norwegians who came to Canada in the 1850s settled there. A small Norwegian settlement was founded on the Gaspé Peninsula along the Saint

Lawrence River in Quebec in 1854, but the settlers moved on to the United States in the early 1860s.

During much of the immigration period, Canada was still a series of British colonies. In 1867 the Dominion of Canada was created, consisting of four provinces: Ontario, Quebec, Nova Scotia, and New Brunswick. Manitoba was formed in 1870, but it was much smaller than it is today, and British Columbia joined in 1871. The provinces where most of the Scandinavians settled were called Northwest Territories, comprising much of the area in present-day Alberta, Saskatchewan, Manitoba, and Ontario, and not to be confused with the area called Northwest Territories today. Alberta and Saskatchewan joined the Dominion of Canada in 1905, and the provinces Ontario, Manitoba, Saskatchewan, and Alberta acquired their present form in 1912. Newfoundland did not join until 1949. In 1931 the British Parliament passed the Statute of Westminster, effectively giving Canada its independence. Canada became a sovereign nation in 1982, but Queen Elizabeth is still the Head of State and Queen of Canada.

As the land in the midwestern United States filled with settlers, the prairie area of Canada opened up and the western provinces in Canada became attractive to Scandinavians. Some of those who went to Canada had already tried their luck in Minnesota, the Dakotas, and Montana, but as these areas filled up and good land became scarce, settlers moved north in search of land that might be more productive or attractive in other ways. Many Scandinavian settlements were established just north of the United States–Canadian border.

Norwegians were the dominant group among the Scandinavian immigrants. Very many of them were migrants from the United States; by 1921 one third of the Norwegian Canadian population had been born in the United States. Norwegian immigrants were mostly farmers and developed a number of rural communities in the western provinces of Manitoba, Saskatchewan, Alberta, and British Columbia. Birch Hills in Saskatchewan was settled in 1894 and was probably the first Norwegian settlement.

Norwegians were often joined by Icelandic settlers, though in much smaller numbers. Icelanders also formed some communities of their own. In 1875 two hundred Icelanders had immigrated to the western shore of Lake Winnipeg in Manitoba and founded a colony. They were joined by twelve hundred new settlers the next year. The Icelanders declared New Iceland to be an independent republic and set about creating a constitution, laws, a government, and schools. Icelandic was the official language. The republic lasted until 1887, when the Canadian government abolished it. The area once called New Iceland has the largest concentration of people of Icelandic descent outside Iceland. Manitoba still has the largest Icelandic Canadian population, but British Columbia, Alberta, and Ontario also have substantial numbers.

By 1910 most of the Norwegian and Icelandic settlements had been established, and these settlers were joined by Swedes, Danes, and Finns. In rural areas Scandinavians often dominate even today, comprising up to 90 percent of the population. In towns and incorporated villages, the Scandinavian population is much less.

Early Swedish settlements were Scandinavia in Manitoba, established in 1885, and Stockholm in Saskatchewan, settled in 1886. But most of the Swedes arrived in the late 1890s, and by World War I the first wave had ended. Many of the Swedes also migrated across the U.S. border from Swedish communities in the Midwest. A second and larger wave of Swedish immigrants came into Canada in the 1920s, and a third one started in the 1950s and has continued up until today. Winnipeg became the first Swedish capital of Canada, but in the 1940s, Vancouver took over. Today, the largest Swedish Canadian populations are found in British Columbia, Alberta, and Ontario. As is the case in the United States, we find a good many Swedish Canadians in cities, including Winnipeg, Calgary, Edmonton, Vancouver, and Toronto. Whereas the majority of the immigrants to the United States were from south-central Sweden, most of the immigrants to Canada came from the Stockholm area and northern Sweden.

Danes joined Norwegians and Swedes in the same areas, but in smaller numbers. An important Danish settlement was established in the eastern province of New Brunswick in 1872, and it became the largest Danish colony in Canada, called New Denmark. The Danish Canadian population of New Brunswick today is not very significant, however; in the 2006 census only 3,875 of the 719,650 people in New Brunswick claimed Danish heritage. Another Danish colony grew up at Dickson, Alberta. Alberta, British Columbia, and Ontario became the core area for Danish Canadians.

The influx of Finns to Canada began in the 1880s, as a result of economic depressions and the Finnish Civil War of 1918. A good many so-called Red Finns who fostered socialist convictions came to Canada after the civil war and up to the 1940s, when Canadian immigration policy gave preference to the conservative "White Finns." Canada was a popular destination for Finns, as it offered a climate similar to that at home, and the land was well suited to logging and farming. Like the other Scandinavians, Finns also migrated from the United States. Thunder Bay in Ontario, which has the largest Finnish ethnic population outside of Finland, became the capital of Finnish Canada, and Sudbury in northern Ontario is another important Finnish Canadian city. Ontario retains the honor of having the largest Finnish population, followed by British Columbia and Alberta.

As was the case in the United States, Scandinavian Canadians soon established churches, cultural institutions, athletic clubs, newspapers, and magazines in their new surroundings. Scandinavian Lutheran churches were established in the settlements during the early twentieth century, serving enclaves of Norwegians, Swedes, or Danes. Finnish Canadians were pioneers in establishing cooperatives, most notably

Canada's largest, the Consumers' Co-operative Society. Finnish Canadians were also notable for being active in political organizations, many of which were left-wing in their orientation. Following World War II, a conservative wind blew over Canada, and the political radicalism of the Finnish Canadian community rapidly lost ground.

Scandinavian Ancestry in Canada Today

In the 2006 Canadian census 4.1 percent of the population, about 1.3 million people out of a population of 31,612,897, claimed Scandinavian background. The Norwegian Canadians are the largest group, followed by Swedish Canadians, Danish Canadians, Finnish Canadians, and Icelandic Canadians. Because Iceland is a country with a very small population, the Icelandic Canadian group of close to ninety thousand is quite significant. There is also a group of unspecified Scandinavians that are not included in the other groups.

Canadians of Scandinavian Ancestry by Country in the 2006 Census

	Number	Percentage of Canadian Population
Denmark	200,035	0.7%
Finland	131,045	0.4%
Iceland	88,875	0.3%
Norway	432,515	1.6%
Sweden	334,765	1.1%
Unspecified Scandinavian	36,140	0.1%

Most Scandinavian Canadians live in the western provinces of Alberta, Saskatchewan, and British Columbia, with a good many also in Ontario. In the table below, Manitoba is also included. One third of the Icelandic Scandinavian population lives in Manitoba.

Scandinavian Canadians in the Provinces with the Largest Populations, 2006 Census

	Saskatchewan	Alberta	British Columbia	Ontario	Manitoba
Danish	10,445	58,825	56,125	51,650	8,210
Finnish	3,960	15,670	29,875	72,990	3,520
Icelandic	6,445	16,870	22,115	11,140	30,555
Norwegian	68,650	144,585	129,425	53,840	18,395
Swedish	33,135	93,810	104,020	67,240	21,825

Naming Traditions in Scandinavia

The subject of this book is Scandinavian *given* names. However, there is a close relationship between a Scandinavian given name and the patronymic name, often used today as a last name, or surname. In order to gain a perspective on naming practices, we need to take a brief look at the larger context of naming in Scandinavia by looking at both given names and surnames.

A Note on the Scandinavian Alphabets

The Scandinavian languages have several letters that are not used in the English twenty-six-letter alphabet. Danish, Norwegian, and Swedish have three extra vowels at the end of the alphabet, and thus their alphabets have twenty-nine letters. The pronunciation of these vowels is the same, but the written forms differ somewhat. Danish and Norwegian use the order æ, ø, and å, while the order in Swedish is å, ä, and ö. The Danish and Norwegian order is followed below.

Æ/æ and Ä/ä are pronounced as the 'a' in English 'cat.' Ø/ø and Ö/ö are pronounced by rounding your lips to say 'oh' and saying 'ee' at the same time. Å/å is pronounced 'oh.' Å/å is written Aa/aa in older documents.

The Icelandic alphabet has a total of thirty-four letters. Vowels with accents account for six of the additional letters: á, é, í, ó, ú, ý. Á/á is the only one that we will comment on here, as it corresponds to Å/å in the other languages. Icelandic also has the letter Æ/æ.

Á/á is pronounced like 'ow.' Æ/æ is pronounced like 'I.'

In Icelandic and Old Norse there are also two extra consonants: Ð/ð and Þ/þ. These letters are no longer used in modern Danish, Norwegian, or Swedish, and the sounds have mostly developed into 'd' or 't.' Where Icelandic spells a word with Ð/ð, modern Danish, Norwegian, and Swedish have replaced it with D/d; for example, Icelandic *Ingiríður* is *Ingrid* in the other languages. Where Icelandic spells a name with Þ/þ, modern Danish, Norwegian, and Swedish have replaced it with T/t; for example, the Icelandic name *Þór* is *Tor* in the other languages. Note that sometimes Tor is spelled Thor, but the name is always pronounced 'Tor' in Danish, Norwegian, and Swedish.

Ð/ð is pronounced in Icelandic like the 'th' in 'that.'

Þ/þ is pronounced in Icelandic like the 'th' in 'think.'
You will find many Old Norse words and elements in the dictionary entries. They are in most cases spelled the same way as in Icelandic. Note that Old Norse ǫ (o with ogonek) is represented by ö in modern Icelandic.

The table below gives a summary of the extra letters, as well as the adapted spelling conventions in the English-speaking environment. See also the pronunciation guide at the front of the book.

Language	Æ/æ or Ä/ä	Ø/ø or Ö/ö	Å/å or Á/á	Ð/ð and Þ/þ
Danish	Æ/æ	Ø/ø	Å/å (aa before 1948)	
Norwegian	Æ/æ	Ø/ø	Å/å (aa before 1917)	
Swedish	Ä/ä	Ö/ö	Å/å	
Icelandic	Æ/æ	Ö/ö	Á/á	Ð/ð and Þ/þ
Adapted spelling	A/a or Ae/ae Sabo (Sæbø) Saether (Sæther)	O/o or Oe/oe Rolvaag (Rølvåg) Odegaard (Ødegård) Oefstedal (Øfstedal)	A/a, Aa/aa or O/o Rolvaag (Rølvåg) Osa (Åsa)	D/d and Th/th Sigrid (Sigríður) Thor (Þór)

Given Names, Patronymics, Matronymics, and Surnames

It is typical of naming patterns in all cultures that a new baby receives a given name or names. In the Scandinavian countries, from the Viking Age and up to the nineteenth century, it was most common to give the child only one given name. In addition to the given name, the parentage of the children was marked by an additional type of name called a *patronymic*, or occasionally a *matronymic*. A patronymic is the name of the father in the possessive form with the addition of the appropriate suffix meaning 'son' or 'daughter'; for example, Olavsson or Olavsdotter would be the son or daughter of Olav. The spellings of the suffix vary according to language. Danish: *sen* or *søn* and *datter*; Norwegian: *sen, son,* or *søn,* and *dotter* or *datter*; Swedish: *son* and *dotter*; Icelandic: *son* and *dóttir*. A matronymic name is a corresponding form based on the given name of the mother, such as Gunnhildson (the son of Gunnhild) or Aslaugsdotter (or the daughter of Aslaug). The resulting patronymic often has a double s, especially in Swedish: Andersson, Nilsson, and so forth. Many of these forms have been simplified in the United States by leaving out one s: Anderson, Nilson, and so on.

It is not known why the Norsemen used a patronymic rather than a matronymic name, but it is possible that the custom was related to the old Germanic laws governing inheritance. According to those laws, each spouse had his or her own property and assets, and spouses did not inherit directly from each other. Instead, the children inherited from each of their parents, and all children accepted into the clan, including illegitimate ones, had the right to inherit from both parents. The maternity of a child would usually not be questioned, but the paternity might. The Swedish historian Birgit Sawyer has studied a certain fashion of inscriptions on rune stones from about the year 1000 that provide detailed information about children and their parentage. According to her theory, the Catholic Church was challenging the Norse laws of inheritance, and children had these monumental stones carved to be sure that they got their rightful inheritance. Perhaps the patronymic was a way of ensuring a child's rights in regard to his or her father.

In the Old Norse and Icelandic sagas, there are several references to the procedure by which a newborn child was accepted as a member of the family. The baby was first brought to her or his mother and then presented to the father, who received the child into the clan by placing him or her on his knee. Those who have read *The Saga of Gunnlaugur Snake's Tongue* may recall that due to a foreboding dream, the father of the heroine Helga the Fair refused to receive her into the clan and ordered his wife to expose the child, that is, to place her outdoors to die. The mother couldn't bear to expose her, so she sent Helga to a relative to be brought up in secret. A few years later, the foster mother told the father what had happened, and he was pleased that his beautiful daughter had been saved. He accepted his parentage and took Helga home to be brought up with great honor and the love and esteem of her father, mother, and kinfolk.

It is important to remember that the patronymic was originally not a surname. Today, it may or may not be a person's last name. If the name is a "true" patronymic (or matronymic), that is, the name of the father (or mother) plus the suffix, we call it a *primary patronymic*. A primary patronymic changes every generation. For example, Einar Gerhardsen (1897–1987), Prime Minister of Norway for most of the period from 1945 to 1965, was the son of Gerhard Olsen. Up until 1923, many Norwegians used a primary patronymic. But Einar Gerhardsen's own children were born after a law was passed to end the use of the primary patronymic, so Einar's politician son, Rune Gerhardsen, does not go under the name Einarsen. If as in this case the name once was a patronymic, but has become a hereditary surname at some point in time, we call it a *secondary patronymic*. A secondary patronymic is passed on from generation to generation. And Rune Gerhardsen's children are also named Gerhardsen.

Most of the Scandinavians who immigrated to the United States did so in the nineteenth century, when the system of using primary patronymics was still dynamic. This is particularly true for Norwegian immigrants, as well as the relatively few from Iceland. In connection with genealogical research on family members, the patronymic will often provide the name of the father, and will be the key to tracing a family back in time. It may also be the key to finding other types of information on a person.

Times have changed, and modern Scandinavians have a surname. Despite the fact that the Scandinavian languages and cultures are so similar, there are major differences in the types of names used as family names or surnames. In addition to the secondary patronymic, there are several other types of names that Scandinavians have adopted as surnames. These will be treated in the sections below.

The table below shows how Denmark, Norway, and Sweden formed each country's five most common patronymics.

Denmark		Norway		Sweden	
Given Name	*Patronymic*	*Given Name*	*Patronymic*	*Given Name*	*Patronymic*
Jens	Jensen	Hans	Hansen	Johan	Johansson
Niels	Nielsen	Johan	Johansen	Anders	Andersson
Hans	Hansen	Ola(v) or Ole	Olsen	Karl	Karlsson
Peder	Pedersen	Lars	Larsen	Nils	Nilsson
Anders	Andersen	Anders	Andersen	Erik	Eriksson

Surnames in Iceland

Iceland is the only country that has maintained an unbroken tradition of using the primary patronymic. In the same way that Erik the Red's sons and daughter were called Leif Erikson, Thorvald Erikson, and Freydis Eriksdottir (the spellings are adapted to English), the son of a contemporary Icelander named Gunnar will be known as Gunnarsson and his daughter Gunnarsdóttir. In 1925 Iceland passed a law requiring all citizens to use a primary patronymic (that is, surnames were forbidden). The most frequently used man's name in Iceland today is Jón Jónsson: Jón tops the list of given names, and as a result Jónsson tops the list of patronymics.

Since the patronymic name changes with each generation, the majority of Icelanders do not have a surname. A good example of this is the Icelandic singer-actress Björk, who follows the old Scandinavian custom of only having one given name. She is also Guðmundsdóttir, but this is only a marker that tells who her father is. If you want to look up an Icelandic friend in the phone book, you will have to look up him or her under the given name. Most given names will have many different listings. For example, if you look up the telephone number of the president of Iceland, Ólafur Ragnar Grímsson, you will find over 2,700 entries for "Ólafur." So you hope that you will remember the person's occupation, the name of the father, or the address, in order to find the right person! If your friend is among the 10 percent of all Icelanders who had a surname, such as Laxness or Blöndal before 1925, and have therefore been allowed to keep using it, your friend will be somewhat easier to find.

When Icelanders go abroad, the patronymic does serve as a kind of surname. In the international community, everyone would assume that Stéfansson is the surname of the geneticist Kári Stéfansson, famous for founding the company deCODE Genetics in 1996. But according to the system, the patronymic will change with each new generation. In Iceland Kári's children would bear the patronymic Kárason rather than Stéfansson. But once Icelanders emigrate from their home country for good, most of them certainly choose to use a secondary patronymic as a hereditary surname for the family.

Icelandic Surnames in North America

Most people of Icelandic ancestry in the United States and Canada have adopted a patronymic name as a hereditary surname, and most of these names cannot be easily distinguished from patronymics originating from the other Scandinavian countries. The name Helgason formed from Helgi, with about three hundred bearers in the United States, is an exception.

Surnames in Denmark

Due to its proximity to Germany, Denmark was greatly influenced by German culture during the Middle Ages. Under the influence of German naming fashions, Denmark was the first Scandinavian country to begin to abandon the use of the primary patronymic. By the end of the Middle Ages, one third of the Danish aristocracy had taken hereditary surnames, and in 1526 the king encouraged the nobility to adopt surnames. The trend spread to the middle class in the towns, and by the end of the eighteenth century half of the urban population had also adopted a surname. Some of these surnames were secondary patronymics, but a large number of Danes took ethnic names, such as Friis (the Frisian) or Holst (person from Holstein), or occupational names like Møller (miller) or Koch (cook) modeled on the German pattern. The use of the primary patronymic held out in the countryside, but as early as 1828 Denmark sent out a directive requiring everyone to have a set surname. Thus, all the children of Hans Jensen would now use the surname Jensen, rather than the primary patronymic Hansen or Hansdatter, and the male children would carry Jensen on down through the generations. The female patronymic ending *datter* was abolished in 1829.

Most Danes have been quite satisfied to use a patronymic as a surname. In fact, 70 percent of all Danes today have surnames ending in *sen*, with Jensen, Nielsen, and Hansen topping the list. In a list of the hundred most frequent surnames, there are seventy-nine patronymics! Another curiosity of Danish surnames is the fact that no other country has so few surnames used by so many citizens. Patronymics often make it difficult to tell people apart, and a number of Danes have added a middle name that functions as part of their surname. The well-known Danish politicians

Anders Fogh Rasmussen and Uffe Ellemann-Jensen have followed this custom, adding Fogh and Ellemann to distinguish themselves from the many others named Anders Rasmussen or Uffe Jensen.

Danish Surnames in North America

Compared to Norway and Sweden, the number of Danish immigrants to North America was relatively small, around three hundred thousand people and only about 5 percent of the population of Denmark during the immigration period. By the time they came to the new country, most Danes had adopted a surname, and these names were largely absorbed into the North American body of surnames. A patronymic could be readily Americanized by changing *sen* to its common English cognate *son*. Some retained the suffix *sen*, and a common misconception is that a name ending in *sen* in America is Danish. In fact, it is almost impossible to distinguish a Danish patronymic from a Norwegian one. Only if the personal name in the patronymic is rarely used in Norway can you be reasonably certain that the surname is of Danish origin, and vice versa. An example of this is Thygesen, which has three thousand bearers in Denmark, but fewer than three hundred in Norway.

Surnames in Norway

In Norway most people prefer not to use a secondary patronymic. There is a long tradition in Norway of using a farm name as a family marker. When the patronymic was in active use, a child would receive a given name and a patronymic, and the name of the farm where the family lived would be tacked on to the rest—for as long as the family lived there. Johannes Endresen Søndenå was the son of Endre and lived on Søndenå Farm. His wife, Helga Larsdotter Håland, was the daughter of Lars and lived on Håland Farm. This pattern is quite clear in church records and other official documents, where the given name, the patronymic, and the farm name are listed, and the system can be an invaluable aid for people doing genealogical research. If the family moved to another farm, they would adopt that name as the family name. As we will see below (see page 182), Johannes Endresen Søndenå and Helga Larsdotter Håland replaced their farm names Søndenå and Håland with Hanakam when they took over that farm.

A Norwegian woman did not adopt her husband's family name upon her marriage. The farm name was always interchangeable. If the couple above had lived at Helga's farm Håland, they would have used this name. And of course, the fact that she married Johannes did not change the fact that she was Lars's daughter!

For about four hundred years, from the fourteenth century until the end of the Napoleonic Wars in 1814, Norway was a part of Denmark. In the Middle Ages the relatively small Norwegian aristocracy followed the Danish trend of adopting a surname. During the seventeenth and eighteenth centuries, the custom filtered down into the urban setting, and merchants, craftspeople, and laborers also adopted surnames. Norwegian towns were much more provincial than Danish or Swedish ones, and the new custom had little influence on naming practices in the countryside until the late nineteenth century. Only after the naming law was passed in 1923 did surnames come into common use. Instead of adopting the patronymic as a surname, most people in the countryside took the farm name. Now, when they moved to a new farm, they took the old farm name with them, or adopted the name of the new farm after a few years. During this period the Industrial Revolution had come to Norway, and many petty farmers and tenant farmers moved to the towns. Farm people usually took the farm name with them as a surname, whereas craftspeople and laborers most often took a patronymic. It is curious to note that the naming law of 2001 again provides for the use of primary patronymics. So far, however, the law change has not led to a wide-scale revival.

As a result of this process, the most common surname type in Norway today is the farm name. Of the hundred most common Norwegian surnames, forty-two are farm names and fifty-eight are secondary patronymics. About 70 percent of Norwegians bear farm names as a surname, and 26 percent have secondary patronymics. The vocabulary of the farm names is quite descriptive and finely tuned to the varied Norwegian landscape, and the number of farm names in use is quite large, about forty thousand. The secondary patronymics number about two thousand. With its large proportion of farm names, the surnames of Norway are almost unique in an international perspective.

Norwegian Surnames in North America
As we have seen, at least 850,000 Norwegians immigrated to North America, most of them in the late nineteenth century. At the time of their immigration, most Norwegians did not have hereditary surnames. The American bureaucracy required a surname, however, and Norwegian immigrants were therefore faced with a number of choices. Should they take a surname in a Norwegian form? Should it be a patronymic or a farm name? Should they adjust it to American naming practices? Or should they take an entirely new name? Individuals would make different choices, and as a result, members of the same family might be known under different names. For example, most of the members of a family from Buringrud in Ringerike adopted the surname Jacobson, which was the primary patronymic of the father, Tron Jacobsen Buringrud. But some of them chose to use the farm name Buringrud.

The first organized Norwegian immigration took place in 1825, and up to the 1870s many of the immigrants adopted a patronymic, usually in an Anglicized form ending in *son*. But toward the end of the nineteenth century it became common to take a farm name. Since so many of the immigrants lived in rural communities where most of the people were Norwegian, it was no problem to use a farm name in its original form. In Lutheran cemeteries in Green County, Wisconsin, there are quite a few gravestones bearing the name Ildjarnstad, a farm name from Valdres. In mainstream American society this name would certainly be a novelty, and probably hard to pronounce. But in this Norwegian American community it was not a problem.

In the late nineteenth century influential people were agitating for and defining a Norwegian national identity. Farm names were important markers of Norwegian identity and placed the bearer in a Norwegian geographical and social setting. An important result of the nationalistic movement was Norwegian independence from Sweden in 1905, an event that did not go unnoticed in Norwegian America. Contrary to the earlier years when it was important to be assimilated into American society, it now became relevant to show your Norwegian background. Surnames like Fisketjon (Norwegian Fisketjøn) and Tufteskog, which might have been considered a problem earlier, were not considered too foreign sounding in the American setting.

It could also be practical to have a surname that was more "exclusive" and readily identified the bearer. In one Midwestern village, 54 out of 312 men were named Olsen at some point. Understandably, many of them felt the need to change their surname.

A large number of Norwegian farm names are in active use in the United States and Canada today, and many can be readily identified by looking at the ending. Frequent markers are names that end in *em* or *um* (developed from *heim*, 'home,' e.g., Fossum), *land* ('land,' e.g., Helland), *stad* ('farmstead,' e.g., Harstad, Hemstad), *rud* ('clearing,' e.g., Rud, Evinrude), *mo* ('sandy heath,' e.g., Sandmo, Moen), *li* ('slope,' e.g., Haugli), *bakke* ('hill,' e.g., Sandbakke, Bakken), *haug* ('mound,' e.g., Haug), *seth* ('outfarm,' e.g., Herseth). Many of these endings will also occur as independent names, often in an Anglicized form.

Norwegian Form	Americanized Form
Eide	Eade, Eddy
Haug, Hauge, Haugen	Houg, Houge, Hougen
Hervik	Harwick
Li, Lie	Lee
Lunde	Lundy
Rud, Ruud	Rood, Rude
Vetrhus	Vettrus, Winterhouse
Østebø	Ostebee
Østerhus	Easthouse

It is not easy to distinguish patronymics used as surnames in the Norwegian American community from those used by Danish Americans and Swedish Americans. As mentioned above, a few may be distinguished based on how common the personal name is in Norway, Denmark, or Sweden. Halvorsen/Halvorson is most likely Norwegian, as there are twelve thousand bearers of Halvorsen in Norway, but only four hundred in Denmark and thirty named Halvorsson in Sweden.

Surnames in Sweden

In Sweden the most frequent surnames are secondary patronymics, with Johansson, Andersson, and Karlsson topping the list. Patronymics are so common that "John and Jane Doe" are called Lars and Anna Medelsvensson ("middle class Svensson")—even though the name Svensson is in ninth place on the list of the most frequently used surnames (2008). But Swedes have other types of surnames that are uncommon in both Denmark and Norway.

Both Denmark and Sweden were influenced by German naming traditions, but the greatest influence was on Swedish names. The nobility were the first to adopt hereditary surnames, and these were created from the symbols on the family coat of arms; for example, *Silver* ('silver,' e.g., Silverstjärn) and *Gyllen* ('gold,' e.g., Gyllenhammar). Others were modeled on a German name such as Morgenstern. In the seventeenth and eighteenth centuries members of the middle class adopted names of two syllables, often ending in *man*: Bergman, Björkman, Nyman. One or both parts of the name were also taken from the natural surroundings, especially from the Swedish flora; for example, Lindberg was formed from *lind* and *berg* ('linden tree' and 'mountain' or 'hill'). Gradually, it became fashionable to use other endings such as *sjö* ('sea,' e.g., Bergsjö), *berg* ('mountain,' e.g., Söderberg), *ström* ('river,' e.g., Hellström), *holm* ('island,' e.g., Lindholm), *lund* ('grove,' e.g., Eklund), *gren* ('branch,' e.g., Lundgren), *kvist* ('twig,' e.g., Bergkvist), and *stedt* ('homestead,' e.g., Norstedt). Such names may appear to describe a specific landscape, but in fact the parts of the names are arbitrarily combined and are therefore called *ornamental* names, meaning that they are made up. This name type is not found in any other Scandinavian country.

Surnames that were originally nicknames are another name type peculiar to Sweden. Often these names were acquired by a young man when he was serving in the military, such as Rask ('the fast one') or Stark ('the strong one'), and these were later adopted as family names.

Another marker of a Swedish surname is the use of Latin suffixes such as *ell* (Forsell), *én* (Lidén), *ér* (Modér), *lin* (Mellin), *ius* (Sibelius), and *aeus* (Petraeus). Even though none of these names has made it into the list of the top one hundred surnames, there are several thousand different surnames ending in these suffixes.

A very large number of Swedish surnames are secondary patronymics ending in *son*. When 730,000 Swedes bear the names Johansson, Andersson, and Karlsson, it can be a problem. Some years ago, the Swedish government manufactured a list of surnames that were considered appropriate for Swedes and put them up for grabs, hoping to encourage families with the commonest *son* names to adopt something more exclusive. There has been no mass movement to adopt new names, so the total picture is unchanged.

The double *s* in patronymics has been largely preserved in the spelling of Swedish names, while Danish and Norwegian patronymics are written with a single *s*. Andersson, Johansson, Nilsson, and Svensson will most often mark someone as Swedish or of Swedish descent. The ending *sen* is not used in Swedish patronymics. In Scandinavia, but not necessarily in North America (see below), the form will help you to distinguish between Swedish and Danish or Norwegian patronymics.

Swedish Surnames in North America

In 1901 Swedes were required by law to adopt a hereditary surname, but by this time most of them probably already had. Thus, a good many Swedish immigrants brought a surname with them. Particularly in the early years of immigration, Swedish farmers were likely to have a primary patronymic. A good many set the patronymic as a surname and passed it down to the next generations.

The dominant surname of Swedish origin in North America today is the secondary patronymic. The Swedes brought with them the ending *sson*. Names like Andersson and Pettersson could easily be Americanized by removing an *s* and perhaps a *t*, creating Anderson and Petterson or Peterson. But a large number of the ornamental names could also be used in North America without problems. Names such as Forsberg, Forsell, Forsgren, Forslund, Forsman and Forstrom, and Lindberg and Lindstrom all have a significant number of bearers today, and they all signal a Swedish heritage.

Summary of Surname Types

The first table below gives a summary of surname types in use today in the various countries. As we can see, the secondary patronymic surnames are a typical feature of Scandinavian names. The next table shows the most frequent secondary patronymics in Denmark, Norway, and Sweden as of 2009.

	Primary patronymic	Secondary patronymic	Farm Name	Ornamental	Occupational
Denmark	none	predominant	some	few	some
Norway	none	26%	70%	none	few (imported)
Sweden	none	very common	rare	common	some
Iceland	90%	rare	rare	none	none

Denmark		Norway		Sweden	
Secondary patronymic	*Bearers 2009*	*Secondary patronymic*	*Bearers 2009*	*Secondary patronymic*	*Bearers 2009*
Jensen	275,113	Hansen	55,732	Johansson	261,898
Nielsen	272,804	Johansen	52,023	Andersson	260,250
Hansen	228,503	Olsen	51,795	Karlsson	198,747
Pedersen	171,768	Larsen	39,187	Nilsson	176,880
Andersen	164,783	Andersen	38,247	Eriksson	141,399
Christiansen	124,119	Pedersen	36,168	Larsson	127,912
Larsen	121,598	Nilsen	36,143	Olsson	112,543
Sørensen	116,267	Kristiansen	24,190	Persson	110,347
Rasmussen	98,527	Jensen	23,725	Svensson	105,435
Jørgensen	92,275	Karlsen	22,073	Gustafsson	73,628

How Common Are Scandinavian Surnames in the United States?

In connection with the U.S. Federal Census, statistics are collected that can tell us something about the most common surnames. The surnames of Scandinavian origin that figure highest on the list are of the patronymic type. Among the surnames that may indicate a Scandinavian heritage, we find that Johnson ranks number 2, Anderson 11, Nelson 39, Olson 175, Hansen 222, Hanson 244, and Jensen 259.

Namesakes in the Scandinavian Tradition

Modern American naming books encourage parents to choose a name for their child that is trendy, cute, or distinctive. In contemporary Scandinavia we can see a similar tendency. But up until quite recently, such motives were a very far cry from what Scandinavian parents were up to when they chose a name for a new baby. What mattered was the family. Names were chosen from a limited palette of family names and according to a quite rigid system. In its simplest form the system worked like this: the first male child was given the name of the father's father, the first female child the name of the father's mother; the second male child got the name of the mother's father, and the second female child the name of the mother's mother. Sometimes, the system was reversed, so that the mother's parents were honored first, but by and large the system traditionally favored the father's family first in this respect.

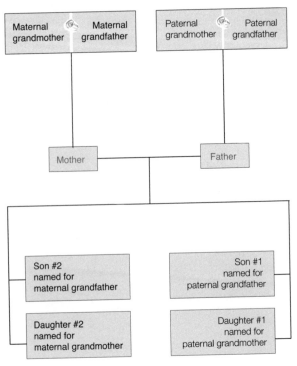

This tradition was practiced in Denmark, Norway, and Sweden for centuries, but it died out first in Sweden. In Denmark it is no longer common practice, but the custom is still carried on in many Norwegian families, particularly in rural communities.

We can illustrate this system by following the naming pattern in our own Norwegian family (see figure below). In order to see the pattern, it is not necessary to list all the children born to the various couples. This family can be traced back a long time, and we begin in 1720, when Johannes Endresen Søndenå was born. Johannes was the son of Endre, a name we can trace back to Old Norse Eindriði. Endre, pronounced *ehn*-dreh, is one of the names of the god Thor, and it means "the lone rider." Readers familiar with Norse mythology will remember that when it thunders, Thor is riding alone across the sky in a wagon pulled by his two billy goats. As we will see, Endre is the name with the longest tradition in this branch of the family.

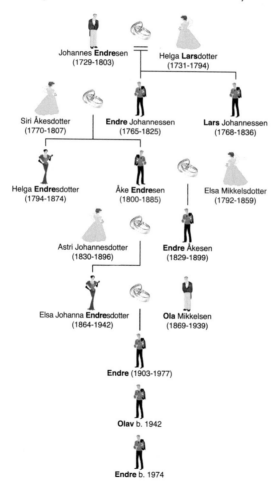

Johannes Endresen married Helga Larsdotter Håland. The couple settled at a farm called Hanakam in Suldal County in 1756. They now used the farm name Hanakam after their names, but it was more like an address to indicate where the family was living than a surname in the modern sense. As we can see from the patronymics of the parents, their first sons should receive the names Endre and Lars. And to be sure, Endre Johannessen Hanakam was born in 1765, and his brother Lars was born in 1768. We can follow the naming traditions through Endre. Endre married Siri Åkesdotter Hiim in 1793, and their first daughter born in 1794 was named Helga after her paternal grandmother. Their first son was Åke (b. 1800), in this case named after his maternal grandfather, and the second was named Johannes (b. 1804) after his paternal grandfather.

Åke Endresen Hanakam married Elsa Mikkelsdotter Brommeland in 1828. Their first son (b. 1829) was named Endre after Åke's father, the second (b. 1834) was named Mikkel after Elsa's father.

In the next generation we follow Endre Åkesen Hanakam. In 1860 he married Astri Johannesdotter Neset. One child is of interest here: Elsa Johanna Endresdotter, born in 1864 and named for both her paternal grandmother Elsa and maternal grandfather Johannes. At this time it was rare to have two given names. Elsa married Ola Mikkelsen Veka in 1895, and true to the pattern, their sons were named Mikkel (b. 1896) and Endre (b. 1903), and a daughter was named Astrid. Endre's eldest son received the name Olav (b. 1942), named for his paternal grandfather Ola Mikkelsen Veka. Olav's eldest son was named Endre (b. 1974) after his paternal grandfather.

But it wasn't always that simple, of course. Quite often a child would die, leaving a void in the naming pattern. But naming traditions had this covered as well. If a child died, the next one of the appropriate sex would be given the same name that the deceased child had had. When doing genealogical research, many people have certainly been puzzled to discover that an ancestor had two or three children named Anna or Lars. How could they keep them apart? And why give children the same name? A look at the life span of the children will usually confirm that they reused a name after a child died.

Another problem could arise if a couple had too many children of the same sex to fit the naming pattern. Then names of grandparents could be feminized or masculinized. A daughter could be named Kristina after grandfather Kristian, or Andrina after grandfather Anders. A son could be named Malenius after grandmother Malena, Randius after grandmother Randi, or Elenius after grandmother Elen.

Anders Andersen and Valborg Kristensdotter Helland were faced with this problem in the late nineteenth century. Following the normal pattern, their children would be named Anders, Anna, Kristian, and Guri. Their first four children, however, were all girls. So they named the first two after Anna and Guri, and the next two Alida and Kristina after Anders and Kristian. Eventually, they did have an Anders and a Kristian. But it was only on the third try that a Kristian survived infancy (see figure below).

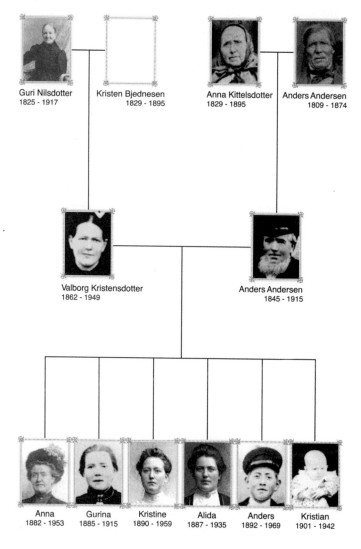

Guri Nilsdotter 1825 - 1917

Kristen Bjednesen 1829 - 1895

Anna Kittelsdotter 1829 - 1895

Anders Andersen 1809 - 1874

Valborg Kristensdotter 1862 - 1949

Anders Andersen 1845 - 1915

Anna 1882 - 1953

Gurina 1885 - 1915

Kristine 1890 - 1959

Alida 1887 - 1935

Anders 1892 - 1969

Kristian 1901 - 1942

If a man's wife had died and he remarried, the system required that the first female child be named after the deceased wife (see figure below). In the example above, we saw that Åke Endresen Hanakam married Elsa Mikkelsdotter Brommeland in 1828. Elsa died in 1859, and the next year Åke married Sissela Larsdotter Vetrhus. Their first child was duly named Elsa after the first wife. Another family member, Tormod Tormodsen Helland lost his wife in 1911. His new wife's first daughter was named Anna Karina after the deceased first wife. We can imagine that many second or third wives were not very happy to have a constant reminder of their predecessors about the house!

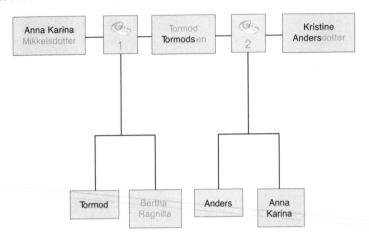

If the father of a child died before it was born, the system required that the child, regardless of its gender, be named after him. This contributed to the "feminization" of men's names already mentioned. Hendrikke Hendriksdotter, for example, was named after her deceased father Hendrik.

But what happened after the names of the grandparents and deceased spouses were used up? Additional children might be named after brothers and sisters of the parents, particularly those who had died without heirs or had no children themselves. Or the family could look back a generation and name children for great-grandparents.

Adapting Names in
Scandinavian North America

What did Scandinavian immigrants do when they had children in the New World? With such a rigid naming system and tradition, it is reasonable to assume that families in the New World felt obliged to carry on with it. The pressure was certainly most strongly felt in the Norwegian communities, as Norwegian immigrants tended to settle together in rural areas and quickly established Norwegian Lutheran churches and organizations to preserve native customs. In Sweden and Denmark the old namesake system was already loosening its grip, and given their settlement patterns there was less group pressure to follow the system in North America. Many Swedes settled in ethnic communities, but not on the scale of the Norwegians. Danes were more likely to settle in the cities, and as a result, few Danish communities grew up.

Sometimes the name could create a problem for a child in North America, but often it did not. A large number of given names do just as well in the United States as in a Scandinavian setting, even though the pronunciation differs a bit. There is no problem with names like Anna, Erica, Helga, and Linda or Alfred, Anton, Arnold, Eric, Gustav, and Norman. First names like Iver, Lars, Ole/Ola, or Alida might be less familiar, but could also be kept with an Americanized pronunciation.

We will first approach the important question of how Scandinavian families adapted their naming traditions to the new surroundings by looking at some examples. Names in our own Norwegian American families indicate that the naming traditions were followed—with certain modifications and adaptations to English and the local environment—for the first generation and possibly for one or two more.

Tron Jacobsen Buringrud and his wife, Hendrikke Hendricksdotter, immigrated to the United States in 1850. Their eldest daughter was born in Norway and named Anne Marie after their mothers, Anna and Mari. Anne Marie Tronsdotter met and married Nels Nelson (or Nils Andersen Stokset as he was known in Norway) in the United States. The couple had eight daughters and three sons. The first child was a girl, and she was named Henrietta Mathilda, no doubt after Anne Marie's mother Hendrikke and Nels's mother Martha Hansdotter. They may have been surprised by the seven additional daughters born in succession, and they later christened a daughter Martha. When they finally had a son, he was named Thomas Albert for their fathers, but Thomas was used for Tron and Albert for Anders. Using replacement names such as these was a typical practice among Norwegian immigrants. But Anne Marie and Nels did use Tron as the middle name of their second son.

When Thomas Albert Nelson married Lulu Belle Norton in 1912, it appears that they used names that began with the first letters of their parents' names to create appropriate names for their children. This is called *alliteration*, and it is also the way words rhymed with each other in the Old Norse lays. The Nelson daughter was named Alberta Louise, using the A for Anne and Louise for her maternal grandmother Lydia Louisa. They may also have taken into consideration the Anglo-American tradition of naming children for their parents: Alberta for Albert and Louise for Lulu Belle. Their son was named Norton, using the N for Nels and also following the tradition in many American families to use the mother's maiden name as a given name for a son.

If by now you are wondering whether the naming pattern could produce numer-

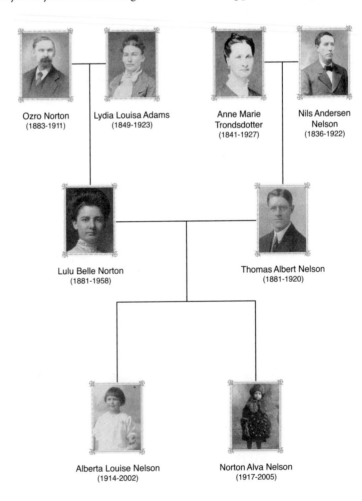

Ozro Norton
(1883-1911)

Lydia Louisa Adams
(1849-1923)

Anne Marie
Trondsdotter
(1841-1927)

Nils Andersen
Nelson
(1836-1922)

Lulu Belle Norton
(1881-1958)

Thomas Albert Nelson
(1881-1920)

Alberta Louise Nelson
(1914-2002)

Norton Alva Nelson
(1917-2005)

ous family members with the same name, the answer is yes! Here is an example from the family of Anna Kittelsdotter and Anders Andersen Helland. Four of their six children immigrated to the United States: Anna, Kittel, Brønla, and Knut. All of them married and had children, and they mostly followed the naming pattern. Anna Iverson (named for her paternal grandmother, not her mother) named a daughter Amalia. The reason she did not use her mother's name is probably that she was a second wife, and her husband had a daughter named Anna, whom she brought up. Both Kittel and Brønla had daughters named Anna, and Knut named a son Anton, no doubt after his mother. He also ran into the problem of having too many children of the same sex.

The Helland family replaced Anders with Andrew, rather than Albert, but the "real" name Anders turns up on some of the gravestones. Anna Iverson had two boys named Andrew, who both died as small children. Kittel replaced Anders with Ahlef (see dictionary). Knut's first son was also named Andrew. For reasons unknown, Brønla did not name anyone after her father, but named her three sons Johan (after her husband's father), Elmer, and Selmer. For the record, the two siblings who stayed in Norway each produced an Anna and an Anders.

The figure below shows the pattern of children named Anna and Anders after

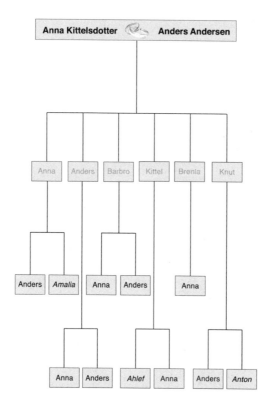

their grandparents. Only children who reached maturity are listed in the figure. As mentioned above, there were other children who died young and who received these two names.

Some Theories and Studies

The Norwegian American professor Einar Haugen did research on naming patterns in heavily Norwegian American areas. Haugen described three stages in the adaptation of Norwegian names to the American setting.

Stage 1

Children of the first immigrants gave their children Norwegian names like Anders, Erik, and Johannes, or Guro, Marte, and Sigrid. Since the communities where the families lived were Norwegian cultural and linguistic enclaves, the names would not be perceived as a problem for the bearers.

Stage 2

In the early period, the ministers in the Norwegian Lutheran churches in the United States were generally Norwegian and just as likely as their parishioners to be isolated from mainstream United States. Gradually, however, they saw it as their duty to urge parents to choose more "elegant" names for their children, or names that belong to the common stock of names with a Germanic origin (i.e., common in English, German, Scandinavian, and other Germanic languages). Names such as Albert, Carl (instead of Karl), and John, or Anne (instead of Anna or Ane), Clara, and Marie (instead of Mari or Maria) became common in the Norwegian American community. If the parents wanted to keep up the naming pattern, they could choose an American name that alliterated with the Scandinavian one, such as Albert for Anders or Asbjørn, and Ben for Bjørn or Bjarne.

In an article on naming influences in the United States and Norway, Anne Svanevik uses an example from an 1894–95 school class in Minnesota to show the development from stage 1 to stage 2 (Svanevik, 193–94). The class consists of twelve girls and thirteen boys. Six of the children have Norwegian names: Gine, Bertha, Andar (a form of Annar), Engebret, Anton, and Olaf. Three have American names: Josie, Nettie, and Tom. The rest have names common to both languages: Anna, Clara, Regina, Elisa, Martin, Oscar, Peter, Albert, John, and Emil. It is also worthy of note that several children are bearers of the same names. Four of the girls are named Anna and two are named Clara. Three of the boys are named Albert.

Stage 3

In the third stage, parents give their children American names like Betsy, Joyce, Tom, and Gilbert. For women, Betsy, Julia, Sarah, and Susie were early favorites. For men, favorites included Albert, Charlie, Louis, and Edward, Eddie, or Ed. Parents may have chosen names that alliterated with the names of their parents and relatives. We have seen examples in our own families to suggest that the parents chose names that were not entirely freed from the practice of namesaking. A granddaughter of Borgilla (Borghilda) is named Beverly, for example, and a grandson of Nels is named Norton.

Some Strategies

If a person's given name or surname was so unfamiliar to English speakers that it caused problems, there were a number of strategies that could be used in North America. A farm name that was easily pronounced in English could be used as a surname without any changes. Helland, Kaupang, Eklund, and Lindberg were no problem. Many chose to use the patronymic in its masculine form, such as Olsen, Andersen, or Andersson. The "daughter" forms (dotter, datter, dóttir) were normally abandoned in favor of the masculine forms, but they do turn up on some grave markers and in church records.

Danish-born actress Brigitte Nielsen was christened Gitte Nielsen in 1963. Though Gitte is an excellent Danish name, it sounds unfortunate pronounced in English. After she immigrated, Gitte chose to use another form of her name, Brigitte—which incidentally might remind people of another femme fatale, Brigitte Bardot. In the photo she is flanked by First Lady Nancy Reagan, President Ronald Reagan, and her husband at the time, Sylvester Stallone. Gitte is an extremely popular name in Denmark, where it is the prototype of a typical girls name. Bearers in 2008: Denmark, 23,579; Norway, 564; Sweden, Gitte 570, Gitta 57. (photo courtesy of Ronald Reagan Presidential Library)

Other names could be Americanized by making small changes in the spelling. Knut was spelled Knute or Knudt. It is indicative of the society in which the people lived that they did not use the form Canute, the British English form of that name. Several English kings were named Canute, including King Canute the Great (ca. 995–1035), king of England, Denmark, Norway, and part of Sweden. Scandinavian immigrants were not versed in British history and were no doubt ignorant of the fact that there was an English form of the name Knútr/Knud/Knut. Kari was spelled Carrie; Ni(e)ls and Sivert were spelled Nels and Severt; Serina, Ranveig, and Sigrid were adapted to Serena, Ranveg, and Sigred; and Olav was usually spelled Olaf. Surnames like Ru(u)d, Lie, and Vetrhus were spelled Rood, Lee, and Vettrus. The patronymic Kittelsen was adjusted to Kittleson.

Kittel Andersen Helland (1850–1912) and his sister Brønla Andersdotter Helland (1853–1923) were photographed in Stavanger, Norway, before Kittel immigrated to the United States in 1872. Brønla followed in 1882, the peak year for emigration from Norway. Although there are a good many people in the United States who use the patronymic Kittelson and its variants as their surname, apparently without problems, Kittel seems to have caused problems as a given name. According to the 2000 U.S. Census, there are about 3,320 bearers of the surname Kittelson and related spellings.

In the United States Kittel Helland often used his initials K. A., or the substitute name Charley. Brønla used the alternate spelling Brynla, but we also find the form Brynhild. Kjettel, the name on Kittel's headstone, is a somewhat misspelled version of his original name, whereas the name on Brønla's is correct, but uses the form Brynla. (photos by Nancy L. Coleman)

There are several vowels in the Scandinavian languages that are not a part of the English alphabet: *æ* or *ä*, *ø* or *ö*, and *å* (see page 69). These letters had to be rendered in another way, and English vowels had to be found that would approximate the pronunciation. The surname Sæbø(e) was written Sabo(e), Rønning became Ronning, Østebø became Ostebee, Sævareid became Sevareid, and Åbø became Aaboe. The given name Brønla became Brynla.

Another strategy was to use an English form of the name or to translate the elements of the name. Anders could call himself Andrew, Brønla could use Brynhilda, and Jørgen could use George. The surnames Ås and Åsen could be translated to Hill, Østerhus ('the farm to the east') to Easthouse, and Vetrhus ('winter' and 'house') to Winterhouse.

Other immigrants chose to take an English name that alliterated with their name, or seemed similar to it. Kittel could use the name Charley; Tormod, Tron, Torbjørn, and Torstein could use Thomas or Tom; Malenius could use Martin or Matt; and Bjedne or Bjarne could use Ben. Anders, a cognate to English Andrew, is and was a very common name, but for some reason many an Anders took the name Albert rather than Andrew.

In written records and on cemetery stones, we can see that the spelling of a name may be inconsistent. A family named Iversen may spell the name Iversen or Iverson in different sources. Anders may appear as Andrew, Anders, or Andres, and Kristian as Christian or Kristian. People doing genealogical research need to be aware of spelling fluctuations.

A final strategy was to use a name that looked Scandinavian, such as Ahlef, which is virtually unknown in Scandinavia. Oscar was also a popular name in Scandinavian America. It may have been popularized by James Macpherson's *The Poems of Ossian*, which was widely read in Scandinavia and the United States during the later nineteenth century and was the inspiration for naming traditions in both places.

The tables below show Scandinavian names that could be used in North America as they were or with minor spelling adjustments. Pronunciation might, however, differ. Note that some given names also appear in the list of equivalent names below.

Given Name	*American Form*
Alfred, m.	Alfred
Alida, f.	Alida
Anna, f.	Anna
Anton, m.	Anton
Arnold, m.	Arnold
Eirik, m.	Eric, Erick
Eirikur, m.	Eric, Erick
Erik, m.	Eric, Erick
Erika, f.	Erica, Ericka
Gustav, m.	Gustav, Gustaf
Helga, f.	Helga
Ivar, m.	Ivar
Iver, m.	Iver
Jon, m.	John
Karen/Karin, f.	Karen, Karin, Caren, Carin
Lars, m.	Lars
Linda, f.	Linda
Ola, m.	Ole
Olav, m.	Olaf
Ole, m.	Ole
Tor, m.	Thor

Surname	American Form
Andersen	Anderson
Andersson	Anders(s)on
Eklund	Eklund
Helland	Helland
Kaupang	Kaupang
Nilsen	Nelson
Olsen	Olson
Olsson	Olson
Ru(u)d	Rood

The next table shows the original Scandinavian names and the substitution or equivalent names that were used in the English-speaking setting.

Original Name	Equivalent Name
Aage	Albert
Aasmund/Åsmund	Osmon(d)
Anders	Andrew, Albert
Arne	Orin
Arnfinn	Arnold
Arve	Harvey
Asbjørn	Oscar
Aslak	Isaac
Atle	Adolph
Augun	August
Berit	Betzy
Bernt	Ben
Birgit/Bergit	Betzy
Bjarne/Bjedne	Ben
Bjørn	Burrie, Burnt
Botolf	Butler
Brynhild	Betzy
Brynjulv	Brown, Bronje
Egil/Eigil	Edward
Einar	Elmer, Eddie
Eivind	Edward, Edwin, Elmer
Elias	Ellis
Endre	Elmer
Enok	Ed
Erik	Erick, Edward
Erling	Earl, Elmer

Original Name	Equivalent Name
Fridjof/Fritjof	Fred
Gjert	Julian
Gregor	George
Gro	Julia
Gudbrand	Gilbert
Gudmund	Gilbert
Gulleik	Goodlet
Gunnar	Gilbert, Gust, Hiram
Gunnbjørn	Gilbert
Gunnhild	Julia
Gunnleik	George
Guri	Julia
Guro	Julia
Gustav	Gust, Gus
Haakon	Henry, Harry, Hagen
Hadle	Hadley
Haldor	Hiram
Hallstein	Halfstone
Halvor	Henry, Harry, Howard, Hall, Oliver
Hans	Henry
Helge	Henry
Herman	Hiram
Ingeborg	Betzy, Belle
Ingebrigt	Elmer
Ivar	Ira, Ives, Edgar
Jacob	Jack, Jake
Jens	James, John
Johan	John
Johannes	John
Jørgen	George
Karen	Carrie
Kari	Carrie
Karl	Charlie
Kjetil, Kittel	Charlie
Knut	Newt, Knute, Knudt
Kolbjørn	Cameron
Lars	Lewis, Louis, Lawrence
Leif	Lyman
Levor	Levin, Louis

Original Name	Equivalent Name
Maren	Mary
Margit	Margaret
Mikkel	Milo, Mike, Michael, McCall
Mons	Morris
Narve	Norvey
Nils	Nick, Nels
Nilsine	Nellie
Oddvar	Oscar
Ola	Orland
Olav	Oliver, Oscar, Olaf
Oline	Olive
Orm	Oliver
Ove	Owe
Per	Pete
Rasmus	Roy, Ross, Robert
Rønnaug	Rawley
Signe	Sadie
Sigrid	Sarah, Sigred
Sigurd	Simon, Sam
Siri	Sarah
Steinar	Stanley
Svein	Simon, Sam
Synneva	Susie
Synnøve	Susie
Tjøstolv	Chester
Tobias	Tom
Tor	Theodore, Tom, Thor
Tore	Tom
Torfinn	Tom
Torgeir	Tom
Torkel/Torkjell	Tom
Torleif/Torleif	Tom
Tormod	Tom
Thorvald	Tom
Tron(d)	Tom
Vetle	Victor
Østen, Øystein	Austin

Source: Based on a list compiled by Olaf Huseby, cited in Einar Haugen, *The Norwegian Language in America* (1953).

Scandinavian Names in the United States

As we saw above (page 63), there are about 11 million people in the United States (2000 Census) who claim Scandinavian ancestry, and in the immigration years the Scandinavians made up an even larger percentage of the U.S. population. In this section we will take a look at what impact Scandinavian Americans may have had on naming traditions in the United States. Statistics are available for the top one thousand names in each decade since 1880. Such statistics cannot, of course, tell us much about the parents and children behind them, their ethnic heritage, or the thinking behind the choice of a name. Many of the names in use in the Scandinavian American communities did not belong exclusively to the Scandinavian languages. But we can identify certain names as Scandinavian "markers" or "typical" for the Scandinavian American community.

Using data from the Web site for the Social Security Administration, we can study the popularity of names by decade from the 1880s up to the year 2000 and each year for 2000 to 2008.

Scandinavian Girls Names in U.S. Naming Tradition

The information in this section takes a look at Scandinavian girls names that turn up among the one thousand most popular names in the United States from the 1880s up until the year 2008. We will first discuss names that turn up in the statistics for each decade from the 1880s to 2000s, and then take a closer look at children born in 1980, during the period when ethnic names were revived.

The table below shows the popularity of Scandinavian girls names by decade from the 1880s to the 2000s. A number of the names in the table are not exclusively Scandinavian, and several of them are also common in the German American community. A good many names also have spelling variations, some of which are not common in the Scandinavian countries. Some spelling variations are English forms of the same name, some are Americanized forms to approximate the pronunciation, and still others are forms of the name that have been used in the Scandinavian American community.

Several names that were popular in the Scandinavian community are not included in the table since they were also mainstream American names and typical for many other ethnic groups. Particularly Anna/Anne/Annie and Maria/Marie should be mentioned, as these names were popular among Scandinavian Americans. In the 1880s, Anna ranked number 2, Anne number 11, and Annie number 122; Maria ranked number 137 and Marie number 45. All of these names have held their position as popular names in the United States.

In the discussion of this data some name forms not included in the table will be mentioned. For example, there are several spelling variations of the name Karen/

Scandinavian Names among the Thousand Most Popular Names Given to Girls in the USA, 1880s–2000s.

Name	1880s	1890s	1900s	1910s	1920s	1930s	1940s	1950s	1960s	1970s	1980s	1990s	2000s
Alva	492	399	432	478	576	617	835	—	—	—	—	—	—
Astrid	—	—	997	968	—	—	—	—	—	—	—	—	—
Berta	383	461	502	696	674	657	—	—	—	—	—	—	—
Bertha	8	12	—	43	70	116	157	246	395	611	990	—	—
Carla	—	—	—	—	979	438	225	138	79	118	193	337	472
Karla	—	—	—	—	—	—	430	242	195	237	272	223	202
Clara	9	11	23	40	55	79	137	227	369	545	551	422	267
Dagmar	904	887	—	—	—	—	—	—	—	—	—	—	—
Dana	920	—	—	—	827	600	303	188	82	253	77	164	384
Danica	—	—	—	—	—	—	—	—	—	—	813	913	691
Erica	—	—	—	—	—	—	767	373	59	36	58	173	—
Erika	—	—	—	—	—	—	—	414	127	76	95	192	—
Ericka	—	—	—	—	—	—	—	—	—	—	375	469	957
Freda	253	176	173	190	218	257	333	406	593	980	—	—	—
Freeda	—	—	782	811	768	968	—	—	—	—	—	—	—
Frida	—	—	—	—	—	—	—	—	—	—	—	—	797
Greta	—	702	697	701	677	383	705	603	518	687	—	—	710
Gusta	894	913	—	—	—	—	—	—	—	—	—	—	—
Hanna	426	531	802	—	—	—	—	—	—	—	709	219	229
Hannah	113	146	188	252	341	457	574	788	835	450	91	11	4
Hedwig	548	—	—	566	865	—	—	—	—	—	—	—	—
Helga	780	634	942	—	—	—	—	—	—	—	—	—	—
Hilda	163	103	99	111	142	197	262	340	505	629	904	—	—
Hildur	—	647	953	—	—	—	—	—	—	—	—	—	—
Hulda	203	225	351	580	905	—	—	—	—	—	—	—	—
Huldah	621	719	991	—	—	—	—	—	—	—	—	—	—
Inga	451	441	751	—	—	—	—	—	—	—	—	—	—
Ingrid	—	—	—	—	—	—	557	561	439	503	703	765	660
Karen	960	—	—	—	—	138	16	8	4	25	84	131	159
Karin	—	—	—	—	—	—	453	366	306	376	720	—	—
Kari	—	—	—	—	—	—	—	642	268	155	163	414	—
Karrie	—	—	—	—	—	—	—	—	685	480	938	—	—
Cari	—	—	—	—	—	—	—	—	589	455	626	—	—
Carrie	22	40	56	98	136	165	203	196	132	41	80	269	774
Katrina	—	—	—	—	—	—	965	465	252	126	101	172	310
Kirsten	—	—	—	—	—	—	—	—	366	302	286	176	321
Kristi	—	—	—	—	—	—	962	390	204	107	162	462	—
Kristin	—	—	—	—	—	—	590	404	159	74	43	116	459
Kristen	—	—	—	—	—	—	933	541	193	72	38	61	247
Kristina	—	—	—	—	—	—	849	506	247	99	60	119	319
Christina	200	243	310	332	349	399	236	174	161	16	18	40	118
Christena	519	668	—	—	—	—	—	—	—	—	—	—	—
Kristine	—	—	—	—	—	—	—	233	161	143	201	404	—
Christine	165	160	153	122	123	129	51	31	27	22	45	102	345
Lena	44	48	60	78	118	181	263	367	422	443	473	542	504
Mari	—	—	—	—	—	—	803	514	570	811	837	—	—
Metta	612	789	—	—	—	—	—	—	—	—	—	—	—
Mettie	600	664	929	—	—	—	—	—	—	—	—	—	—

NORTHFIELD PUBLIC LIBRARY
210 Washington Street
Northfield, MN 55057

Scandinavian Names among the Thousand Most Popular Names Given to Girls in the USA, 1880s–2000s (continued).

Name	1880s	1890s	1900s	1910s	1920s	1930s	1940s	1950s	1960s	1970s	1980s	1990s	2000s
Nora	56	69	94	145	174	203	227	241	296	388	413	463	309
Oda	641	638	821	—	—	—	—	—	—	—	—	—	—
Osa	814	861	—	—	—	—	—	—	—	—	—	—	—
Osie	692	864	867	—	—	—	—	—	—	—	—	—	—
Randi	—	—	—	—	—	—	953	484	523	516	264	452	—
Serena	570	698	778	—	—	—	—	—	—	429	426	332	289
Signe	972	615	718	938	—	—	—	—	—	—	—	—	—
Sigrid	—	732	950	—	—	—	—	—	—	—	—	—	—
Sonja	—	—	—	—	—	—	317	417	269	310	604	—	—
Sonia	—	—	—	788	656	420	474	363	242	183	270	372	576
Sonya	—	—	—	—	—	—	576	478	170	149	300	644	—
Thelma	—	169	41	28	34	63	136	238	392	700	—	—	—
Thora	—	758	—	845	—	—	—	—	—	—	—	—	—

Note: The numbers in the columns indicate the rank of the name for each decade, from 1 to 1000, 1 being the most popular. The numbers do not indicate the number of bearers.

Karin, but it is not likely that all of them would be used in the Scandinavian American community. The spellings Caryn, Caron, Karon, and Karan would seldom be chosen by Scandinavian Americans. But when different spellings of a name achieve high popularity, the sum of their rankings tells us more about the popularity than the rank of an individual spelling form. For this reason some of these variations are mentioned below.

To better understand this data, it is useful to divide the decades into three periods. The first one is from the 1880s to the 1920s, the period during which immigration from Scandinavia was at its high point. The second one is from the 1930s to the 1970s, a period when Scandinavians assimilated into American society. The third period is from the 1980s to the 2000s.

During the first period, the 1880s to the 1920s, the most popular Scandinavian names are Bertha, Clara, Carrie, Lena, and Nora, all of which rank among the top one hundred names. A good many of the other names found in the early period have spelling variations, and these increase the total popularity of these names. For example, Berta is quite popular and adds to the total popularity of Bertha, and the spelling variations Birtha and Birtie (not included in the table) turn up sporadically among the top thousand names during this period. Similarly, Freda/Freeda, Hanna/Hannah, Hulda/Huldah, Christina/Christine/Christena, Metta/Mettie, and Osa/Osie are all fairly popular names.

Statistics do not tell us anything about the origin of a name, and Osa and Osie deserve a closer look. Despite the fact that these were among the top thousand names in the United States for several decades, the names and their meanings have eluded authors of name books and Web resources, which for the most part do not mention Osa/Osie. The Web site Nameberry.com lists Osa in an article titled "The Lost Names of 1880," but there are no suggestions as to its origin or meaning. A search for bearers of Osa and Osie in the United States census for 1880 turns up women in states with few Scandinavian Americans, such as Indiana, Tennessee, Kentucky, and Georgia, as well as a good many in states with significant Scandinavian American populations. For example, there is an Osa Bertelson, born in Norway and living in Rush City, Minnesota. Her husband is listed as Osul Bertelson, and these names are certainly Americanized spellings of Åsa and Åsulv. We include Osa and Osie, which most likely also are Americanized spellings of Åsa/Åse.

Both Hannah and Huldah are uncommon spellings in Scandinavia, but since it was common to spell the name "Hannah" in the United States, this spelling caught on in the American Scandinavian community, and the spelling "Huldah" may have come into use on the analogy of Hannah. The table also shows that other alternate spellings such as Kari/Karrie and Kristina/Kristine did not become common until the later decades.

Other names that are popular in the early decades are Alva, Astrid, Dagmar, Greta, Gusta, Hedwig, Helga, Hilda, Hildur, Inga, Karen, Nora, Oda, Serena, Signe, Sigrid, Thelma, and Thora. The name Thelma, which was virtually unknown in Scandinavia and the United States, bursts onto the scene in the 1890s, a short time after the book *Thelma* by Marie Corelli came out and immortalized the name of the heroine. Thelma ranked among the hundred most popular names up to the 1930s. Dana turns up in the 1880s, but disappears for a few decades. Then it experiences a comeback with high rankings in the later decades. Dana may be a marker name of Danish identity, but it is not a typical Scandinavian name. Karen is another name that makes a brief appearance in the 1880s, but disappears until the later decades when it gains very high rank.

It is possible to associate certain names with Danish, Norwegian, or Swedish ethnic groups in the United States. Birtha/Birtie (occur sporadically, not included in the table) and Dana would most likely be used by Danish Americans; Carrie, Signe, and Sigrid by Norwegian Americans; and Alva, Christina/Christena, Gusta, Inga, and Metta by Swedish Americans. Mettie *could* be an Americanized spelling of Mette, the Danish and Norwegian form of the name. A look at the women named Mettie in the census for 1880 reveals that this name was also used by many non-Scandinavians. But there are Scandinavian American bearers in the census, for example, Danish American Mettie Andreason in Manti, Utah. But the 1880 census also shows that most of the women with a Danish or Norwegian background who were named Metta/Mettie or Osa/Osie used the spellings Metta and Osa.

There are a number of names that disappear from the list of the most popular names during the early twentieth century: Astrid, Dagmar, Hedwig, Helga, Inga,

Metta/Mettie, Oda, Osa/Osie, Signe, Sigrid, and Thora. A reason for this could be that the Scandinavian Americans have reached stage 3 in their choice of names (see page 88), so fewer children are being given the traditional names.

Sonia is a name that enters the list during the 1910s, and by the 1940s the alternate spellings "Sonja" and "Sonya" have contributed to the popularity of the name. Even though the origin of this name is Russian, the fame of Norwegian figure skater and film star Sonja Henie (1912–69) certainly contributed to the popularity of the name, perhaps even to the spellings "Sonja" and "Sonya."

By the period from the 1930s to the 1970s, many of the names from the first period have gone out of fashion. During the first decade of this period, only Clara and Thelma rank among the top one hundred names. New names enter the list from the 1920s to 1940s: for example, Carla, Dana, Ingrid, Karen/Karin, Mari, and Randi. These show growing popularity during the next decades, particularly Karen, which ranks number 16 in the 1940s. And with the support of several alternate spellings of the name, the rank would be even higher: Caren, Caryn, Karon, Karan, and Caron. Karen/Karin is the most popular girls name during the mid-twentieth century. By the 1950s, Karen ranks as high as number 8. This name continues to rank high in the 1970s, but loses ground in the 1980s and 1990s. Statistics for the year 2008 show that Karen ranks number 183, while Karin, Caren, and Carin have all disappeared from the list.

In the 1940s, several Scandinavian forms of names of the Saints Christina and Katarina enter the list: Katrina, Kristi, Kristin, Kristen, and Kristina. Kristin and the alternate spelling Kristen show rapidly rising popularity. In Scandinavia Kristen is a boys name, a form of Kristian, but the Americans are largely not aware of this. By the 1970s, Kristen and Kristin were among the top hundred names. Since the 1990s their popularity has declined, but in 2008 they were still fairly high on the list: the "misspelled" form Kristen holds the lead, ranking number 492, while Kristin is number 883. The popularity of Kristin may have been influenced by the Norwegian author Sigrid Undset, who won the Nobel Prize for her trilogy *Kristin Lavransdatter*. During World War II Undset spent several years as a refugee in the United States, where she was well known for her literary works and her stance against Nazi Germany. Kirsten and the related form Kiersten are also popular. In 2008 Kirsten ranked number 567 and Kiersten 661.

Other names starting with K or a hard C are popular during this period. Karla joins Carla in the 1940s, and both of them show rising popularity. Carla/Karla, a feminine form of Carl/Karl, may mark Swedish identity. Erica/Erika, a feminine form of Eric/Erik, may be associated with the heather plant and is also a popular German name. But its popularity follows the lead of Eric/Erik, and the name has taken on the character of a marker name in the Scandinavian community. Erica/Erika shows high popularity during the last decades of the twentieth century, but then drops sharply.

The Norwegian soprano Kirsten Flagstad (1895–1962) starred at the Metropolitan Opera during the 1930s and 1950s and also toured the United States with concert programs. She is certainly partly responsible for the popularity of the name Kirsten (also spelled Kiersten) in the United States. Bearers in 2008: Denmark, 47,657; Norway, 9,124; Sweden, 1,075; United States, 27,326.

Mari is a Swedish and Norwegian form of Maria, but it may also be an alternative spelling of the English Mary. It is interesting that Randi, a Norwegian form of Ragnfrid, becomes popular during these decades. The name may have other origins in the United States, as other names ending in -i were popular (Sandi, Andi, Brandi). Ingrid is another name that enters the scene in the 1940s, and it has maintained its popularity up until the 2000s, gaining popularity in recent years.

In the final period, the 1980s to the 2000s, Bertha, Freda, Hilda, Karin, Mari, and Thelma drop out of the top one thousand names. In the 2000s, however, the Swedish form "Frida" enters the list. Carrie retains popularity from the 1880s to the 2000s, but its popularity has been steadily declining since the 1980s. (This Scandinavian girls name should not be confused with the Finnish boys name Kari and the Icelandic boys name Kári.) In 2008 this name is no longer among the most popular names. By the 1990s the popularity of both Kari and Carrie had fallen sharply, and in the 2000s only Carrie remained. Kari makes a brief comeback for girls born in 2002, ranking number 976, but since then Kari has dropped off the list.

Similarly, the spellings Sonja and Sonya drop out in the 1990s and 2000s, respectively, while Sonia remains. Even though the spelling Kristine had relatively high rank in the 1990s, it drops out of the list in the 2000s, as do Kristi and Randi.

Names beginning with K or a hard C retain their popularity in the final period, and alternate spellings add to their total popularity. Kristi, for example, has several spellings, all with individual ranks among the top thousand names. We should also mention Danica, an interesting name that enters the list in this period. The alternate spelling Danika also turns up in the years after 2000. This name may be a marker of Danish identity. See the section on Canada on page 113 for further information about this name.

The Scandinavian Names Revival

Whereas the generations in the early and mid twentieth century were most interested in assimilating into American culture, the 1970s brought renewed interest in ethnicity. As a result, it became popular in the American Scandinavian community to take up certain Scandinavian names such as Carrie/Kari, Kristin, Kristina/Christina, and Erica/Erika as a cultural "marker."

Name statistics for children born in 1980 reflect the renewed interest in Scandinavian names. In the table below, we list the Scandinavian-type names that turn up in the one hundred most popular names in states with a significant population of Scandinavian ethnic background. Rank numbers are given for girls names in Iowa, Illinois, Minnesota, Montana, Nebraska, North Dakota, Oregon, South Dakota, Utah, Washington, and Wisconsin, as well as for the United States as a whole.

We have included two names in the table that are not *necessarily* Scandinavian markers, Anna and Kara. Anna/Anne was a very common name among Scandinavian immigrants, and Anna was the most common form. Anna was also a top name in all of Scandinavia during the immigration period, so it is a family name in a large number of Scandinavian American families today. In earlier periods families may have Americanized the name to Ann, Anne, or Annie. During the ethnic names revival, they may have returned to Anna. In any case, Anna has been on the rise during recent decades, while Ann, Anne, and Annie have dropped considerably in popularity. In 2008 Anna ranked 26, Anne 499, Ann 830, and Annie 392 among the one thousand most popular names.

The other name is Kara, which is not a Scandinavian name at all. Kara is a twentieth-century name, a respelling of Cara. It comes from Italian 'beloved' or Gaelic 'friend.' But spelled with a K the name has a Scandinavian feel and appearance, and it could readily be associated with the other Scandinavian girls names starting with a K sound, particularly Karen and Kari. The K names for girls dominate during the Scandinavian ethnic names revival.

If we compare the rankings of the marker names in the core Scandinavian American area with the national rankings, we can see that most of the names turn up in the national lists as well. But there are some interesting differences. Anna is more popular in some of the core area than nationally. Kari does not rank nationally among the top one hundred names, but the rank of Carrie is similar. Neither Kara, Krista, Kristi, or Kristine is among the hundred most popular names nationally, while they are significantly popular in the core area. The rankings for Kristin, Kristina, and Erika are in the same range in the core area as nationally. Katrina is more popular in some of the core states than nationally, but Karen, Christina, Christine, and Erica actually rank *higher* nationally. Christy is a rare spelling in the core area, but it ranks nationally among the top hundred names. If there is any conclusion to be drawn here, it is that the names beginning with K are more popular in the core area, and that given a choice, parents in this area are more likely to use a Scandinavian spelling of a marker name, such as Kari, Kristi, Kristin, Kristine, Erika. In itself, spelling a name with a K instead of Ch seems to be a marker.

Top names given to girls born in 1980, in states with populations including significant numbers of people with a Scandinavian background. (Names with alternate spellings are placed together.)

Name	IA	IL	MN	MT	NE	ND	OR	SD	UT	WA	WI	USA
Anna	52	61	39	33	60	—	35	47	56	31	54	55
Carrie	37	42	—	43	48	37	44	32	55	54	35	46
Kari	55	—	47	59	96	30	94	50	—	—	56	—
Kara	81	—	—	74	80	61	66	54	—	—	—	—
Karen	80	56	61	—	95	—	98	—	69	76	67	54
Katrina	—	73	—	60	92	—	63	75	—	—	98	90
Krista	95	—	58	61	—	78	—	81	78	63	88	—
Kristi	98	—	69	79	81	42	—	49	—	—	99	—
Christy	—	—	—	—	—	—	—	—	73	—	—	83
Kristy	—	84	—	75	—	91	91	—	62	—	71	78
Kristin	30	32	32	38	—	32	39	34	52	50	24	37
Kristen	64	—	52	52	51	25	58	51	43	58	58	39
Christina	29	17	29	19	23	—	—	23	46	18	33	15
Kristina	76	64	50	66	67	65	—	55	82	39	60	73
Christine	70	35	46	72	63	57	—	78	67	—	45	41
Kristine	—	—	76	—	—	66	—	—	—	96	—	—
Erica	49	31	59	—	49	49	49	37	71	48	47	34
Erika	—	94	—	—	—	77	74	93	—	64	84	81

As we can see from the table, the lists of the top one hundred names include only a few Scandinavian names, since many of them are actually spelling variations or different forms of the same name. Thus, the statistics showing the top hundred names in a state do not tell much about the range of Scandinavian names that were in use during the ethnic names revival. Few states have searchable databases for names, but Oregon is an exception. On the government Web site we can find statistics for names given to babies from 1961 to 2008. The next table will give some idea of the Scandinavian names that were given to children born in the state during the period from 1970 to 1989. Statistics for the total number of children given each name from 1961 to 2008 are also included.

Scandinavian Girls Names Given to Children Born in Oregon

Name	1970–1989	Total 1961–2008
Astrid	1	50
Berit	1	9
Birgit	1	2
Birgitta	2	5
Birgitte	2	2
Brigitta	5	13
Brigitte	21	52
Carrie	1,385	1,965
Kari	838	1,268
Christen	46	75
Kristen	1,109	1,876
Christin	63	91
Kristin	1,546	2,368
Kristyn	48	88
Christi	122	197
Kristi	699	1,110
Christie	188	319
Kristie	230	337
Christy	488	700
Kristy	485	666
Christina	2,936	4,423
Kristina	1,445	2,247
Christena	6	12
Kristena	9	16
Christine	1,514	2,819
Kristine	526	974
Erica	1,140	1,855
Erika	662	1,342
Freda	4	10
Frida	—	34
Greta	43	157
Hilda	23	61
Inga	26	38
Inge	4	6
Inger	5	11
Ingri	1	1
Ingrid	82	181
Karen	1,082	3,453
Karin	128	282
Katrina	836	1,460
Kirsten	383	848
Kirstin	91	174
Kirstyn	6	23
Kirsti	9	26
Kirstie	14	45
Kirsty	7	16
Kirstina	2	6
Kirstine	4	9
Lena	113	282

Scandinavian Girls Names Given to Children Born in Oregon (continued)

Name	1970–1989	Total 1961–2008
Liv	7	23
Liva	1	3
Maren	44	118
Signe	18	34
Sigrid	4	13
Siv	3	4
Thora	1	4
Tora	1	6
Tova	5	9
Tove	9	10

In the Oregon table we can see the same tendency as in the previous table. The names beginning with a K sound dominate, whether they are spelled with a K or Ch, and there are several variations for these popular names. Spellings with a K were more popular for several of them. Only Erica/Erika comes close to the number of bearers of the K names. But even the names with few bearers confirm a Scandinavian name trend in Oregon during the ethnic names revival. If we compare the figures for the period 1970 to 1989 with the total number, we can see that for most of the names, bearers born in this twenty-year period represent a large percentage of the children who were given these names between 1961 and 2008.

An interesting name choice turned up in an article in the Norwegian newspaper *Aftenposten* in 2004. An American student named Rennesa was attending summer school at the University of Oslo. Her great-grandfather had immigrated to the United States from the island of Rennesøy near Stavanger. Probably on the analogy of the name Vanessa, her parents had adapted the name of the island to create a distinctive name for their daughter.

Scandinavian Boys Names in U.S. Naming Tradition

This section takes a look at Scandinavian boys names that turn up among the one thousand most popular names in the United States from the 1880s to the 2000s. As we did for the girls, we will first discuss boys names that turn up in the statistics for each decade from the 1880s to the 2000s, and then take a closer look at boys born in 1980.

The table below shows the popularity of Scandinavian boys names by decade from the 1880s to the 2000s. A number of the names in the table are not exclusively Scandinavian; for example, Carl/Karl and Hans are also common in the German American community. Some names not included in the table will be mentioned in the discussion of the data.

Several names that were popular in the Scandinavian community are not included

Scandinavian Names Among the Thousand Most Popular Names Given to Boys in the United States, 1880s–2000s.

Name	1880s	1890s	1900s	1910s	1920s	1930s	1940s	1950s	1960s	1970s	1980s	1990s	2000s
Adolphus	410	456	612	712	833	851	—	—	—	—	—	—	—
Alf	673	798	900	—	—	—	—	—	—	—	—	—	—
Andres	710	847	765	766	637	628	605	583	486	360	238	168	164
Arne	—	—	—	849	—	—	—	—	—	—	—	—	—
Arvid	900	764	964	679	777	818	989	—	—	—	—	—	—
Bo	—	—	—	—	—	—	—	—	—	—	657	721	819
Carl	33	23	26	25	27	29	36	49	57	90	115	204	382
Karl	262	220	220	187	228	179	180	158	154	212	248	390	724
Christian	235	276	377	462	563	635	510	385	234	108	100	32	21
Kristian	—	—	—	—	—	—	—	—	—	527	685	438	461
Dane	—	—	—	—	—	—	785	470	479	564	310	422	410
Einar	—	—	890	939	—	—	—	—	—	—	—	—	—
Eric	545	417	422	423	423	331	151	74	28	14	21	29	62
Erik	—	—	—	—	—	—	700	473	183	87	85	113	176
Erick	—	946	—	—	—	—	967	752	440	277	256	201	184
Erling	—	—	—	988	—	—	—	—	—	—	—	—	—
Finn	—	—	—	—	—	—	—	—	—	—	—	—	540
Gunnar	—	—	—	—	—	—	—	—	—	—	—	636	563
Gunner	—	—	—	—	—	—	—	—	—	—	—	906	595
Gustaf	782	832	—	—	—	—	—	—	—	—	—	—	—
Gustav	296	404	583	592	853	—	—	—	—	—	—	—	—
Gus	—	172	204	297	336	388	495	563	644	894	—	—	—
Gust	376	435	824	—	—	—	—	—	—	—	—	—	—
Hans	343	416	567	620	755	679	932	655	514	551	658	842	—
Harold	84	31	19	12	13	19	28	62	99	152	253	416	612
Leif	—	—	—	—	—	—	—	794	771	858	—	—	—
Nels	383	429	747	872	—	—	—	—	—	—	—	—	—
Norman	117	97	78	49	43	40	67	107	138	225	332	562	940
Normand	—	—	—	—	492	456	637	850	—	—	—	—	—
Olaf	478	570	719	742	—	—	—	—	—	—	—	—	—
Ola	882	—	—	—	—	—	—	—	—	—	—	—	—
Ole	301	488	727	—	—	—	—	—	—	—	—	—	—
Sigmund	—	—	821	481	912	—	—	—	—	—	—	—	—
Soren	—	—	—	—	—	—	—	—	—	—	—	—	911

Note: The numbers in the columns indicate the rank of the name for each decade, from 1 to 1000, 1 being the most popular. The numbers do not indicate the number of bearers.

in the table since they were also mainstream American names and typical for many other ethnic groups as well. These include Jon/John, Albert, and Andrew, a popular replacement name for Anders. In the 1880s, John ranked number 1, Albert number 16, and Andrew number 27. In this decade and during the entire period, there are certainly a good many Scandinavian men supporting the popularity of Jon/John, Albert, Andrew, Austin (a replacement name for Øystein/Østen), and Oscar. All of these names have held their popular positions in the United States.

It is interesting that the spelling "Jon" does not turn up in the list until the 1920s. Many would consider this spelling a Scandinavian marker. By the 1930s, Jon ranked 199, and its popularity grew steadily over the next decades: number 125 in the 1940s, 119 in the 1950s, and 83 in the 1960s. It is likely that the Scandinavian American community contributed to its popularity.

The list of names in the table is shorter for the boys than for the girls, and none of the boys names achieves as high a rank as Clara or Bertha. Carl, Christian, Eric/ Erik, Harold, and Norman are the only names among the top one hundred. Harold is the English spelling of Scandinavian Harald, so this name does not have a distinctive Scandinavian flavor. There are only a few boys names with spelling variations.

As with the girls, we can divide the data into three periods. In the early period, the 1880s to 1920s, we find names that were common in Scandinavia at the time: Adolphus, Alf, Arvid, Carl/Karl, Eric, Gustaf/Gustav, Hans, Harold (Harald), Nels, and Olaf/Ola/Ole. Arne, Erling, and Sigmund turn up for a few decades as the period progresses. Andres, another form of Anders, is on the list, and it is popular throughout the entire period. Andres is also a Spanish form of the name of Saint Andrew, so most Americans may not associate this name with Scandinavia. The more common Scandinavian written form, Anders, never makes the list, but surprisingly the patronymic Anderson turns up as a given name during many decades. Christian also makes an early appearance, and it is popular throughout the period. Erick, the American spelling of Erik, turns up in the 1890s, but it disappears again until the 1940s.

A few of these names mark a specific Scandinavian identity. Adolphus, Carl/ Karl, and Gustaf/Gustav are Swedish marker names, and Alf, Harold (Harald), Olaf/Ola, and Sigmund mark a Norwegian identity. Gust was a typically Scandinavian American form of Gustav, and it is known from both Swedish and Norwegian America. Gus is another form of this name, but it probably was used by other ethnic groups as well. Ole was primarily associated with Norwegian Americans, but the form could also mark Danish identity. The name Norman is in a category all by itself. Spelled "Nordmann" the word means a Norwegian, but Norman is not a common Scandinavian name. The spelling "Normand" is close to the Danish spelling *nordmand*, meaning Norwegian. In North America Norman(d) became a name that marked a person as having Norwegian or Scandinavian ancestry. Nels, Christian, and Eric/Erik are common in all of Scandinavia, and would mark a Scandinavian heritage. In the early twentieth century the names that sound most foreign in the American setting—Alf, Nels, Olaf/Ola/Ole—fall in popularity and disappear from the list by the 1910s. However, the patronymics Nelson and Olson have became common given names, and often rank among the top one thousand. These are also marker names of a Scandinavian identity. Somewhat surprisingly, Arvid is popular for a good many decades, from the 1880s to the 1940s.

From the 1930s to the 1970s, Andres, Carl/Karl, Christian, Gus, Hans, Harold, and Norman remain popular names. In the 1940s and beyond, the spellings "Erik" and "Erick" add to the popularity of Eric. By the 1970s, Eric is number 14 and Erik is number 87. The spelling "Normand" enters the list during this period. Dane, a name that could mark Danish identity, turns up in the 1940s and continues to be popular throughout the period. Leif joins the list in the 1960s.

The final period, the 1980s to the 2000s, includes the Scandinavian names revival. Even so, the list of names is quite short, as several of the names to make the top one thousand are forms of the same name: Carl/Karl, Christian/Kristian, and Eric/Erik/Erick. But there are some interesting new names on the list. Bo, a popular Swedish and Danish name, turns up on the list for the 1980s and retains its status in the 1990s and the 2000s. Finn joins the list in the 2000s. This name is fairly common in Denmark and Norway, but in the United States it probably also marks Finnish identity. The popular Scandinavian name Gunnar and the alternate form Gunner turn up in the 1990s. Leif is on the list for the 1970s and 1980s, but in view of the fact that Leif Erikson discovered America around 1000, and is therefore a popular figure in the Scandinavian American community, it is strange that his name has not been a significant one on the list of popular names. Perhaps this is related to the fact that Americans find it difficult to pronounce and sometimes spell it wrong. Finally, the Danish Norwegian name Soren (Søren) joins the list for the 2000s.

Of the Scandinavian marker names, only Andres, Carl/Karl, Christian, Eric, Harold, and Norman have an unbroken record of popularity since the 1880s among the one thousand most popular names. Harold ranked number 12 in the 1920s, but has been consistently losing ground, ranking number 737 for children born in 2008. Carl has fared somewhat better, ranking 490 in 2008. Norman was on the list for children born in 2006, but has since disappeared. Eric was very popular in the period of ethnic revival during the 1970s, ranking number 12. Among boys born in 2000, Eric had dropped to 42 and in 2008 to 86. But the alternate spellings also retain popularity: Erick 179 and Erik 213 in 2008. Of the Scandinavian marker names, only Christian shows rising popularity, but probably not primarily thanks to Scandinavian Americans, as it is also common in other groups. In the 1920s the name ranked number 563, and in most of the decades since its popularity has risen. Most noteworthy is the period from the 1990s, when Christian ranked number 32, and up to the present. By the 2000s, Christian ranked 21 and this ranking has remained stable, supported by the alternate spellings Cristian and Kristian.

The Scandinavian Names Revival

Finally, we will take a look at the statistics for names of boys born in 1980, during the ethnic names revival. It is worth noting that the list of names for the core area of Scandinavian America is shorter for the boys than for the girls (see table above). In the table below, we list the Scandinavian-type names that turn up in the one hundred most popular names in states with a significant population of Scandinavian ethnic background. Rank numbers are given for boys names in Iowa, Illinois, Minnesota, Montana, Nebraska, North Dakota, Oregon, South Dakota, Utah, Washington, and Wisconsin, as well as for the United States as a whole.

Top names given to boys born in 1980, in states with populations including significant numbers of people with a Scandinavian background. (Names with alternate spellings are placed together.)

Name	IA	IL	MN	MT	NE	ND	OR	SD	UT	WA	WI	USA
Andrew	11	21	7	29	9	22	15	23	24	16	9	19
Carl	—	—	86	—	—	—	—	—	—	90	97	—
Christian	—	—	—	—	—	—	—	—	88	—	—	—
Christopher	7	3	6	6	5	6	2	7	6	3	7	2
Kristopher	—	—	96	—	—	92	92	—	—	93	—	—
Eric	14	15	16	17	18	11	18	9	33	20	11	16
Erik	66	57	49	72	66	53	59	71	89	46	52	64
Jon	88	—	68	—	—	76	—	79	—	—	91	—

Three names that are not necessarily Scandinavian are included in the table: Andrew, Christopher/Kristopher, and Jon. Andrew was a common replacement name for Anders, a very common name among Scandinavian immigrants (see the common U.S. surname Anderson/Andersson/Andersen; Anderson is currently number 12 on the list of the most common last names, Andersen 954). Anders/Andrew is therefore no doubt a name found in many Scandinavian American families, and it would be relevant to use it during an ethnic names revival. Christopher/Kristopher has broad appeal among Americans, but particularly spelled with a K it might be interpreted as a Scandinavian marker (in Scandinavia it is spelled Kristoffer or Christoffer). As mentioned above, Jon is the common Scandinavian form of the name John.

In the next table we can see that Carl, Christian, and Jon only turn up in the top hundred names for the Scandinavian ethnic core area. Jon has slipped down from the high national ranking in earlier decades. Andrew ranks higher in some of the core states, but is also quite popular nationally. Christopher is number 2 on the national list, a higher ranking than in any of the core states, but when spelled Kristopher it only turns up among the top hundred names in the core area. The popularity of Eric is within the same range nationally as in the core area, but parents in the core area are somewhat more likely to spell it Erik.

As we did for the girls, we take a look at the Scandinavian names given to boys born in Oregon between 1961 and 2008. The next table gives some idea of the variety of names that parents were choosing for their children during the ethnic names

Scandinavian Boys Names Given to Children Born in Oregon

Name	1970–1989	Total 1961–2008
Anders	17	84
Arne	9	17
Arnie	5	11
Bjarne	1	2
Bjorn	39	78
Carl	542	1,175
Karl	266	572
Christen	20	30
Kristen	15	24
Christian	478	2,869
Kristian	55	175
Christoffer	12	16
Kristoffer	51	77
Einar	3	8
Eirik	5	8
Eric	4,541	8,016
Erick	158	481
Erik	1,234	2,225
Eyvindur	1	1
Gunnar	22	163
Gunner	7	80
Jens	26	47
Lars	52	105
Leif	85	193
Magnus	—	21
Nels	19	38
Niels	4	8
Nils	13	26
Norman	138	377
Odin	7	38
Olaf	9	17
Olav	3	3
Ole	7	18
Olof	1	3
Peder	9	14
Per	5	8
Stein	1	3
Sten	8	16
Svein	—	2
Sven	17	24
Tage	1	5
Thor	26	63
Tor	7	12
Tore	1	2
Torsten	2	8

The Leif Erikson statue at Shishole Marina in Seattle. Leif Erikson, born in Iceland, is credited with discovering America five hundred years before Christopher Columbus, and he is the only Scandinavian to be honored with his own day in the United States. Since 1964, October 9 has been celebrated as Leif Erikson Day. President Barack Obama issued a proclamation in 2009 calling upon Americans "to observe this day with appropriate ceremonies, activities, and programs to honor our country's rich Nordic-American heritage." The name Leif has never been popular enough in the United States to turn up in the statistics for the most popular names, but the name of Leif's father, Erik the Red, who fled Norway and colonized Greenland, has been a top name for many years in the forms Erik, Eric, and Erick. (photo by Nancy L. Coleman)

Bearers of Various Forms of Erik Born in the United States

	Eric	Erik	Erick
1880s	122	—	—
1900s	205	—	44
1920s	2,028	—	—
1940s	15,170	854	345
1950s	53,248	2,444	935
1960s	152,187	14,754	3,294
1970s	211,427	32,084	7,167
1980s	204,045	36,303	8,993
1990s	135,147	33,590	15,666
2000s	64,674	20,803	19,383

Bearers of Various Forms of Erik in Scandinavia (2008)

	Eric	Erik	Erick	Eirik	Eiríkur
Denmark	634	35,824	32	41	—
Iceland	—	—	—	—	694
Norway	923	20,338	43	12,598	—
Sweden	30,834	302,308	278	140	—

Though it is not a top name in the United States, Ivar Haglund's fish restaurants have made Ivar a household name in the Seattle area. Ivar/Iver are well known in Scandinavia: Denmark, Ivar 578, Iver 493; Norway, Ivar 10,251, Iver 1,645; Sweden, Ivar 20,030, Iver 44. (photo by Nancy L. Coleman)

revival. The tendency to use names starting with a K sound is not as marked as for the girls. It is interesting that the Scandinavian spellings of Christopher—Christoffer and Kristoffer—turn up and enjoy their greatest popularity between 1970 and 1989. As we might expect, Eric/Erik has many bearers, and the popularity extends beyond the ethnic names revival. Even the form Eirik turns up with a few bearers, most of them in the period from 1970 to 1989. We can also see that there must have been some Icelanders in Oregon, as one boy was named Eyvindur. The names of the Norse gods Odin and Thor/Tor enjoy a certain popularity. Two other names beginning with Tor are on the list, Tore and Torsten, and there are several others not included in the table that have one or two bearers: Torben, Torbjorn, Torfinn, Torgrim, Torkil, Torvald, Thorr, and Thorsten. The patronymics Torsen, Thorsen, Torson, and Thorson also turn up as first names, as do other patronymics: Andersen, Jensen, Larsen/Larson, Nilsen, Olsen. Nelson is a fairly popular given name (132 bearers), and 58 were named Anderson in the period 1961 to 2008.

Scandinavian Names in Canada

Statistics on names are not as readily available for Canada during the immigration period, which makes it difficult to compare trends in Canada with the material for the United States. Both countries share a similar culture and language, so differences would probably be quite small. Since the Scandinavian Canadian communities were a part of the picture of immigration from Scandinavia to North America, there is every reason to assume that Canadian Scandinavian naming practices were similar to those in the United States. But immigration to Canada took place later than to the United States, and many immigrants migrated to Canada from Scandinavian communities in the United States. Naming trends would therefore be influenced by current naming fashions at home and in Scandinavian United States.

Statistics on names are, however, available for the provinces for the last couple of decades, but each province has its own system, so that the data is not easy to compare. Statistics on the one hundred most popular names are also available for all of Canada for 2008. Since the Canadian Scandinavian community is largely gathered in the western provinces, it is not surprising that few Scandinavian names are popular enough to turn up among the most popular names for the whole country.

There are two girls names on the list, Annika ranked number 89 and Danica/Danika number 90. Annika is one of the most popular girls names in Sweden (ranked number 47 among all Swedish women in 2009), and it probably is a marker name in the Swedish Canadian community. Danica/Danika is rare in Scandinavia (only 56 Danish bearers in 2009), but there is reason to believe that it has become a marker name in the Danish Canadian community. During the Age of the Enlightenment (late eighteenth to early nineteenth centuries), an atlas named *Flora Danica* on the flora of Denmark, Norway, and the Danish colonies was published (1761–1883). Subsequently, Royal Copenhagen, the Danish producer of fine china, created a famous series called Flora Danica. Flora Danica may have been the inspiration for naming girls Danica/Danika. In addition to these two names, we should mention Anna, ranked number 98, and a good number of women in the Scandinavian ethnic community have certainly contributed to its popularity.

Among the one hundred most popular boys names in Canada for 2008, Eric, ranked number 79, is the only real Scandinavian name. Eric has been losing popularity in recent years, however. In 2006 Eric ranked 57, but fell to 70 in 2007. Andrew, ranked number 35, should also be mentioned because it is a popular replacement name for Scandinavian Anders.

Scandinavian Names in the Core Area for Scandinavian Canada
Most of the Scandinavian immigrants to Canada settled in the western provinces of Manitoba, Saskatchewan, Alberta, and British Columbia. All of the provinces have some statistics on popular names, but these are rarely good enough for our purposes. Scandinavian Canadians once dominated many areas in these provinces, but many other ethnic groups have since found homes there. The top twenty-five baby names listed for these provinces are a reflection of a multicultural society and of international trends, as many of the same names that are found all over the western world also top the lists in Canada and its provinces.

Around 1910 Østen (Øystein) Johannesen and Marta Jonesdotter Lie emigrated from Fister in Rogaland, Norway, and settled in Big Beaver, Saskatchewan. They called themselves Austin and Martha Lee in their new surroundings. Marta was the first white woman in the area. Østen and Marta had nine children. They are pictured with their daughters Gertie, who died as a child, and Maria. The boys were Arthur, Østen (or Austin), Magnus, and Oscar. The girls were Gertie, Maria, Olga, Erlinga, and Gjertrud (named for her deceased sister). They chose Scandinavian names for half of their children, but adjusted them when necessary: Østen (Austin), Magnus, Erlinga, and Gjertrud. The names of the other children were popular ones in Scandinavian communities in North America: Arthur, Oscar, Maria, and Olga.

The name data for the provinces of Alberta and British Columbia goes into more depth and lists names given to babies born from the 1990s to 2009. The data from Alberta includes *all* names given to babies, while the data from British Columbia lists all names given to at least five babies during a given year. The data from Alberta in particular gives a picture of the variety of Scandinavian names in use in Canada today. The next two tables document Scandinavian girls and boys names in Alberta and British Columbia for the period from 1997 to 2009. The comment column lists years for when the names with few bearers were used or indicates if a name only shows up in certain years.

In the first table, a few names have been included that are not very typical in the Scandinavian countries themselves, but there is good reason to believe they are considered markers of a Scandinavian identity. As indicated above, Danica/Danika may have become popular in the Danish Canadian community, and Dana could also be

Scandinavian Girls Names Given to Children Born in Alberta and British Columbia

Name	Alberta 1997–2009	Comment: Data based on all babies	British Columbia 1997–2009	Comment: Data based on names with at least 5 bearers
Annika	334		381	
Anika	215		285	
Astrid	17		11	2002, 2005
Bertha	16		—	—
Carrie	34		44	1997–2002, 2008
Kari	21		10	1997, 1999
Christina	342		499	
Kristina	136		156	
Christine	224		267	
Kristine	42		48	1997–2003
Dana	201		126	Few since 2005
Danica	288		339	
Danika	270		327	
Erica	327		289	
Erika	368		307	
Freya	33	1999–2009	21	2007–2009
Greta	32		5	2009
Ingrid	9		5	2001
Karen	152		198	
Katrina	352		250	
Kirsten	250		186	
Kirstin	33		10	1997, 2000
Kristen	293		178	
Kristin	119		70	
Lena	114		76	
Liv	31	2000, 2004–2009	13	2008–2009
Maren	87		23	
Nora	65		68	
Randi	61		5	1997
Serena	248		315	
Sonia	69		106	
Sonja	36		45	
Sonya	44		31	
Tyra	137		113	1997–2005

a marker name of Danish identity, parallel to Dane in the list of boys names. The name Tyra may be inspired by the tenth-century queen of Denmark, consort of King Gorm the Old and mother of Harald Bluetooth. In Scandinavia in 2009 Tyra is most popular in Sweden, where it is a top-ranking name. A girl should be honored to be her namesake, as Tyra's reputation was based on great wisdom and military prowess. But it is also possible that the popularity of the name in Alberta and British Columbia may be attributed to other factors and cultures, such as the African American model and television personality Tyra Banks.

Scandinavian Boys Names Given to Children Born in Alberta and British Columbia

Name	Alberta 1997–2009	Comment: Data based on all babies	British Columbia 1997–2009	Comment: Data based on names with at least 5 bearers
Anders	33		14	2008–2009
Andres	25		—	
Ari	27	2001–2009	22	2006–2009
Bjorn	17		—	
Bo	22		—	
Carl	74		58	1997–2005
Karl	67		91	
Carsten	16		—	
Karsten	26		7	2008
Christian	752		691	
Kristian	119		98	
Dane	188		177	
Eric	1,291		1,164	
Erick	38		19	1998–2000
Erik	346		345	
Finn	148		238	
Gunnar	34		5	1997
Gunner	21		—	
Lars	27		6	2006
Leif	69		83	
Magnus	47		42	
Norman	27		28	
Odin	42		39	2005–2009
Soren	50		55	
T(h)or	20		—	

There is more reason to believe that Nora, Lena, and Sonia/Sonja/Sonya give rise to Scandinavian connotations, even though these are not exclusively Scandinavian names. Nora may be a marker of Norwegian identity, parallel to Norman and inspired by Ibsen's character in the play *A Doll's House*. Lena has a long tradition as the most typical girls name in Scandinavian America (see Norwegian jokes about Ole and Lena). Sonia/Sonja/Sonya was made popular by the Norwegian figure skater and movie star Sonja Henie, and perhaps it still is a Scandinavian marker. Queen Sonja of Norway may also contribute to the use of this name.

Annika is a very typical Swedish name, and it is also quite popular in Canada. Even though Swedes rarely spell it "Anika," statistics for this spelling are included.

Several Scandinavian names beginning with K are also popular choices in these provinces. These include Katrina, Kirsten, Kristin, Kristina, and other forms of these names. It is interesting that Kari and Karen seem to be less popular than in the core area for the United States, and that Christina and Christine seem to be preferred over Kristina and Kristine. Karla (also Carla), the female form of Karl, only has sporadic use, so it is not included in the table. Erika has a slight edge over Erica.

Liv and Freya are new names in the statistics. The international popularity of the name of the goddess of love has no doubt contributed to the use of her name in Canada. The actresses Liv Ullmann and Liv Tyler may have inspired the use of Liv in recent years.

In the statistics for Alberta, there are a number of girls names that turn up sporadically with one or two bearers. These include Annelise, Beata, Berit, Birgitte, Britt, Britta, Dagmar, Dagny, Hilda, Malin, Margareta, Margit, Marit, Mari, Marika, Mette, Signe, Siri, Solveig, Tora, and Tova.

The list of boys names also includes marker names for the different Scandinavian countries. Some of these names are used by other ethnic groups. Ari marks an Icelandic identity, Bo and Carl/Karl are most typical for Sweden, and Norman is mainly associated with Norway. Dane is not a typical Danish name, but it has clear reference to a Danish man, while Soren (Søren) is a genuinely typical Danish name. Since there are a good many Finns in Canada, it is likely that Finn has become a marker name for Finnish Canadians, even though the name is common in Denmark and Norway.

Anders is a typical name in all the Scandinavian countries. In the Scandinavian

Norwegian actress and film director Liv Ullmann has lived many years in the United States. She is well known for her roles in Ingmar Bergman's *Persona* (1966) and *Scenes from a Marriage* (1973), as well as her role as Kristina in Jan Troell's film *The Emigrants* (1971). (photo by Jarl Fr. Erichsen / SCANPIX, used by permission)

In 1977 Bebe Buell, the mother of actress Liv Tyler, saw Liv Ullmann on the cover of *Time* magazine, and she named her baby Liv after her. (photo by Daniel Dormann, used by permission)

In July 2009 the toy company Spin Master Ltd. released the Liv dolls, called "a bold new fashion doll line that celebrates what's cool about being a real teen girl." The name Liv has never made the lists of the most popular names in North America, but in Oregon, Alberta, and British Columbia a good many girls are named Liv. Perhaps the doll series will spark a new name fashion. (photo courtesy of Andrew Wagar, Spin Master Ltd.)

community, Andrew was often used as a replacement name, and some of the hundreds of Andrews in the statistics are certainly Scandinavian Canadians. Andres is another form of the same name, statistically most common in Sweden. But it corresponds to the pronunciation of the name in some Norwegian dialects, even though the standard spelling "Anders" is used in the written form. Anders could be a Norwegian or Swedish marker in Canada as well.

It is interesting that Andersen and Anderson, the patronymics corresponding to

Anders, turn up as first names with a few bearers for most years. The same is true of the patronymics Nelson, Jensen, and Hansen.

As in the United States, Eric/Erick/Erik is the most popular of the Scandinavian names. Canadians are more likely to spell it Eric than Erik, and the Anglicized spelling Erick has only a few bearers and has lost popularity. The spellings Carl and Christian are also preferred over Karl and Kristian, but most of the men named Carsten/Karsten spell it with a K. As in Scandinavia, Gunnar takes precedence over Gunner, though this somewhat archaic spelling is used by a good percentage of the Canadian bearers.

The name of the Norse god Odin is a newer addition to the name list, and parallel to Freya in the list of girls names it seems to be gaining popularity. By contrast, it is surprising that the name of the god T(h)or is not very popular, as this god is certainly as well known in Canada as is Odin. T(h)or has not made the list for British Columbia, and there are only one or two bearers in Alberta most years.

In the statistics for Alberta, there are a number of other Scandinavian names with a small number of bearers. These include: Birk, Dag, Dagur, Eirik, Eldar, Endre, Erling, Gustav, Haakon, Ivar, Iver, Joran (Jøran), Jussi, Kjell, Loki, Mats, Niall, Nels, Nils, Olaf, Ole, Osten (Østen), Sten, Tage, Torsten, and Thorvald.

Austin has a high frequency in Alberta and British Columbia. There are several known examples of men named Øystein/Østen who used the name Austin in North America. This name is probably also fairly common among Scandinavian Canadians, but since it is not a Scandinavian name, it is not included in the list.

Kai is another name that turns up with a good many bearers in the statistics for both provinces. There are a good many bearers of the name in Norway and Denmark, and Kai enjoyed considerable popularity from 1940 to 1980. It is doubtful, however, that Kai is a name used primarily by the Scandinavian community, as it is common in many other languages as well.

Scandinavian Given Names
in Historical Perspective

Names in Scandinavia have come into use in different historical periods. As we will see, naming practices have undergone fairly radical changes due to historical developments. But older names have largely not disappeared as a result of expanding the corpus of names. Since the history of the Scandinavian countries is not a common series of events, the history of names differs somewhat from country to country. But there are still basic similarities, and for our purposes we can divide the name types into the following groups:

- Pre-Christian names derived from the older forms of the Scandinavian languages, Old Norse–Icelandic (ca. 700–1350), Old Danish (ca. 800–1100), and Old Swedish (ca. 800–1225)
- Christian names derived from the names of Christian saints, largely from the English forms of the names, and eventually adapted to the Scandinavian languages (beginning ca. 1000)
- Names borrowed from German (fifteenth to seventeenth centuries), and French (eighteenth century)
- The Scandinavian Names Renaissance (ca. 1850–1950)

Naming traditions since 1950 will be discussed in the next chapter.

Names in the Viking Age (750–1050)

A great many Scandinavian names can be traced back to the Viking Age, and a few of them even to the earlier linguistic period called Proto-Nordic (200–700). The Proto-Nordic language was common to all the Scandinavian tribes, but by the Viking Age the language had developed into the variants Old Norse (Norway and its colonies Iceland, the Faroe Islands, Greenland, and parts of the British Isles), Old Danish, and Old Swedish. Despite small differences in form, names that stem from the Viking Age are still so similar that it can be difficult to distinguish between Danish, Norwegian, and Swedish names.

One of the oldest names documented in Scandinavia was found on one of the two ill-fated Golden Horns discovered in Denmark in 1639 and 1734. These beau-

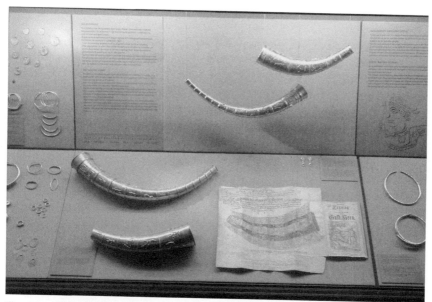

The copies of the Gallehus Golden Horns in Nationalmuseet, Copenhagen, and Ole Worm's drawing from 1641. The runic inscription, found on the smaller horn, contains one of the earliest documentations of a Scandinavian name, HlewagastiR. The runes are written in Proto-Nordic, the earliest form of the Scandinavian languages. (photo by Jan Mehlich, used by permission)

tiful horns from the Iron Age were stolen in 1802 by a goldsmith and melted down to make several very ordinary items, but copies were made from the original drawings. The inscription is in the Proto-Nordic language, and the name of the man who made the horn is mentioned in the inscription. His name was HlewagastiR, which is composed of the words for "shelter" and "guest." The last part of the name, *gastiR*, is a name we can recognize today in the form Gjest. A man named Gjest Baardsen (1791–1849) has become the Norwegian equivalent of Robin Hood. The name Gjest is to be found in several lists of Norwegian emigrants during the nineteenth century. But in 2008 there were only six men in Norway named Gjest.

Many names from the Viking Age are documented on rune stones. The inscriptions on the famous stones from Jelling in Denmark contain the names of King Gorm (Gorm den Gamle, ca. 875–960), his wife Queen Thyra (Thyra Danebod), and their son Harald Bluetooth (Harald Blåtand, ruled ca. 960–985). Harald's wife Tova is named on another rune stone.

Sweden has a great many rune stones. Some of them are from the pre–Viking Age, such as the Järsberg Stone from the sixth century. The name Ravn (or Hrafn) 'raven' is documented on this stone. Around the year 1000, it seems to have been quite fashionable to carve rune stones, and thanks to these monuments, men's names such as

Many Viking Age names are documented on rune stones. The Jelling Stone in Denmark mentions King Gorm the Old, Queen Thyra, and their son Harald Bluetooth. All of these names are in use today. The runic inscription reads: "King Harald had these runes carved to honor his father Gorm and his mother Thyra. The same Harald who conquered all of Denmark and Norway, and turned the Danes into Christians." (photo by Malene Thyssen, used by permission)

Bluetooth, the protocol for exchanging data over short distances, was named for King Harald Bluetooth. The Bluetooth symbol is a so-called bind rune, composed of the runes for 'h' and 'b.'

Gunnar, Helge, Torsten, and Björn, and women's names such as Sigrid, Ragnhild, and Ingegärd, have been documented. The Vikings were travelers and raiders, and many of their names have been carved on rune stones in the Viking colonies and other places the Vikings traveled to. In the spectacular Christian cathedral Hagia Sophia in Istanbul (later a mosque and now a museum), you can find the names Halvdan, Are, and Arne. These names were carved in runes on a balustrade about the year 1000!

In Norway the names Astrid and Gunvor are found on the Dynna Stone, and in 2007 a new stone found under the floor of a church documents the names Halvard and Åsolv. Many of the names from the Viking Age are still in use today, most in Iceland, followed by Norway, Sweden, and Denmark in that order. Many immigrants,

The Dynna Stone in Norway (from ca. 1050) mentions Gunnvor, daughter of Trydrik, and her daughter Astrid: "Gunnvor built a bridge, Trydrik's daughter, in memory of Astrid her daughter; she was the cleverest maiden in Hadeland." Both Gunnvor and Astrid are names that have many bearers today, whereas Trydrik is no longer in use. (© Museum of Cultural History, University of Oslo, Norway, Eirik Irgens Johnsen)

The Bure Stone in Sweden (eleventh century) tells about Bergsven, Sigfast, Fride, Bure, and Fartägn: "Bergsven and Sigfast and Fride erected this stone to honor Bure, their father. But Fartägn carved the runes." The names Bergsven, Sigfast, and Fartägn are no longer found in Sweden, but in 2008 there were 36 Norwegians named Bergsvein and 58 Norwegians bearing the form Fartein. There were 207 Swedish men named Fride and 78 named Bure in 2008. (photo by Bengt A. Lundberg, courtesy of Riksantikvarieämbetet)

especially those from Norway, came from isolated rural communities and bore names such as Bjug or Kleng for the men, and Brønla or Borghild for the women. Such names were disappearing due to the urbanization of the Scandinavian societies, but they were preserved for a time in the Scandinavian American communities.

When looking up the meanings of the old Scandinavian names, the reader will be struck by several things. Some of the names are very short, consisting of only one syllable, and these will often be the same words as the names of animals or objects in the landscape, such as the men's names Bjørn (bear), Orm (snake), Ulv (wolf), Ørn (eagle), and Stein/Sten (stone). The shortest women's names have less concrete meanings, for example Liv (protection, shelter), Aud (wealth, prosperity), and Siv (relationship, kinship).

Longer names are typically composed of two syllables, such as Torstein and Astrid. The meanings of these names may give the impression of a quite "vicious" naming vocabulary, as they very often include elements meaning battle or that are associated with warriors and valkyries. Despite the warlike meanings of the parts in the name composition, many people find these names pleasant sounding and even poetic!

Some scholars think that parents hoped a name would give certain powers or traits to the child. This may have been the case at one time, but by the Viking Age the names didn't really mean anything. The elements were put together rather arbitrarily, with little thought to what the combination might mean. The name Hallstein is an example of a rather meaningless name, comprising two elements that both mean "stone."

Viking Age names are documented in several sources. *Landnámabók*, a history of the settlement of Iceland, and Snorri Sturluson's *History of the Norwegian Kings* are two important sources. Other names are found in the Icelandic sagas and Norse mythology. In the list below, the modernized forms of the names are used, rather than the Old Norse–Icelandic forms.

Viking Age Women's Names (contemporary spellings)

Aldis	Bera	Geirhild
Alvhild	Bergdis	Gerd
Arnbjørg/Arnbjörg	Bergliot	Gro
Arndis	Bergtora	Groa
Arnfrid	Bjørg, Björg	Gudlaug
Arngerd	Brynhild	Gudny
Arngunn	Dyrfinna	Gudrid
Arntrud	Fridgerd	Gudrun
Astrid	Gauthild	Gunnhild
Aud	Geirbjørg, Geirbjörg	Gunnvor

Gyda	Oddny	Torlaug
Halldora	Ragna	Torny
Hallfrid	Ragnfrid	Torunn
Hallgerd	Ragnhild	Tova
Hallveig	Rannveig	Turid
Heid	Ravnhild	Tyra
Helga	Revna	Ulvhild
Herdis	Salbjørg, Salbjörg	Unn
Hertrud	Salgerd	Valgerd
Hervor	Signy	Valgjerd
Hild	Sigrid	Vedis
Hildegunn	Solveig	Vigdis
Idun	Steinunn	Vilborg
Ingebjørg, Ingebjörg	Steinvor	Yngvild
Ingegjerd	Svanhild	Øydis
Ingerid	Svanlaug	Ålov
Ingunn	Sæhild	Åsa
Jarngerd	Tjodhild	Åsdis
Jodis	Tora	Åsgerd
Jofrid	Torbjørg, Torbjörg	Åshild
Jorunn	Tordis	Åsta
Liv	Torgerd	Åsvor
Malmfrid	Torhild	
Oddfrid	Torkatla	

Viking Age Men's Names (*contemporary spellings*)

Alv	Bård	Gudtorm
Are	Dag	Gunnar
Arne	Egil/Eigil	Gunnlaug
Asbjørn/Asbjörn	Einar	Gunnstein
Atle	Eindride	Gyrd
Audun	Eirik	Halldor
Bergtor	Erling	Hallgrim
Bjarne	Frode	Hallvard
Bjørn/Björn	Gaute	Halvdan
Bodvar	Gisle	Harald
Bork	Gjest	Hauk
Botolv	Grim	Helge
Brage	Gudbrand	Håkon
Brynjolv	Gudleiv	Håvard

Inge	Ragnvald	Torgrim
Ingemar	Ravnkjell	Torkjell
Ingjald	Reidar	Torleiv
Ivar	Roald	Tormod
Jostein	Roar	Torolv
Jørund, Jörund	Rolv	Torstein
Kjartan	Sigmund	Torsten
Kjetil	Sigurd	Torvald
Knut	Skjalg	Trond
Kolbein	Skule	Tryggve
Kolbjørn, Kolbjörn	Snorre	Ulv
Kåre	Stein	Valdemar
Leiv	Steinar	Vemund
Magnus	Svein	Vigleik
Odd	Sveinung	Yngve
Olav	Sølve, Sölve	Øyolv
Olve	Teit	Øystein, Östen
Orm	Torarin	Øyvind
Ottar	Torbjørn, Torbjörn	Åke
Ragnar	Torgeir	Åsmund

The Influence of Christianity

Christianity came to Scandinavia during the tenth century, toward the end of the Viking Age. As a result, the names of the Christian saints were introduced as given names, and the trend had a lasting influence on the naming traditions. But in Norway the first imported name of note was Magnus. Snorri Sturluson tells how this name came to Norway in his *History of the Norwegian Kings*. King Olav had a servant woman named Alvhild, who was of good family and was also his mistress. She was expecting a child, and it was common knowledge that King Olav was the father. When the child was born, Alvhild almost died, and her son just barely survived. There was a priest present, and he insisted that the child be christened without delay, as the boy would be "the devil's man" if he died a heathen. The king was asleep, and he never liked it when anyone woke him up. Sigvat, the king's poet, said, "I would rather take it upon myself to christen the child than to wake the king." So the child was christened Magnus, the best name Sigvat could think of. The king was quite angry when he woke up the next morning and heard what had happened during the night. "The King said, 'Why did you give the boy the name Magnus? We don't use that name in our family.' Sigvat replied, 'I named him after King Charlemagne; he is the most worthy man I could think of in the whole world.' Then the King said, 'You are a man who brings luck with him, Sigvat, and everyone thinks that luck and intelligence go hand in hand. But strangely enough, it sometimes happens that luck follows the witless, so a witless piece of advice may be turned to the best.' Then the king was extremely pleased. The boy was brought up, and it was soon clear that he was clever and talented" (*The Saga of Saint Olaf*, chapter 122, our translation).

The conversion to Christianity soon led to the introduction of many new names. We find evidence on rune stones and documents from as early as the year 1000 that children were being named for Biblical figures and the saints John, Lawrence, Nicolas, Peter, and Stephen, as well as Agnes, Catherine, Cecilia, Elizabeth, and Margaret. Names of the disciples and other important Biblical names, particularly Maria, Anna, Eva, and Jacob contributed to this picture. The name Christian itself became a name for men and women: Christian, Kristian, and Kristen for men; Kristina and Kristin for women. The Christian names gradually replaced many of the Norse names in popularity. Scandinavians did not start honoring Anna, mother of Virgin Mary, until about 1400, but once parents started honoring her by naming their daughters after her, Anna and other forms like Ane and Anne would become the most frequently used girls name over time in Denmark, Norway, and Sweden, and also one of the top 5 names in Iceland.

In their original forms, or forms corresponding to their English cognates, these names are not of great interest for this book. But many of them have developed forms

Birgitta, the Exalted One. Statue from 1435 in Vadstena Cloister Church, Sweden. Saint Birgitta of Sweden (1303–73) popularized the name Birgitta in all of the Scandinavian countries. There are several modern forms of the name, and all of them have many bearers in 2008: Denmark, Birgit 22,547, Birgitte 15,450, Berit 5,251, Birgitta 312; Norway, Berit 19,568, Birgit 3,874, Birgitte 2,691, Birgitta 232; Sweden, Birgitta 177,613, Birgitte 684, Berit 32,931, Birgit 23,386.

Brit Kari, born in 1958 in Wisconsin. Her names are typical Scandinavian forms of the names of the saints Birgitta and Katarina. Brit may be written Brit or Britt. Britt is the most popular spelling in Sweden and Denmark, while both spellings are popular in Norway. Both Brit(t) and Kari are found in the United States, and Kari ranked among the most popular American girls names during the twentieth and early twenty-first centuries (see page 97). Bearers in 2008: Denmark, Brit 554, Britt 3,059, Kari 478; Norway, Brit 6,448, Britt 7,775, Kari 28,031; Sweden, Brit 211, Britt 39,710, Kari 915; Oregon (children born 1961–2008), Brit 7, Britt 47, Kari 1,268. (photo by Nancy L. Coleman)

that are considered typical Scandinavian names as good as any: Hans, Jens, Lars, Mats, Nils, Per, and Pål for the men, and Agneta, Elsa, Karen, Kari, Lise, Marit, and Merete for the women. The table below shows some of the most important names in their different forms.

Borrowed Names

German Names

The Protestant Reformation came to Scandinavia in the sixteenth century, and this led to changes in naming patterns. Now that they were Protestants, many objected to the practice of naming children after Catholic saints, but since many of the old Scandinavian names had not been in use for a long time, there seemed few alternatives. Particularly in Denmark, German names such as Hans, Claus, Amalie, and Gertrud seemed a good alternative, even though several of these are actually other forms of the names of the same saints that had been honored with Scandinavian forms of these names. The upper class led in this fashion, and German even became the everyday language of communication in polite society. As a consequence, the German forms of the names of saints replaced the Scandinavian forms where the upper classes were concerned, while the farmer classes kept the Danish forms. For example, an upper-class man would be named Johannes, Peter, or Nicolaus, while a

Variants of the Names of Christian Saints

Form ca. 1000	Modern Danish Forms	Modern Norwegian Forms	Modern Swedish Forms	Modern Icelandic Form
Johannes (Saint John the Baptist)	Johannes, Jens, Johan, Hans, Jan, Jo(h)n	Johannes, Johan, Hans, Jan, Jon, Jonny, Jo, Jens	Johannes, Jo(h)an, Jo(h)n, Jonne, Jusse, Jussi	Jóhannes, Jóhann, Jón
Nicolaus	Nicolai, Niels, Claus	Nikolai, Nils, Klaus	Nikolaus, Niklas, Nils, Klas	Nikulás, Níels
Paulus	Poul	Pål, Paul	Povel, Pål, Palle	Páll
Petrus	Peter, Peder, Per, Pelle	Petter, Peder, Per	Pet(t)er, Pär, Pelle	Pétur
Laurentius	Laurids, Laurens, Lorens, Lars, Lasse	Lavrans, Laurits, Lars	Laurens, Lars, Lasse	Lárentsíus, Lárentíus, Lárus
Agnes	Agnet(h)e	Agnete	Agnet(h)a	Agneta
Birgitta	Birgitte, Birthe, Berit, Bitten, Gitte, Bibi	Birgitte, Birgit, Berit, Bergit, Brit(t), Brit(t)a	Brigitta, Birgitta, Berit, Britt	Birgitta, Birgit
Cecilia	Cecilie, Sidsel	Sissel, Sissela	Sissila, Sissa	Sesselja
Elizabeta	Else, Elise, Lis, Lise, Lisbeth, Ilse	Elisabet(h), Elsa, Else, Lisa, Lise, Lisbet, Ellisiv	Elisabet(h), Elisa, Lisbet, Lisbetta, Elsa, Bettan, Lisa, Lisen	Elísabet, Elísa, Ellisif, Lísa
Katarina	Kathrine, Karen, Karna, Karina, Trine	Katrine, Karina, Kari, Trine	Katarina, Karin, Kari	Katrín, Karína
Margaretha	Margarethe, Merete, Meta, Mette, Grethe	Margit, Marit, Margritt, Merete, Gret(h)e	Margareta, Margit, Greta, Magga, Märt(h)a	Margrét

farmer would bear the name Jens, Per, or Niels. At the same time, many skilled laborers were moving into Danish towns from Germany, and this migration had an impact on naming traditions in the towns.

In Norway, also due to trade and contact with Germany, German names had already entered the naming vocabulary during the Middle Ages. These names had been given appropriate Old Norse spellings and declensions: Arnold (Arnaldr), Didrik (Didrikr), Fredrik (Friðrekr), Hermann, and Vilhelm (Vilhjalmr); Bodil (Bóthildr), Mechthild (Magnhildr), and Valborg. By the time of the Protestant Reformation in 1536, Norway had become a part of Denmark. Since most of the Norwegian population still lived in the rural areas, the tendency to take German names was not as widespread as in Denmark, but German names came into use in some places, particularly in Bergen, which was a part of the Hanseatic League and home to many tradesmen and shipping agents from Germany, and in mining areas dependent on German technology, such as Røros (copper) and Kongsberg (silver).

In the seventeenth and eighteenth centuries Sweden became a significant European power, and there was much contact between Germany and Sweden. German names had already made an impact on the vocabulary of Swedish names, but while names had been borrowed from Low German in the earlier period, new names came in from the High German area. Many of these names came into use through Sweden's ties to the Baltic area. Names such as Bernhard, Gerhard, and Adolf replaced Bernt, Gert, and Alf, and girls were given names like Amalia, Emma, Hedvig, and Ida. Following the Thirty Years' War (1618–48), German names had a marked effect in Scandinavia, and they increased in number for the next two hundred years.

Some of the names mentioned here have had a lasting effect on Scandinavian naming traditions. These include for boys Hans, which has enjoyed high frequency for several centuries, Klaus, and Fredrik; Hedvig, Emma, and Ida for girls. The latter two have topped the ranking list in recent years for the most popular girls names.

French and English Names

Between the Reformation and mid-nineteenth century the most important influence on Scandinavian naming traditions came from France and England. Influence was greatest in Sweden and Denmark. During the eighteenth century Sweden had close ties to France, and King Gustav III even preferred to converse in French with his court. French names became particularly fashionable for girls: Antoinette, Charlotte, Frédérique, Henriette, Jeanne, Jeanette, Louise. The names Désirée and Joséphine came in through the royal family. Following the Napoleonic Wars (ending in 1814), a French marshal named Jean-Baptiste Bernadotte was chosen to succeed the childless Swedish king. In 1818 he was crowned King of Sweden and Norway, and he was known as King Carl XIV Johan of Sweden and King Karl III Johan of Norway. The fact that this popular king never learned to speak Swedish or Norwegian—or even needed to—bears witness to the ease with which the ruling classes communicated in French. Carl Johan's wife, Queen Désirée, was also French, as was Queen Joséphine, the wife of the next king, Oscar I (see also page 169).

Frenchified spellings of names already in use in other forms were adopted: Marie instead of Maria, Sophie instead of Sofia, Christine instead of Kristina. French has also had a lasting effect on the pronunciation of certain names. For example *Marianne*, a name common in Denmark, Norway, and Sweden, is pronounced without the final *e* in Sweden, while it has been retained in Denmark and Norway.

English names came into fashion during the nineteenth century. In Sweden the influence was regional, with the western coastal area around Gothenburg, where there are a number of families intermarried with Scottish families, leading the way.

Names such as Alfred, Allen, Arthur, Charles, Edgar, Edwin, Henry, John, and Oswald came into use for men, and Alice, Annie, Edith, Fanny, Jane, Jenny, Mary, Nancy, Nelly, and Pamela for women. English names also became fashionable in Denmark and Norway during this period, often inspired by names used in the novels by Charles Dickens and other popular English authors.

A quirky feature of the English-inspired name fashion was that English names that are nicknames, and seldom found on birth certificates in England at this time, were used as given names: Kate, Kitty, Lizzie, Maggie, and Peggy for girls; Benny, Billy, Eddie, Harry, Jonny, Teddy, Tommy, and Willy for boys. The use of nicknames as given names has persisted up to the present, with Jonny/Jonnie and Tommy/Tommie achieving high rank among the top names.

The Scandinavian Names Renaissance

By the early nineteenth century the borrowed names, in particular those from the Catholic saints, had made significant inroads into the vocabulary of names in all of the Scandinavian countries. The tendency was greatest in Sweden, where many families abandoned the strict tradition of naming children for their grandparents during the eighteenth century and where the resulting void was filled with fashionable names from various sources, but it was also strong in Denmark. Norway was a European outpost and a much more rural society, and the old naming traditions persisted. But parents in Norway were often under pressure from clergymen, many of whom were Danes, to abandon the "heathen" names, as well as those taken from the names of wild animals, such as Bjørn (bear) and Orm (snake), in favor of good and pious Christian names. As a result, the Norse names lost ground. Professor Kristoffer Kruken at the University of Oslo has studied this development. His findings show that by 1800, around 39 percent of the men's names in Norway were of Scandinavian origin, whereas about 56 percent were Christian and 5 percent were of German origin. The tendency to use Christian names was even stronger for the women: about 28 percent had names of Scandinavian origin, 67 percent of Christian origin, and 4 percent of German origin (see Kruken and Stemshaug, 61).

Since most of the immigrants to the United States came from rural areas, there are more names of Scandinavian origin among the emigrants than in the general Norwegian population during the immigration period. Names on the ships' lists and the emigrant protocols bear witness to this fact. And if we look at the statistics for the different areas, we see that Scandinavian names held a strong position in the areas where the immigrants came from. For example, large numbers of the Norwegian immigrants came from Hedmark, Oppland, Telemark, Buskerud, and Rogaland, and by 1800 these provinces all have a much higher frequency for men's names of Scandinavian origin than in other parts of the country: Hedmark 45 percent, Oppland

46 percent, Telemark 61 percent, Buskerud 45 percent, and Rogaland 50 percent. For the women there is much less variation from the national averages, but Telemark is an exception with 43 percent of the women bearing Scandinavian names.

But by the mid-nineteenth century the picture changed, due to what is called the Scandinavian Names Renaissance. There were several causes for this movement. In the larger European picture, it was influenced by the Romantic Movement (mid-eighteenth to early nineteenth centuries) in art and literature, which encouraged artists to look for the essence of their people in folk art. As a result, the Old Norse–Icelandic sagas were rediscovered, and translations into modern Swedish and Danish started to appear (Danish was the written language in Norway at this time). Inspired by the sagas, men's names like Arne, Egil, Gunnar, Helge, and Torbjørn, and women's names like Gudrun, Hallgjerd, Helga, and Hervor came back into use. Renewed interest in Norse mythology inspired the use of the names of the Norse gods and goddesses, including Odin, Tor, Frøy, Njord, Brage, and Balder for boys; Frigg, Frøya, and Siv for girls, and names of the warrior women called valkyries popularized names like Brynhild and Sigyn.

Contemporary literature also inspired naming, as authors used themes and characters from Old Norse literature in their own works. The Danish author Adam Oehlenschläger (1779–1850) seems directly responsible for the restoration of many names to the Danish tradition, among them Gudrun, Signe, Thora, Thyra, and Valborg for the women, and Ejnar, Hagbard, Harald, Helge, Kjartan, and Olaf for the men. In Sweden, Esaias Tegnér's poems "Frithiofs saga" (1825) and "Svea" (1811) inspired parents to use the men's names Fritjof, Helge, Hilding, and Viking, and the women's names Ingeborg and Svea.

In Norway, the European Romantic Movement developed into the movement called National Romanticism (ca. 1840–60), which had a profound impact on naming traditions. The historian Peder Andreas Munch and the linguist Ivar Aasen encouraged parents to revive the old Norwegian names, and they wrote articles to raise people's awareness of the origins of different names. As in Denmark and Sweden, contemporary literature played an important part. Translations of the Icelandic sagas and Snorri Sturluson's *History of the Norwegian Kings* brought names like Håkon, Sverre, Tryggve, and Øyvind, as well as Astrid, Gyda, Ragnhild, and Åsa into the limelight. Contemporary authors did their part as well. Bjørnstjerne Bjørnson's peasant tales and poems in the 1850s popularized the names Arne, Arnljot, and Torbjørn for boys, and Bergljot, Ingrid, and Synnøve for girls. Henrik Ibsen's plays, particularly the historical dramas and *Peer Gynt*, also contributed to the renewed interest in Scandinavian names.

The new fashion of using Scandinavian names hit the urban areas first. As mentioned above, the rural areas had retained many Scandinavian names, and many of the "new" names were not new in this setting. However, the old names had changed over the years, and new forms had evolved, such as Sjur for Sigurd, Tosten for Torstein, Østen for Øystein, Guro for Gudrun, Siri for Sigrid, and Synne for Synnøve. As a result of the new naming trend, dialect forms were now abandoned in favor of the older spellings.

Most Frequently Used Men's Names in the 1920s

If we look at the top names for this period, we can see that the Scandinavian Names Renaissance had the greatest impact in Norway and Sweden during the 1920s. In Denmark, there are only 4 Scandinavian names among the top 10. In Norway, 9 out of the top 12 are Scandinavian; in Sweden, 10 out of 12. Another interesting thing is that the saints' names have entirely disappeared from the top names used in Sweden. In the table below, the names of Scandinavian origin are listed in bold type.

Rank	Denmark (1920–29)	Norway (1925–29)	Sweden (1925)
1	**Erik**	**Arne**	**Karl**
2	Hans	**Kåre**	**Erik**
3	Christian	**Olav, Olaf**	**Sven**
4	**Svend**	**Odd**	Olof
5	**Aage**	Jon	**Gunnar**
6	Jørgen	Per	**Gustav**
7	Poul	**Leiv, Leif**	Lennart
8	Peter	**Rolv, Rolf**	**Rune**
9	Jens	**Gunnar**	**Arne**
10	**Knud**	Kjell	**Stig**
11		Knut	Bertil
12		Hans	**Åke**

Most Frequently Used Women's Names in the 1920s

For the women, the percentage of Scandinavian names in use in the 1920s is much less than for the men: only 1 of the top 10 names in Denmark and 3 of the top 12 in Sweden, but 8 out of 12 in Norway.

Rank	Denmark (1920–29)	Norway (1925–29)	Sweden (1925)
1	Marie	**Solveig**	Maria
2	Margrethe	**Gerd**	Margareta
3	Anna	**Inger**	Anna
4	Else	Rut(h), Rutt	Elisabet
5	**Inger**	**Ing(e)rid, Ingri**	**Ingrid**
6	Karen	**Bjørg**	Linnea
7	Ruth	Else	**Ingegerd**
8	Grethe	**Astri(d)**	Karin
9	Kirstine	**Åse**	Viola
10	Ellen	Anna	Brit(t)a
11		Anne	Kristina
12		**Liv**	**Ingeborg**

Given Names Today

In the early Viking Age (ca.700–800), the elements of names could be quite freely combined to produce a large number of different names. Even so, the flora of names used in Scandinavia has certainly never been greater than in our own time. Thanks to the Scandinavian Names Renaissance, the old names were rediscovered and came back into use. In addition, the names of Catholic saints have had a continuous tradition since about the year 1000, and many of these names have numerous alternate forms, all of which are still in use: for example, Hans, Jens, Johan, Johannes, Jon, and Jonny; and Bettan, Elisabet(h), Ellisiv, Elsa, Else, Lisbet, Lisa, and Lise. And thanks to modern mass media, names of celebrities and internationally popular names have been added to the store. In addition, recent immigration from non-Western countries to the Scandinavian countries has added names such as Ali, Mohammed, Aber, and Fedia.

Name Laws

In contrast to the United States, some countries feel that name giving should be regulated by law. This is true for Denmark, Norway, and Sweden. To meet the needs of a multicultural society, these laws have been revised in recent years.

Denmark

In Denmark a child must be given a name by the time she or he is six months old, and both parents must sign the form. Very many couples live together without being married, and many children are therefore born "out of wedlock." Whether the parents are married or not, the child does not automatically receive the surname of its father. The parents must agree on a surname, but if they have not decided by the time the child is six months old, it will automatically receive the *mother's* surname. There is an interesting twist to this. As mentioned above, the Danes abandoned the custom of using a patronymic name in the nineteenth century, but the new law gives the practice new potential. If no name has been agreed upon and the mother's name is a patronymic type name, the child will be given a *matronymic* name; that is, the mother's given name with the ending *søn* for a boy and *datter* for a girl. For example, Birthe Jensen's child would be given the surname Birthesøn or Birthesdatter, rather than Jensen.

The selection of a child's given name is also governed by law in Denmark, and the Department of Family Affairs publishes lists of approved names for boys and girls. In 2007 there were 6,754 names approved for boys and 8,974 names approved for girls. It is not permissible to give a boy a girls name or vice versa. If the parents want to use a name that is not on the list, they must apply to the local government and be granted approval in order to use the desired name.

Norway

The Norwegian law is quite similar. The name of a child must be registered by the time the baby is six months old, and if the parents have not done so, the child will be given the mother's surname. If the mother has no surname, the surname of the child will be given her name "with an ending that shows the relationship of mother and child," that is, a matronymic name. Unlike Denmark, Norway does not have lists of approved names, but it is not permissible to give a boy a girls name or vice versa. The use of a surname as a given name is restricted, unless it has a tradition of being used as both a given name and a surname. For example, a child cannot be named Andersen, Helland, or Vik, since they are surnames.

Under the old law, a person was not allowed to have more than one last name, and hyphenated last names were also not permitted. But this rule has now been revoked. Since many women keep their last names after marriage, some will welcome the chance to give their children the surnames of both parents. If a child was given the surnames of both of the parents under the old system, only the final name would officially be a surname, and the other one would be a middle name. For example, a daughter of Jorunn Undset and Harald Arnestad might be named Solveig Undset Arnestad, but Undset would be a middle name, and the child's last name would be Arnestad; the parents would also not be able to give her the hyphenated name Undset-Arnestad. Under the new law they may do just that.

But other parents look ahead to when a child with a lengthy last name might marry a person with another lengthy last name. For example, Solveig Undset-Arnestad might marry Håvard Solstad-Jensen, and it would be a problem if they wanted their children to have all the names: Elsa Solstad-Jensen-Undset-Arnestad. And the problem would potentially multiply with each new generation. In order to prevent endless surnames, some couples choose to give their children only one surname. The new law also allows the use of a patronymic or matronymic name.

Before the new law was passed in 2006, the Norwegian government also issued lists of names that were not allowed. Parents could not name their daughter Kiss, Norgia, Nuppe, Røy, or Valkyrie, or their son Burre, Fnorre, Gay, Gnomen, Jesus, Junior, or Musa. Jesus was not allowed, even though it is a popular name in Latin America and other Catholic countries, and there are a number of immigrants from Latin America. Immigration to Norway probably explains the fact that it is no longer forbidden. In 2007 there were thirty-six men named Jesus living in Norway. The name Drita was also not approved, due to its associations with the toilet (drit=shit). However, this name came to Scandinavia with refugees from the Balkans, and in 2007 there were eighteen bearers in Norway and over a hundred in Sweden. Such names are no longer prohibited under the new Norwegian law, but such a name will definitely be a burden in Norway.

Sweden

A Swedish child will automatically be given the surname of the parents, if they have a common surname. But if the parents have different surnames, they must make a decision on the surname of the child within three months after its birth. If they

Typical Names in Scandinavia

Norway

Girls
1. Kari
2. Solveig
3. Berit
4. Bjørg
5. Gerd
6. Jorun/Jorunn
7. Hege
8. Reidun/Reidunn
9. Sissel
10. Mari

Boys
1. Svein
2. Odd
3. Geir
4. Terje
5. Rune
6. Olav
7. Espen
8. Magnus
9. Frode
10. Kjetil

NO

SE

Sweden

Girls
1. Birgitta
2. Gunilla
3. Siv
4. Ulla
5. Kajsa
6. Svea
7. Alva
8. Saga
9. Ylva
10. Ronja

Boys
1. Carl/Karl
2. Olof/ Olov
3. Gustaf/Gustav
4. Bo
5. Göran
6. Christer/Krister
7. Ingemar/Ingmar
8. Gösta
9. Bror
10. Sture

DK

Denmark

Girls
1. Helle
2. Inge
3. Birte/Birthe
4. Pia
5. Lone
6. Jette
7. Gitte
8. Jytte
9. Dorthe/Dorte
10. Pernille

Boys
1. Søren
2. Niels
3. Jesper
4. Poul
5. Sven/Svend
6. Flemming
7. Torben
8. Henning
9. Mogens
10. Preben

© Geoatl/Kart&grafikk

cannot decide, the child will be given the mother's surname. If the paternity of the child is undetermined, it will also be given her surname. The law also requires that the child have an approved given name within three months, but the choice of name has few restrictions. A name that is considered inappropriate or a potential problem for the child will, however, be denied.

Modern Scandinavian names have a great deal in common, and the vocabulary of names in one country still has a great influence on that of its neighbors. This will be evident in the tables to be found in the next chapter, which show the top 20 names used in 2008.

What's In a Name—Danish, Norwegian, or Swedish?

Can you tell by a person's name whether they are likely to be Danish, Norwegian, or Swedish? To a certain extent you can. There are certain names that will mark a person as a Dane, Norwegian, or Swede. It is easy to recognize an Icelandic name, as the forms, with their characteristic endings and accent marks, are markers in themselves.

Top Names in Scandinavia Today

Following the Christianization of the North about 1000, more men's names of Scandinavian origin have remained in use than women's names. Naming girls seems to be more prone to follow fashion and trends. Due to this phenomenon, the dictionary section of this book contains many more boys names than girls names: around 1,000 boys names as opposed to about 550 girls names. In recent years, however, the Scandinavian naming vocabulary has undergone globalization, and a large number of international names has been added.

The most recent lists of the top twenty names (2008) in Denmark, Norway, and Sweden contain almost no names of Scandinavian origin for either girls or boys! As can be seen in the table of boys names below, only Erik, Gustav, Magnus, and Ole qualify as Scandinavian. Even Magnus is questionable, as it does not come from a Scandinavian word but from Carolus Magnus, the Latin name of Charlemagne (see page 126). As for the girls names, only Inge, Inger, Ingrid, Tuva, and Vilde qualify, and the first three all start with the same element, so there is little variation.

The Scandinavian countries have followed the international trend of using Biblical names for boys. Lucas/Lukas (English Luke) tops the list for 2008 in Norway and Sweden. Top names in Sweden often forecast what will happen to Norwegian name fashions. But the tendency to use names deriving from the Christian religion is most marked in Norway and Denmark. However, the forms are quite different. In Norway, Lucas/Lukas is followed by two other names of Jesus' disciples, Mathias and Markus (English Matthew and Mark), and none of these forms is adapted to the Norwegian language. The most recent name fashion in Denmark shows a different trend, marking a return to the Scandinavian forms of the names of Christian saints, such as Jens and Hans (John the Baptist), Lars (Laurence), Niels (Nicholas) and Per (Peter), to the top twenty list. This is a new development, since in 2006 the Danish list contained many of the same names to be found among the top twenty in Norway and Sweden in 2008: Lucas, Mathias, Markus, Noah, Jonas, Sebastian, Alexander, Tobias, Viktor, Oliver, and Emil. In the globalized world of today, such a pronounced return to traditional Danish names is an unusual phenomenon. It will be interesting to see whether it lasts, and also whether it is a prediction of how the top twenty names will look in the other Scandinavian countries in the next few years.

Three of the four members of the well-known Swedish pop group ABBA are bearers of popular Scandinavian names: Agnetha, Bjørn, and Benny. Norwegian Swedish Anni-Frid has a much less common name. In June 2008 the group got together with the cast for the opening of the film *Mamma Mia!* From left to right: Benny Andersson, Pierce Brosnan, Amanda Seyfried, Meryl Streep, Agnetha Fältskog, Anni-Frid Lyngstad, Christine Baranski, Colin Firth, Catherine Johnson, Phyllida Lloyd, Judy Craymer, Björn Ulvaeus, and Dominic Cooper. Bearers of the ABBA names in 2008—*Agnetha*: Denmark, Agnete 2,279, Agnetha 9; Norway, Agnete 550, Agnetha 48; Sweden, Agneta 34,995, Agnetha 1,028. *Bjørn/Björn*: Denmark, 5,298; Norway, 40,266; Sweden, 61,137. *Benny*: Denmark, 8,626; Norway, 273; Sweden, 10,761. *Anni-Frid*: Denmark, fewer than 5; Norway, fewer than 5; Sweden, Anni-Frid 9, Annifrid 21. (photo by Daniel Åhs Karlsson, used by permission)

Biblical names are not as popular for the girls, but in Denmark, Scandinavian forms of the names of saints are also among the top twenty: Mette (Margaret), Else (Elizabeth), and Karen (Catherine), as well as Anne and Anna (Ann, mother of Virgin Mary) and Maria (Virgin Mary). Kirsten (Christian woman), one of the most popular Danish girls names in the twentieth century, makes a strong comeback as number 2 on the list. Bente (from Latin Benedictus) also makes its return. Of these Christian names, only Anna ranked among the top twenty Danish names in 2006.

A characteristic of currently popular girls names in Norway and Sweden is that many of them end in *a* or *ah*. In Denmark the preferred ending is *e*. When names of Scandinavian origin were in widespread use, most of the girls names would end in a consonant, such as *d* (Astrid, Gerd, Ingrid, Turid), *g* (Bjørg, Ingebjørg), or *s* (Tordis, Vigdis).

For a long time Iceland has kept the old Scandinavian names alive, but Icelandic naming traditions have also changed radically in recent years. Until 2006, a majority of the top twenty names originated from Old Norse, and the rest were Icelandic forms of Christian names. In 2008, seven of the top twenty boys names and only three of the twenty most popular girls names are of Scandinavian origin. In addition to Icelandic forms of the names of saints, new Biblical names in their international forms have joined the list: Daniel and Aron, Sara and Rakel.

Teachers in particular will notice that certain names dominate in different age groups of students. Ida, for example, has been a top name in Denmark, Norway, and Sweden in recent years. In a small class of eighteen-year-olds in 2006–7, three of the five girls were named Ida! And in other classes there might be two or three students named Nina, Thomas, or Aleksander. But the list of top names is also somewhat misleading. As mentioned above, there is now a very large corpus of names, and many Scandinavian names are to be found among the top hundred names for 2008.

Popular Boys Names in Scandinavia

Below are the top twenty names for boys born in 2008. Names of Scandinavian origin are in bold type.

Top 20 Names for Boys Born in 2008

	Denmark	Norway	Sweden	Iceland
1	Jens	Lucas, Lukas	Lucas	Jón
2	Peter	Mathias	Oscar	Daniel
3	Lars	Markus	William	Aron
4	Michael	Emil	Elias	Viktor
5	Henrik	Kristian, Christian	Hugo	Alexander
6	Søren	Jonas	Alexander	**Arnar**
7	Thomas	**Magnus**	Erik	**Guðmundur**
8	Niels	Oliver	Isak	Gabríel
9	Hans	Tobias	Filip	Kristján
10	Jørgen	Alexander	Emil	Tómas
11	Jan	Andreas	Viktor	Stefán
12	Martin	Henrik	Oliver	**Magnús**
13	Christian	Daniel	Liam	**Sigurður**
14	**Ole**	Noah	Anton	Mikael
15	Anders	Adrian	Axel	Ísak
16	**Erik**	William	Leo	Kristófer
17	Morten	Kristoffer	**Gustav**	Andri
18	Per	Sebastian	Albin	**Ólafur**
19	Jesper	Martin	Edvin	**Einar**
20	Poul	Jakob	Simon*	**Gunnar**

* *Simon* is a Biblical name, but the spelling may also be a form of Scandinavian Sigmund.

If we look at the top hundred names for boys born in 2008, we find more Scandinavian names. Names are listed alphabetically.

- Denmark: Arne, Bjarne, Bo, Carl and Karl, Carsten and Karsten, Erik, Erling, Finn, Kjeld, Knud, Leif, Magnus and Mogens, Ole, Ove, Rune, Steen, Svend, Torben, Vagn

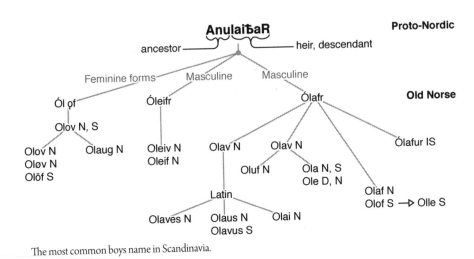

AnulaibaR — Proto-Nordic

ancestor —⏞⏞— heir, descendant

Feminine forms — Masculine — Masculine — **Old Norse**

Ól of — Óleifr — Ólafr

Olov N, S

Olov N — Olaug N — Oleiv N — Olav N — Olav N — Ólafur IS
Oløv N — — Oleif N — — Oluf N — Ola N, S
Olöf S — — — — — Ole D, N

Olaf N
Olof S ⟶ Olle S

Latin

Olaves N — Olaus N — Olai N
— Olavus S

The most common boys name in Scandinavia.

King Olav Dies by Halvdan Egedius (1877–99). The popularity of the name can be traced back to King Olav of Norway (995–1030). As a Catholic saint, he is celebrated in many countries on July 29. Bearers in 2008: Denmark, Ole, 35, 870, Olav, 857; Norway, Ole, 32,570, Olav, 16,226, Ola, 9,221; Sweden, Olof, 119,668, Olov, 37,800, Ola, 20,619; Oregon (boys born 1961–2008), Olaf, 17, Olav, 3, Ole, 19, Olof, 3.

- Norway: Amund, Brage, Eirik and Erik, Eskil, Eivind and Even, Erlend, Håkon, Håvard, Iver, Magnus, Odin, Olav, Ola and Ole, Sindre, Sigurd, Simen and Simon, Sivert, Sondre, Stian (may also be a Scandinavian name or a short form of Kristian), Storm, Sverre, Trym, Vegard, Vetle
- Sweden: Arvid, Carl, Erik, Hjalmar, Loke, Måns, Olle, Sigge, Sixten, Svante, Vidar, Viggo

At the same time, a good many typical Scandinavian names that were among the top hundred before 2008 have disappeared from the list:

- Denmark: Bjørn, Ejnar and Ejner, Gunnar, Harald, Helge, Tage, Thorvald, Valdemar, Viggo
- Norway: Ask, Audun, Bjørn, Bjørnar, Einar, Harald, Ivar, Knut, Sigmund, Tor, Torbjørn, Vebjørn
- Sweden: Alf, Birger, Björn, Bo, Bror, Erik, Gunnar, Håkan, Inge, Ingemar and Ingmar, Ingvar, Ivar, Kjell, Leif, Olof and Olov, Ragnar, Rolf, Sten, Stig, Sven, Torsten, Ulf, Åke

Among the hundred top names for boys born in 2008, we find several names of Catholic saints in their Scandinavian forms. Names are listed alphabetically.

- Denmark: Anders, Christian, Hans, Jan, Jens, Jeppe, Jørgen, Lars, Lasse, Laurits, Niels, Niklas, Per, Peter, Poul
- Norway: Anders, Andreas, Hans, Jens, Kristian, Kristoffer, Lars, Mats, Nils, Per, Petter, Pål
- Sweden: Hannes, Hampus, Johan, Johannes, Nils

But we can see the same tendency as observed above. Many of the Scandinavian forms that have been so typical have disappeared from the top hundred names. Denmark is an exception in this respect, as 2008 was a revival year for such names, and several of them ended up among the top twenty names.

Popular Girls Names in Scandinavia

Below are the top twenty names for girls born in 2008. Names of Scandinavian origin are in bold type.

Top 20 Names for Girls Born in 2008

	Denmark	Norway	Sweden	Iceland
1	Anne	Linnea	Maja	Sara
2	Kirsten	Emma	Emma	Anna
3	Hanne	Sara	Julia	Emilía
4	Mette	Thea	Ella	Katrín
5	Anna	Nora	Elsa	Eva
6	Helle	Ida	Alice	María
7	Susanne	Sofie	Alva	**Gudrún**
8	Lene	**Ingrid**	Linnea	Kristín
9	Karen	Leah	Wilma	Margrét
10	**Inge**	Julie	Klara	Júlía
11	Marianne	Hanna	Nellie	**Helga**
12	Maria	Mia	Ida	Telma
13	**Inger**	Anna	Elin	Viktoría
14	Bente	Maria	Ebba	Rakel
15	Lone	Emilie	Amanda	Aníta
16	Else	Mathilde	Isabelle	Elísabet
17	Pia	Amalie	Agnes	Lilja
18	Jette	**Vilde**	Molly	**Hildur**
19	Camilla	**Tuva**	Hanna	Ísabella
20	Charlotte	Malin	Emilia	Karen

As is the case for the boys names, we find more Scandinavian names among the top hundred names for girls born in 2008. Names are listed alphabetically.

- Denmark: Astrid, Bodil, Freja, Gerda, Inga and Inge, Inger, Ingrid, Nanna, Tove, Aase
- Norway: Alva, Astrid, Frida, Ingeborg, Ingrid, Sigrid, Solveig, Signe, Live, Erika, Tiril, Tuva, Vilde
- Sweden: Astrid, Freja, Frida, Hilda, Ingrid, Linn, Liv, Moa, Saga, Siri, Signe, Svea, Tuva, Tyra

Girls names derived from the names of Catholic saints are also among the top hundred names for girls born in 2008. Names are listed alphabetically.

- Denmark: Anne, Anna, Anja, and Anni, Bente, Birgit, Birthe, Britta, Camilla, Cecilie, Christina, Else, Eva, Gitte, Grethe, Hanne, Johanne, Kirsten and Stine, Karen, Karin, and Karina, Katrine and Trine, Lis, Lisbeth, Maria and Marie, Margit, Mette
- Norway: Ane, Anne, and Anna, Camilla, Elise, Eva, Johanne, Johanna, and Hanna, Kristina and Kristine, Malin, Maren, Mari, Maria, and Marie, Marte, Stine, Sunniva, Synne

- Sweden: Anna, Elsa, Eva, Hanna, Johanna, Lena, Margareta, Margit, Maria, Märta

At the same time, we see that a number of distinctively Scandinavian names that were popular up until very recently have disappeared from the list. Again, Denmark has lost fewer, and is an exception.

Names from Norse Mythology

Until the end of the Viking Age (ca. 750–1050), the Scandinavian peoples had their own religion. By the year 1000, all of the countries were in the process of adopting Christianity. While the old religion was still being practiced, it was not common to give children names of the gods and goddesses. However, there were a number of given names that *contained* a holy name, especially combinations starting with *Tor* (Old Norse Þór-). But the gods and goddesses had a number of alternative names, and it was common to give boys in particular names like Yngve or Endre, which were alternative names for the gods Frey and Thor.

The most important of the Norse gods were Odin, Thor, and Frey, and the most important of the goddesses were their wives or consorts, Frigg, Sif, and Freyja, as well as Gerðr, who was Frey's beautiful giantess wife. In modern times, these names have enjoyed some degree of popularity as given names. Gerðr and Sif in their modern forms are by far the most popular of the goddess names, and Thor has also enjoyed exceptional popularity. Gerd and Gerda were among the most popular girls names in the mid-twentieth century, but even though there are many women named Gerd alive today, the name has disappeared from the lists of the most popular names. A few other gods and goddesses have joined the modern vocabulary of names. These include Odin's sons Bragi and Balder, Njord (father of Frey and Freyja), and Balder's wife Idunn. It is interesting that Frigg, the name of Odin's wife, is not among the mythological names in use in our day. We also find the name Freydis, a name connected to Frey and Freyja, though not the name of an independent goddess. Tjalvi, the son of a peasant couple, is servant to the god Thor. According to Norse mythology, the first human beings were Ask and Embla, and these names have also become fairly common given names.

It is interesting that Freya is enjoying considerable popularity in English speaking countries. In England and Wales the name was ranked number 31 in 2003, moved up to number 23 in 2006, and was number 25 in 2007. In Scotland it ranked number 32. In North America there are also a good many women named Freya. In Oregon, for example, 63 girls were named Freya in the years 1961–2008. In Alberta 33 girls were named Freya from 1999 to 2009, and 21 were given the name in British Columbia between 2007 and 2009 (see page 115).

Freya Seeking Her Husband by the Swedish painter Nils Blommér (1816–53). Freya was the Norse goddess of love and fertility. Freja has become a very popular name for girls, especially in Denmark. The name is also popular in English-speaking countries. Bearers in 2008: Denmark, Freja 6,112, Frøya 4; Iceland, Freyja 297; Norway, Frøya 287, Freya 38; Sweden, Freja 2,139. (illustration © The National Museum of Fine Arts, Stockholm)

Tor/Thor is the most popular mythological name for boys. The story of Thor's journey to Jotunheimen to get his stolen hammer back from the giant Trym is well known. *Trym's Wedding Feast* by W. G. Collingwood (1854–1932) shows Trym kissing his bride, Thor, who is dressed up to look like Freya.

There are nine worlds in the cosmos of Norse mythology. Most of the gods and goddesses live in Ásgarðr, but Njord, Freyja, and Frey live in Vanaheim. The other worlds are inhabited by elves, dwarfs, fire, ice, human beings—and giants. The giants are usually at odds with the gods, and much of the lore in Norse mythology is built around the various conflicts between gods and giants. It would be reasonable for people to shun the names of giants, but nevertheless, there are a couple of giants' names that are popular today: Trym for the boys and Gerd for the girls. In all probability, few associate the name Trym with the simple-minded giant who stole Thor's hammer, or Gerd with the beautiful giantess with whom Frey falls madly in love.

Loki is another name to note. He is a half-god in the Norse cosmos, and one who makes a lot of trouble for the other gods and goddesses. Loki can also be helpful, as he is in the story about how Thor gets his hammer back, in which he finds out who stole the hammer and even dresses up as a woman to help Thor get it back.

Girls Names from Norse Mythology

Old Norse Form	Modern Scandinavian Forms	Bearers in Denmark, Norway, and Sweden (2008)
Gerðr	Gerd, Gerda	59,575
Sif	Siv, Siw	52,377
Freyja	Frøya, Freyja, Fröja, Freja, Freya	9,923
	Frøy, Frey (actually masculine forms)	70
Freydís	Frøydis, Freydis, Frejdis	3,003
Embla	Embla	1,269
Iðunn	Idun, Idunn	1,262
Frigg	Frigg	66

Boys Names from Norse Mythology

Old Norse Form	Modern Scandinavian Forms	Bearers in Denmark, Norway, and Sweden (2008)
Þórr (Thor)	Tor, Thor	39,977
Þrymr	Trym	2,008
Bragi	Brage	1,815
Óðinn	Odin	1,624
Loki	Loke	1,502
Askr	Ask	887
Baldr	Balder	375
Narfi	Narve	313
Njǫrðr	Njord	41
Þjálfi	Tjalve	26
Ægir	Ægir, Ägir	14

Name Days

In Sweden, Norway, and Finland (but not in Denmark) there is a calendar of name days. The custom of celebrating name days has its roots in the early Catholic Church. Each day of the year, except Christmas Day and a few others that were considered too holy, was dedicated to a Christian saint or martyr. Early Christians thought that celebrating birthdays was a barbarian custom, due to their belief in original sin. Since children were born into original sin, a birthday was not much to celebrate. Instead, the Church encouraged parents to celebrate their children's day of baptism or the name day of the saint or martyr for whom the child was named.

During Catholic times in Scandinavia, however, it was not common to celebrate either birthdays or saints' days. But after the Protestant Reformation the custom of celebrating name days turned up in Sweden among the upper classes. In 1749 the first almanac with name days was published, and the custom of celebrating name days gradually spread to the common people in Sweden and Finland.

The Swedish lists of names are still quite traditional and have undergone fairly minor changes over the years. The days considered the holiest are still not designated as name days. A major revision took place in 1901, and this list was valid until 1972. In the oldest list, there was only one name per date, but since 1972 the lists have included two or three names for each date, often both boys and girls names. Through the years a good many dates have retained the original connection to the name of a Christian saint, even though most bearers of these names certainly do not associate themselves with a saint! In 2001 a new list was adopted, and it was agreed that the list would be revised every fifteen years; the next revision should come in 2016. In Finland the lists are regularly updated to keep up with shifting naming fashions, and the underlying philosophy seems to be to distribute the names so that most people will have a name day to celebrate. In Norway there was no almanac of name days until 1988. The list is updated from time to time.

Despite the efforts to work out a list, it has not become common for Norwegians to celebrate their name days. But name days have become a media stunt, as newspapers list the names for each day and explain their origin. They usually give examples of well-known bearers of the names, sometimes with an interview, or they find a local person to congratulate on their name day. There are often tables that show the popularity of the name over time. These columns have certainly raised the awareness among the Norwegian people of names and naming traditions, and even though people do not celebrate their name days, they are avid readers of these columns.

Other countries in Europe also celebrate name days; they are probably most important in Greece, where big celebrations are held for people who are named after the saints and martyrs honored on name days.

In the calendars below, you will find the name days for Norway and Sweden. Boys names appear in bold type, girls names in italic.

January	Norway	Sweden
1	New Year's Day—no names on this date	
2	**Dagfinn**, *Dagfrid*	*Svea*
3	**Alfred, Alf**	**Alfred**, *Alfrida*
4	**Roar, Roger**	*Rut*
5	**Hanna, Hanne**	*Hanna, Hannele*
6	*Aslaug, Åslaug*	**Kasper, Melker, Baltsar**
7	**Knut**, *Elbjørg*	**August**, *Augusta*
8	**Torfinn**, *Turid*	**Erland**
9	**Gunnar**, *Gunn*	**Gunnar, Gunder**
10	**Sigmund**, *Sigrun*	**Sigurd**, *Sigbritt*
11	**Børge, Børre**	**Jan**, *Jannike*
12	**Reinhard, Reinert**	**Fridolf**, *Frideborg*
13	**Gisle**, *Gislaug*	**Knut**
14	**Herbjørn**, *Herbjørg*	**Felix**, *Felicia*
15	**Laurits**, *Laura*	**Lorentz**, *Laura*
16	**Hjalmar, Hilmar**	**Hjalmar, Helmer**
17	**Anton, Tønnes, Tony**	**Anton, Tony**
18	*Hildur, Hild*	*Hilda, Hildur*
19	**Marius**, *Margunn*	**Henrik**
20	**Fabian, Sebastian, Bastian**	**Fabian, Sebastian**
21	*Agnes, Agnete*	*Agnes, Agneta*
22	**Ivan**, *Anja*	**Vincent, Viktor**
23	**Emil**, *Emilie, Emma*	**Frej**, *Freja*
24	**Joar, Jarle, Jarl**	*Erika*
25	**Paul, Pål**	**Paul, Pål**
26	**Øystein, Espen**	*Bodil, Boel*
27	**Gaute**, *Gurli, Gry*	**Göte**, *Göta*
28	**Karl**, *Karoline*	**Karl**, *Karla*
29	**Hermod, Hermann**, *Herdis*	*Diana*
30	*Gunhild, Gunda*	*Gunilla, Gunhild*
31	**Ivar**, *Idun*	**Ivar, Joar**

February	Norway	Sweden
1	Bjarte, *Birte*	Max, Maximilian
2	Jomar, Jostein	Candlemas—no name day
3	Ansgar, Asgeir	*Disa, Hjördis*
4	*Veronica, Vera*	Ansgar, Anselm
5	*Agate, Ågot*	*Agata, Agda*
6	*Dortea, Dorte*	*Dorotea, Doris*
7	Rikard, *Rigmor, Riborg*	Rikard, Dick
8	*Åshild, Åsne*	Bert, *Berta*
9	*Lone, Leikny*	*Fanny, Franciska*
10	*Ingfrid, Ingrid*	*Iris*
11	Ingve, Yngve	Yngve, Inge
12	Randolf, *Randi, Ronja*	*Evelina, Evy*
13	Sveinung, *Svanhild*	Agne, Ove
14	Jardar, *Hjørdis*	Valentin
15	*Sigfrid,* Sigbjørn	*Sigfrid*
16	Julian, *Juliane, Jill*	Julius, *Julia*
17	Sondre, *Aleksandra, Sandra*	*Alexandra, Sandra*
18	Frode, *Frøydis*	Fritiof, *Frida*
19	*Elin, Elna*	*Gabriella, Ella*
20	Haldor, *Haldis*	*Vivianne*
21	Samuel, *Selina, Celine*	Hilding
22	Tim, *Tina*	*Pia*
23	Torstein, *Torunn*	Torsten, *Torun*
24	Mattias, Mattis, Mats	Mattias, Mats
25	Viktor, *Viktoria*	Sigvard, Sivert
26	*Inger, Ingjerd*	Torgny, Torkel
27	*Laila, Lill*	Lage
28	*Marina, Maren*	*Maria*
29	Leap Year day—no name day	

March	Norway	Sweden
1	Audun, *Audny*	Albin, *Elvira*
2	Ernst, *Erna*	Ernst, *Erna*
3	*Gunnbjørg, Gunnveig*	*Gunborg, Gunvor*
4	Adrian, *Ada*	Adrian, *Adriana*
5	Patrick, *Patricia*	*Tora, Tove*
6	Andor, *Annfrid*	Ebbe, *Ebba*
7	Arild, Are	*Camilla*
8	*Beate, Betty, Bettina*	*Siv*
9	Sverre, Sindre	Torbjörn, Torleif
10	*Edel, Edle*	*Edla, Ada*
11	Edvin, *Tale*	Edvin, Egon
12	Gregor, *Gro*	*Viktoria*
13	*Greta, Grete*	Greger
14	*Mathilde, Mette*	*Matilda, Maud*
15	Christer, Chris, *Christel*	Kristoffer, *Christel*
16	Gudmund, *Gudny*	Herbert, *Gilbert*

March	Norway	Sweden
17	Gjertrud, Trude	Gertrud
18	**Aleksander, Sander, Edvard**	**Edvard, Edmund**
19	**Josef,** Josefina	**Josef,** Josefina
20	**Joakim, Kim**	**Joakim, Kim**
21	**Bendik, Bengt, Bent**	**Bengt**
22	Paula, Pauline	**Kennet, Kent**
23	Gerda, Gerd	Gerda, Gerd
24	Ulrikke, Rikke	**Gabriel, Rafael**
25	Maria, Marie, Mari	Feast of the Annunciation (Maria)
26	**Gabriel, Glenn**	**Emanuel**
27	**Rudolf, Rudi**	**Rudalf, Ralf**
28	Åsta, Åste	**Malkolm, Morgan**
29	**Jonas, Jonatan**	**Jonas, Jens**
30	**Holger,** Olga	**Holger,** Holmfrid
31	**Vebjørn, Vegard**	Ester

April	Norway	Sweden
1	**Aron, Arve, Arvid**	**Harald,** Hervor
2	**Sigvard, Sivert**	**Gudmund, Ingemund**
3	**Gunnvald,** Gunvor	**Ferdinand,** Nanna
4	Nanna, Nancy, Nina	Marianne, Marlene
5	Irene, Eirin, Eiril	Irene, Irja
6	**Åsmund, Asmund**	**Vilhelm,** Helmi
7	Oddveig, **Oddvin**	Irma, Irmelin
8	**Asle, Atle**	Nadja, Tanja
9	Rannveig, Rønnaug	**Otto,** Ottilia
10	**Ingvald,** Ingveig	**Ingvar,** Ingvor
11	**Ulf,** Ylva	**Ulf,** Ylva
12	**Julius,** Julie	Liv
13	Asta, Astrid	**Artur, Douglas**
14	Ellinor, Nora	**Tiburtius**
15	**Odin, Odd,** Oda	Olivia, **Oliver**
16	**Magnus, Mons**	Patrik, Patricia
17	Elise, Else, Elsa	**Elias,** Elis
18	**Eilert,** Eilen	**Valdemar, Volmar**
19	**Arnfinn, Arnstein**	**Olaus, Ola**
20	Kjellaug, Kjellrun	Amalia, Amelie, Emelie
21	Jeanette, Jannike	Anneli, Annika
22	**Oddgeir,** Oddny	**Allan, Glenn**
23	**Georg, Jørgen, Jørn**	**Georg, Göran**
24	**Albert,** Olaug	Vega
25	**Markus, Mark**	**Markus**
26	Terese, Tea	Teresia, Terese
27	**Charles,** Charlotte, Lotte	**Engelbrekt**
28	Vivi, Vivian	**Ture,** Tyra
29	**Toralf, Torolf**	**Tyko**
30	Gina, Gitte	Mariana

May	Norway	Sweden
1	**Filip**, *Valborg*	*Valborg*
2	*Åsa, Åse*	**Filip**, *Filippa*
3	**Gjermund**, *Gøril*	**John**, *Jane*
4	*Monika, Mona*	*Monika, Mona*
5	**Gudbrand**, *Gullborg*	**Gotthard, Erhard**
6	*Guri, Gyri*	*Marit, Rita*
7	*Maia, Mai, Maiken*	*Carina, Carita*
8	**Åge, Åke**	**Åke**
9	**Kasper, Jesper**	**Reidar**, *Reidun*
10	**Asbjørn, Espen**, *Asbjørg*	**Esbjörn, Styrbjörn**
11	**Malvin**, *Magda*	*Märta, Märit*
12	**Normann, Norvald**	*Charlotta, Lotta*
13	*Linda, Line, Linn*	*Linnea, Linn*
14	**Kristian, Kristen, Karsten**	**Halvard, Halvar**
15	**Hallvard, Halvor**	*Sofia, Sonja*
16	*Sara, Siren*	**Ronald, Ronny**
17	**Harald**, *Ragnhild*	**Ruben**, *Rebecka*
18	**Eirik, Erik**, *Erika*	**Erik**
19	**Torjus, Torje, Truls**	*Maj, Majken*
20	**Bjørnar**, *Bjørnhild*	*Karolina, Carola*
21	*Helene, Ellen, Eli*	**Konstantin**, *Conny*
22	**Henning**, *Henny*	**Hemming, Henning**
23	**Oddleif**, *Oddlaug*	*Desideria, Desirée*
24	*Ester, Iris*	**Ivan**, *Vanja*
25	*Ragna*, **Ragnar**	**Urban**
26	*Annbjørg, Annlaug*	*Vilhelmina, Vilma*
27	**Cato**, *Katinka*	*Beda, Blenda*
28	**Vilhelm, William, Willy**	*Ingeborg, Borghild*
29	**Magnar**, *Magnhild*	*Yvonne, Jeanette*
30	**Gard, Geir**	*Vera, Veronika*
31	*Pernille*, **Preben**	*Petronella, Pernilla*

June	Norway	Sweden
1	*June, Juni*	**Gun, Gunnel**
2	**Runar, Rune**, *Runa*	**Rutger, Roger**
3	**Rasmus**, *Rakel*	**Ingemar, Gudmar**
4	*Heidi, Heid*	*Solbritt, Solveig*
5	**Torbjørn, Torben**, *Torbjørg*	**Bo**
6	**Gustav**, *Gyda*	**Gustav, Gösta**
7	**Robert, Robin**	**Robert, Robin**
8	**René**, *Renate*	*Eivor, Majvor*
9	**Kolbein, Kolbjørn**	**Börje, Birger**
10	**Ingolf**, *Ingunn*	**Svante, Boris**
11	**Borgar, Bjørge**, *Bjørg*	**Bertil, Berthold**
12	*Sigfrid, Sigrid, Siri*	**Eskil**
13	*Tone, Tonje, Tanja*	*Aina, Aino*
14	**Erlend, Erland**	**Håkan, Hakon**
15	**Viggo**, *Vigdis*	*Margit, Margot*

June	Norway	Sweden
16	Torhild, Toril, Tiril	**Axel**, Axelina
17	**Botolv**, Bodil	**Torvald**, Torborg
18	**Bjarne, Bjørn**	**Björn, Bjarne**
19	**Erling, Elling**	**Germund**, Görel
20	**Salve, Sølve**, Sølvi	Linda
21	**Agnar, Annar**	**Alf, Alvar**
22	**Håkon**, Maud	Paulina, Paula
23	Elfrid, Eldrid	**Adolf**, Alice
24	**Johannes, Jon, Hans**	St. John's Day—no name day
25	**Jørund**, Jorunn	**David, Solomon**
26	**Jonny**, Jenny	Rakel, Lea
27	Aina, Ina, Ine	Selma, **Fingal**
28	**Leo, Leon**, Lea	**Leo**
29	**Peter, Petter, Per**	**Peter**, Petra
30	Solbjørg, Solgunn	**Leif, Elof**

July	Norway	Sweden
1	**Ask**, Embla	**Aron**, Mirjam
2	**Kjartan**, Kjellfrid	Rosa, Rosita
3	**André**, Andrea, Andrine	Aurora
4	**Ulrik**, Ulla	Ulrika, Ulla
5	Mirjam, Mina	Laila, Ritva
6	**Torgrim**, Torgun	**Esaias**, Jessika
7	**Håvard**, Hulda	**Klas**
8	Sunniva, Synnøve, Synne	**Kjell**
9	**Gøran, Jøran, Ørjan**	**Jörgen, Örjan**
10	Anita, Anja	**André**, Andrea
11	**Kjetil, Kjell**	Eleanora, Ellinor
12	**Elias, Eldar**	Herman, Hermine
13	Mildrid, Melissa, Mia	**Joel**, Judit
14	Solfrid, Solrun	**Folke**
15	**Oddmund**, Oddrun	**Ragnvald**, Ragnhild
16	Susanne, Sanne	**Reinhold, Reine**
17	**Guttorm, Gorm**	**Bruno**
18	**Arnulf, Ørnulf**	**Fredrik, Fritz**
19	**Gerhard, Gjert**	Sara
20	Margareta, Margit, Marit	Margareta, Greta
21	Johanne, Janne, Jane	Johanna
22	Malene, Malin, Mali	Magdalena, Madeleine
23	Brita, Brit, Britt	Emma
24	Kristine, Kristin, Kristi	Kristina, Kerstin
25	**Jakob, Jack, Jim**	**Jakob**
26	Anna, Anne, Ane	**Jesper**
27	Marita, Rita	Marta
28	**Reidar**, Reidun	**Botvid, Seved**
29	**Olav, Ola, Ole**	**Olof**
30	Aurora, Audil, Aud	**Algot**
31	Elin, Eline	Helene, Elin

August	Norway	Sweden
1	**Peder,** *Petra*	**Per**
2	*Karen, Karin*	*Karin, Kajsa*
3	**Oliver, Olve,** *Oline*	**Tage**
4	**Arne,** *Arnhild, Arna*	**Arne, Arnold**
5	**Osvald, Oskar**	**Ulrik, Alrik**
6	**Gunnleiv,** *Gunnlaug*	**Alfons,** *Inez*
7	**Didrik,** *Doris*	**Dennis,** *Denise*
8	*Evy, Yvonne*	*Silvia, Sylvia*
9	**Ronald, Ronni**	**Roland**
10	**Lorents, Lars, Lasse**	**Lars**
11	**Torvald, Tarald**	*Susanna*
12	*Klara, Camilla*	*Klara*
13	*Anny, Anine, Ann*	**Kaj**
14	**Hallgeir,** *Hallgjerd*	**Uno**
15	*Margot, Mary, Marielle*	*Stella, Estelle*
16	**Brynjulf,** *Brynhild*	**Brynolf**
17	**Verner,** *Wenche*	**Verner, Valter**
18	**Tormod, Torodd**	*Ellen, Lena*
19	**Sigvald, Sigve**	**Magnus, Måns**
20	**Bernhard, Bernt**	**Bernhard, Bernt**
21	**Ragnvald,** *Ragni*	**Jon,** *Jonna*
22	**Harry,** *Harriet*	*Henrietta, Henrika*
23	*Signe, Signy*	*Signe, Signhild*
24	**Bertil,** *Belinda*	**Bartolomeus**
25	**Ludvig,** *Lovise, Louise*	*Lovisa, Louise*
26	**Øyvind, Eivind, Even**	**Östen**
27	**Roald, Rolf**	**Rolf, Raoul**
28	**Artur, August**	*Gurli, Leila*
29	**Johan, Jone, Jo**	**Hans, Hampus**
30	**Benjamin, Ben**	**Albert,** *Albertina*
31	*Berta, Berte*	**Arvid, Vidar**

September	Norway	Sweden
1	*Solveig, Solvor*	**Samuel**
2	*Lisa, Lise, Liss*	**Justus,** *Justina*
3	*Alise, Alvild, Vilde*	*Alfhild, Alva*
4	**Idar,** *Ida*	*Gisela*
5	**Brede, Brian, Njål**	*Adela, Heidi*
6	*Sollaug, Siril, Siv*	*Lilian, Lilly*
7	*Regine, Rose*	**Roy,** *Regina*
8	**Allan,** *Amalie, Alma*	*Alma, Hulda*
9	**Trygve, Trym,** *Tyra*	*Anita, Annette*
10	**Tord, Tor**	**Tord,** *Turid*
11	**Dag,** *Dagny*	*Dagny, Helny*
12	*Jofrid, Jorid*	*Åsa, Åslög*
13	**Stian, Stig**	**Sture**
14	*Ingebjørg, Ingeborg*	*Ida*
15	**Aslak, Eskil**	*Sigrid, Siri*

September	Norway	Sweden
16	*Lillian, Lilly*	**Dag,** *Daga*
17	*Hildebjørg, Hildegunn*	*Hildegard, Magnhild*
18	**Henry,** *Henriette*	**Orvar**
19	*Konstanse, Connie*	*Fredrika*
20	**Tobias, Tage**	*Elise, Lise*
21	**Trond,** *Trine*	**Matteus**
22	**Kyrre, Kåre**	**Maurits, Moritz**
23	**Snorre,** *Snefrid*	*Tekla, Tea*
24	**Jan, Jens**	**Gerhart, Gert**
25	**Ingvar, Yngvar**	**Tryggve**
26	**Einar, Endre**	**Enar, Einar**
27	*Dagmar, Dagrun*	*Dagmar, Rigmor*
28	*Lena, Lene*	**Lennart, Leonard**
29	**Mikael, Mikal, Mikkel**	**Mikael,** *Mikaela*
30	**Helge,** *Helga, Hege*	**Helge**

October	Norway	Sweden
1	**Remi,** *Rebekka*	**Ragnar,** *Ragna*
2	*Live, Liv*	**Ludvig, Love**
3	**Evald,** *Evelyn*	**Evald, Osvald**
4	**Frans, Frank**	**Frans, Frank**
5	**Brynjar, Boye, Bo**	**Bror**
6	*Målfrid, Møyfrid*	*Jenny, Jennifer*
7	*Birgitte, Birgit, Berit*	*Birgitta, Britta*
8	*Benedikte, Bente*	**Nils**
9	**Leidulf, Leif**	*Ingrid, Inger*
10	**Fridjof, Frits,** *Frida*	**Harry,** *Harriet*
11	**Kevin, Kennet, Kent**	**Erling, Jarl**
12	**Valter,** *Vibeke*	*Valfrid,* **Manfred**
13	**Torgeir, Terje, Tarjei**	*Berit, Birgit*
14	**Kai,** *Kaia*	**Stellan**
15	*Hedvig, Hedda*	*Hillevi, Hedvig*
16	**Flemming, Finn**	**Finn**
17	*Marta, Marte*	*Antonia, Toini*
18	*Kjersti, Kjerstin*	**Lukas**
19	**Tore,** *Tora*	**Tore, Tor**
20	**Henrik, Heine,** *Henrikke*	*Sibylla*
21	**Birger,** *Bergljot*	*Ursula, Yrsa*
22	*Karianne, Karine, Kine*	*Marika, Marita*
23	**Severin, Søren**	**Severin, Sören**
24	**Eilif,** *Eivor*	**Evert, Eilert**
25	*Margrete, Merete, Märta*	*Inga, Ingalill*
26	**Amandus,** *Amanda*	*Amanda,* **Rasmus**
27	**Sturla, Sture**	*Sabina*
28	**Simon, Simen**	**Simon,** *Simone*
29	**Noralf,** *Norunn*	*Viola*
30	**Aksel, Ånund, Ove**	*Elsa, Isabella*
31	*Edit, Edna*	**Edgar,** *Edit*

November	Norway	Sweden
1	**Vetle**, *Veslemøy*	All Saints' Day—no name day
2	*Tove, Tuva*	**Tobias**
3	**Raymond, Roy**	**Hubert, Hugo**
4	**Otto, Ottar**	**Sverker**
5	**Egil, Egon**	**Eugen**, *Eugenia*
6	**Leonard, Lennart**	**Gustav, Adolf**
7	**Ingebrigt**, *Ingelin*	*Ingegerd, Ingela*
8	*Ingvild, Yngvild*	*Vendela*
9	**Teodor**, *Tordis*	**Teodor**, *Teodora*
10	*Gudbjørg, Gudveig*	**Martin**, *Martina*
11	**Martin, Morten**, *Martine*	**Mårten**
12	**Torkjell, Torkil**	**Konrad, Kurt**
13	*Kirsten, Kirsti*	**Kristian, Krister**
14	**Fredrik, Fred, Freddy**	**Emil**, *Emilia*
15	*Oddfrid*, **Oddvar**	**Leopold**
16	**Edmund, Edgar**	*Vibeka, Viveka*
17	**Hugo, Hogne, Hauk**	*Naemi, Naima*
18	**Magne**, *Magny*	*Lillemor, Moa*
19	*Elisabeth, Lisbet*	*Elisabet, Lisbet*
20	**Halvdan**, *Helle*	**Pontus**, *Marina*
21	*Mariann, Marianne*	*Helga, Olga*
22	*Cecilie, Silje, Sissel*	*Cecilia, Sissela*
23	**Klement, Klaus**	**Klemens**
24	*Gudrun, Guro*	**Rune**, *Gudrun*
25	*Katarina, Katrine, Kari*	*Katarina, Katja*
26	**Konrad, Kurt**	**Linus**
27	**Torleif**, *Torlaug*	*Astrid, Asta*
28	**Ruben**, *Rut*	**Malte**
29	*Sofie, Sonja*	**Sune**
30	**Andreas, Anders**, *Andrea*	**Andreas, Anders**

December	Norway	Sweden
1	**Arnold, Arnljot, Arnt**	**Oskar, Ossian**
2	**Bård**, *Borghild, Borgny*	*Beata, Beatrice*
3	**Sveinung, Svein**	*Lydia*
4	*Barbara, Barbro*	*Barbara, Barbro*
5	**Ståle**, *Stine*	**Sven**
6	**Nils, Nikolai**	**Nikolaus, Niklas**
7	**Hallstein**, *Hallfrid*	*Angela, Angelika*
8	**Morgan**, *Marlene, Marion*	*Virginia*
9	*Anniken, Annette*	*Anna*
10	*Judit, Jytte*	*Malin, Malena*
11	**Daniel, Dan**	**Daniel**, *Daniela*
12	*Pia, Peggy*	**Alexander**, *Alexis*
13	*Lucia, Lydia*	*Lucia*
14	**Steinar, Stein**	**Sten, Sixten**
15	*Hilda, Hilde*	**Gottfrid**
16	**Oddbjørn**, *Oddbjørg*	**Assar**

December	Norway	Sweden
17	*Inga,* **Inge**	**Stig**
18	**Kristoffer,** *Kate*	**Abraham**
19	**Isak,** *Iselin*	**Isak**
20	**Abraham, Amund**	**Israel, Moses**
21	**Tomas, Tom, Tommy**	**Tomas**
22	**Ingemar, Ingar**	**Natanael, Jonatan**
23	**Sigurd, Sjur**	**Adam**
24	**Adam,** *Eva*	*Eva* (Christmas Eve)
25	Christmas Day—no name day	Christmas Day—no name day
26	**Stefan, Steffen**	**Stefan, Staffan**
27	**Narve,** *Natalie*	**Johannes, Johan**
28	*Unni, Une, Unn*	**Benjamin**
29	**Vidar, Vemund**	*Natalia, Natalie*
30	**David,** *Diana, Dina*	**Abel, Set**
31	**Sylfest,** *Sylvia, Sylvi*	**Sylvester**

Naming Traditions in the Royal Families

Denmark, Norway, and Sweden are all constitutional monarchies, whereas Finland and Iceland are republics. In this section we will take a look at the naming practices of the royal families in the three monarchies.

Even though the Scandinavian monarchies are challenged in today's society and are in many ways an anachronism, the reigning regents and their heirs apparent are all very popular among their subjects. The christening of a new prince or princess, or the death of a monarch, often sparks a naming fashion. Perhaps a royal name is an attractive alternative for your next child? In this chapter we will also give you some advice on the choice of a royal name.

Denmark

The Danish monarchy is the oldest in the world. It can be documented through historical records since the reign of Gorm the Old, who died during the Viking Age ca. 960. Up until 1660, when the principle of divine monarchy was introduced into Denmark, the king was elected. For all practical purposes, however, the throne was passed to the oldest son of the former king. The old royal family died out in 1448 and was succeeded by the House of Oldenburg, which occupied the throne until 1863, when King Frederik VII died childless. At that point, another branch of the royal family, the House of Glücksborg, took over. The first king in this family was Christian IX, who was given the nickname "father-in-law of Europe" because his children and grandchildren took over, or married into, most of the thrones in Europe.

In the early period, several of the kings are of interest for English speakers. The nickname of Harald Bluetooth (Harald Blåtand) has been preserved for posterity by naming Bluetooth technology after him. He was chosen for this honor because he was an early exponent of diplomatic relations, so that people could communicate and trade with each other.

Several Danish Viking kings raided and eventually conquered England. Sweyn Forkbeard became king of England in 1013 and served one year before he died. He was also overlord of Norway after King Olav Tryggvason was killed. His son, Knud (or Canute) I the Great, served as king of Denmark 1018–35, as king of Norway 1029–30, and king of England 1016–35.

Members of the Danish Royal Family gathered for the christening of Princess Isabella in 2007. Seated left is Crown Princess Mary (b. 1972), holding Isabella. Seated right is Crown Prince Frederik (b. 1968), holding Prince Christian (b. 2005). Standing from left are Susan Elizabeth and John Donaldson, Queen Margrethe II (b. 1940), and Prince Henrik (b. 1934). (photo by Steen Brogaard, courtesy of Steen Brogaard and Helga Wæver, Colourpress)

There have been two queens to rule Denmark, both of them named Margrethe. In 1665 a law was passed giving the right to ascend the throne to the first-born son of a king; if there were no sons, the oldest daughter would inherit the throne. A new law was passed in 1853 in which there was no provision for a daughter to inherit the throne. When it became evident that the children of King Frederik IX would all be daughters, the law was again changed in 1953 so that the present queen could succeed her father. Queen Margrethe II has only sons, and the oldest child of Crown Prince Frederik is also a boy, so should the monarchy survive, it is unlikely there will be another woman regent for some time to come.

From the list of regents below, we can see that the vocabulary of names is fairly small. In the early period, names like Harald, Svend, Knud, Erik, Valdemar, and Christoffer dominate, but they do not form a stringent alternating pattern like the one we see in modern times. Starting with Christian II, the Danish regents have adhered to a strict pattern of naming the heir apparent Christian or Frederik, alternating with each generation and broken only by Queen Margrethe. In many cases, the old Scandinavian custom of naming the first son for the father's father has been followed. We can see this pattern repeated in the name chosen for Margrethe's son

Frederik, who was named for her father. Frederik has opted to keep up the old tradition in kingly names by naming his firstborn Christian. This is not, however, his father's name. Queen Margrethe's royal consort is French and was christened Henri Marie Jean André, but he is known as Prince Henrik of Denmark. Since Frederik will owe his kingship to his mother's line, it was expected that he would choose the name Christian for the child in line for the throne. Since royal children in Denmark are given a number of names, young Prince Christian was also given the name of his grandfathers, Henri and John, as well as another royal name, Valdemar.

Queen Margrethe II was christened Margrethe Alexandrine Þórhildur Ingrid: Margrethe after her maternal grandmother (see below), Alexandrine after her paternal grandmother, Ingrid after her mother. At the time of her birth, Iceland was still a part of the Kingdom of Denmark, and Margrethe was princess of Iceland until Iceland became independent in 1944—thus her Icelandic name, Þórhildur.

Despite the fact that the Danish royal family traces its lineage back to the Viking Age, they have not chosen to perpetuate the old Danish king names: Gorm, Harald, Svend, Knud, and Erik. Erik VII of Pomerania (d. 1439) was the last Danish king with a Scandinavian name. The only name that has a continuing tradition in the royal naming practices is Valdemar. Valdemar is a Scandinavian form of Russian Vladimir, and the name dates back to Valdemar the Great (1131–82), who was named after his Russian maternal grandfather. Prince Christian, his uncle Prince Joachim, and Joachim's son by his first wife, Felix Henrik Valdemar Christian, each bear this name. Since Christoffer III of Bavaria became king in 1440, all of the kings have had names that reflect the Christian heritage in Denmark (Christoffer, Christian, Margrethe, and Hans, which is a form of Johannes), or the close proximity to Germany and intermarriage with nobility there (Frederik).

Another thing that is interesting about the Danish royal names is that royal children have four (sometimes five) given names, although they use only the first one. This practice is common in other European royal families, and it is a way to show status and the fact that they are in a class by themselves. Ordinary people, especially those living in the countryside, would normally have only one given name. People in the bourgeoisie, the upper- and upper-middle classes, showed their elevated status by giving their children two or three names. And the royal family would top it all off with four to six names. Perhaps the record for the number of names is held by the children of Prince Knud (1900–1976). Princess Elisabeth (b. 1935) has eleven names: Elisabeth Caroline-Mathilde Alexandrine Helena Olga Thyra Feodora Estrid Margarethe Désirée. Her brother Ingolf, Count Rosenborg (b. 1940), has ten: Ingolf Christian Frederik Knud Harald Gorm Gustav Viggo Valdemar Aage. Prince Knud was designated heir to the Danish throne before the 1953 law that gave women the right to inherit the throne.

Recommended Danish Royal Names (with adjusted spelling)

For Boys	For Girls
Erik	Amalia
Gorm	Bodil
Harald or Harold	Dagmar
Knude or Knute	Estrid
Svend or Sven	Ingrid
Valdemar	Margreta
	Tova
	Tyra

Advice on Using Danish Royal Names

If you are considering using a Danish royal name for your child, we would suggest you choose one that also reflects the Danish language heritage. The names of the recent kings are not names that do this. Both Christian and Frederik are names that originated in other cultures (in this case northern Germany). A better choice would be to go back to the older kings and consider Gorm, Svend, Knud, Erik, Harald, or Valdemar. Margrethe would also be a good choice.

You should also consider adapting the spelling so that the name will accommodate approximate pronunciation in English. Erik, Gorm, Harald, and Valdemar may each be used as they are. But you might use the spellings Sven, Knute (or Canute), and Margreta. Spelling the name "Margreta" will preserve the Danish heritage and allow for the final syllable to be pronounced. It should not be written with an *h*, that is, "Margrethe" or "Margretha," as the sound is "t," not "th."

The Danish Royal Family regularly follows the practice of using Danish name forms. Queen Margrethe II was named for her maternal grandmother, Princess Margaret of Connaught. The form of the name was adjusted to the Danish language, just as Queen Margrethe's consort, Prince Henrik, took the Danish form of his name.

Danish Regents from Gorm the Old to Margrethe II

died 960	Gorm the Old (Gorm den Gamle)
950–85	Harald Bluetooth (Harald Blåtand)
985–1014	Sweyn I Forkbeard (Svend Tveskæg)
1014–18	Harald II
1018–35	Knud I the Great (Knud den Store)
1035–42	Hardeknud
1042–47	Magnus the Good (Magnus den Gode)
1047–74	Svend II Estridsen
1074–80	Harald III Grindstone (Harald Hen)

1080–86	Knud II the Holy (Knud den Hellige)
1086–95	Oluf I Hunger
1095–1103	Erik I the Kind-hearted (Erik Ejegod)
1104–34	Niels
1134–37	Erik II the Memorable (Erik Emune)
1137–46	Erik III the Lamb (Erik Lam)
1146–57	Svend III Grathe
1146–57	Knud III
1146–82	Valdemar I the Great (Valdemar den Store)
1182–1202	Knud IV
1202–41	Valdemar II the Victor (Valdemar Sejr)
1241–50	Erik IV Plowtax (Erik Plovpenning)
1250–52	Abel
1252–59	Christoffer I
1259–86	Erik V Glipping
1286–1319	Erik VI Menved
1320–26	Christoffer II
1326–30	Valdemar III
1329–32	Christoffer II (second time)
1332–40	Interregnum
1340–75	Valdemar IV Atterdag
1375–87	Oluf II
1387–1412	Margrete I Valdemarsdatter
1396–1439	Erik VII of Pomerania (Erik af Pommern)
1440–48	Christoffer III of Bavaria (Christoffer af Bayern)
1448–81	Christian I
1481–1513	Hans
1513–23	Christian II
1523–33	Frederik I
1533–34	Interregnum
1534–59	Christian III
1559–88	Frederik II
1588–1648	Christian IV
1648–70	Frederik III
1670–99	Christian V
1699–1730	Frederik IV
1730–46	Christian VI
1746–66	Frederik V
1766–1808	Christian VII
1808–39	Frederik VI

1839–48	Christian VIII
1848–63	Frederik VII
1863–1906	Christian IX
1906–12	Frederik VIII
1912–47	Christian X
1947–72	Frederik IX
1972–	Margrethe II

Norway

The Norwegian monarchy traces its roots back to King Harald Fairhair, who united the petty kingdoms of Norway in about 872. But as the list below shows, there were periods during which there were several regents and many short reigns. In contrast to Denmark, Norway has had a turbulent royal history. During the Viking and Middle Ages, several kings were Danish, and from 1380 to 1814 Norway was in a union with Denmark. Following the dissolution of the Kingdom of Denmark and Norway in 1814, Norway was in a union with Sweden for about ninety years. For those interested in the names of regents during the periods under Danish and Swedish rule, we refer to the lists for Denmark and Sweden.

As an ancestor, King Harald Fairhair has special status. A quick look at genealogy Web pages for Norwegians and others with Norwegian ancestry reveals that many people trace their ancestry back to him. According to the Norse historian Snorri Sturluson (1179–1241), Harald was descended from the Norse god Frey himself, so being a descendant of a good king with such an exclusive ancestry is a wonderful thing! When King Olav V announced the engagement of his son Harald to the commoner Sonja Haraldsen in 1968, some of the media immediately set to work to "prove" that Sonja Haraldsen was a direct descendant of Harald Fairhair, and therefore of royal blood. King Harald Fairhair had an extremely active sex life, and according to the historical sources he fathered twenty-three children with seven women. Considering the ease with which such men received or forced sexual favors, the number was probably even greater, so his genes no doubt spread over a wide area. Unfortunately, such ancestry is impossible to prove today, as there are no official records that have survived. Even though Scandinavians in the Viking Age were diligent about recording their family lineage, and this can sometimes be documented in historical records, the official role of keeping family genealogy became the responsibility of the Catholic Church after Christianity was introduced around the year 1000. When the Protestant Reformation came to Norway in 1536, the revelers burned church record books. Families can now at best only trace their genealogy back to the late sixteenth century. Be that as it may, Harald Fairhair made his name popular as a royal name and also in the general populace.

The most notable thing about the names of the regents in Norway is that they almost always have a name of Norse origin: Harald, Eirik, Håkon, Olav, Svein, Øystein, Sigurd, Sverre, and Inge. An exception is the name Magnus, which is one of the early imported names. The only woman regent in Norwegian history, Queen Margrete, shows the Christian influence on naming traditions.

Since it is only a little over a hundred years ago that the union with Sweden was dissolved, it is especially interesting to look at how the present royal family have addressed name giving. When Christian Frederik Carl Georg Valdemar Axel, otherwise known as Prince Carl of Denmark, became king of Norway in 1905, he chose the name Haakon. For the little crown prince, two-year old Alexander Edward Christian Frederik, the name Olav was chosen. Thus, the new royal family revived two kingly names with a long tradition. The name of Olav's son, Harald, revived another name. While the daughters of Olav's colleagues in the other Scandinavian countries were given names reflecting general European naming styles, such as Benedikte, Anne-Marie, Desirée, and Christina, Olav's daughters were given Norse names after

The Crown Prince of Norway and his family on May 17, 2009, the Norwegian National Holiday. Prince Sverre Magnus (b. 2005), Crown Princess Mette-Marit (b. 1973), Princess Ingrid Alexandra (b. 2004; heir to the throne), Crown Prince Haakon (b. 1973), Marius Borg Høiby (b. 1997; Mette-Marit's son from an earlier relationship). (photo by Stian Lysberg Solum / SCANPIX, used by permission)

distinguished consorts of the old kings: Ragnhild and Astrid. In Denmark and Sweden royal children are given a whole slew of names, but King Olav and his wife followed the Norse custom of giving their son, the heir apparent, only one name. Their daughters were given two or three: Ragnhild Alexandra and Astrid Maud Ingeborg. This stands in contrast to the practice in other royal families, where royal children are given about four names, with only one or two used on a daily basis.

The present regent, King Harald, named his daughter Märtha Louise after his mother, a Swedish princess, and his son Haakon Magnus after his grandfather and a series of Norwegian kings. Crown Prince Haakon does not use his second name, and he will certainly use Haakon VIII when and if he becomes king. Crown Prince Haakon and his wife, Crown Princess Mette-Marit, have also given their children two names: Ingrid Alexandra and Sverre Magnus.

The Norwegian royal family seems to be committed to keeping the Norse names alive. An exception might be the young princess, Ingrid Alexandra. Alexandra is of Greek origin. But the naming process is in keeping with the tradition of namesaking. Ingrid Alexandra is named after her great-grandfather, King Olav, who was originally Prince Alexander; her great-great-great-grandmother, Queen Alexandra, consort of King Edward VII of England; and her great aunt, Ragnhild Alexandra. But her first name, Ingrid, is Scandinavian, and has a tradition in the Scandinavian royal families, as well as in the family of her commoner mother.

Advice on Using Norwegian Royal Names

If you are looking for a kingly Norwegian name for your child, you are fortunate. In contrast to Denmark, all of the names in the Norwegian Royal Family are readily identified with Norway and the Norse tradition. Most of them will be no problem when used for a child in an English-speaking environment. In some cases small adjustments in the spelling may be advisable. Håkon/Haakon may be written

Recommended Norwegian Royal Names (with adjusted spelling)

For Boys	For Girls
Eirik	Astrid
Hokon, Hakon, Haakon	Gudrun
Harald or Harold	Gunnhild
Knute	Ingeborg
Magnus	Ingrid
Olav or Olaf	Kristin
Oystein	Margreta
Sigurd	Metta
Svein	Marit
	Sonja
	Ragnhild

"Hokon" and Øystein does fairly well written "Oystein." Inge is not as easy to adapt to English, as the spelling "Inga" is readily identified with the girls name. To ensure that the final syllable is pronounced, Margrete may be written "Margreta."

Norwegian Regents from Harald Fairhair to Harald V

At times during the Middle Ages two kings ruled simultaneously, thus some reigns overlap.

ca. 872–933	Harald Fairhair (Harald Hårfagre)
ca. 933–35	Eirik I Haraldsson Bloodaxe (Eirik Blodøks)
930s–ca.960	Håkon I Haraldsson, the Good (Håkon Adalsteinsfostre, den gode)
ca. 960–70	Harald II Eiriksson Greycloak (Harald Gråfell)
970–95	Earl Håkon Sigurdsson (Håkon Ladejarl, Danish)
995–1000	Olav I Tryggvason
1000–1015	the earls Eirik and Svein Håkonsson (Eirik og Svein Håkonsson, Ladejarler, Danish)
1015–28	Olav II Haraldsson, Saint Olav (Olav den Heilage)
1028–29	Earl Håkon Eiriksson (Håkon Eiriksson Jarl, Danish)
1029–30	Knut the Great (Knut den Store, Danish)
1030–35	Svein Knutsson
1035–47	Magnus I Olavsson, the Good (Magnus den Gode)
1045–66	Harald III Sigurdsson Hardrule (Harald Hardråde)
1066–69	Magnus II Haraldsson
1067–93	Olav III Haraldsson the Mild (Olav Kyrre)
1093–95	Håkon Magusson (Håkon Toresfostre)
1093–1103	Magnus III Olavsson Barefoot (Magnus Berrføtt)
1103–5	Olav Magnusson
1103–23	Øystein I Magnusson
1103–30	Sigurd Magnusson the Crusader (Sigurd Jorsalfare)
1130–35	Magnus IV Sigurdsson the Blind (Magnus Blinde)
1130–36	Harald IV Magnusson Gille
1136–61	Inge I Haraldsson Hunchback (Inge Krokrygg)
1142–57	Øystein II Haraldsson
1157–62	Håkon II Sigurdsson the Broadsholdered (Håkon Herdebrei)
1161–84	Magnus V Erlingsson
1177–1202	Sverre Sigurdsson
1202–4	Håkon III Sverresson
1202–27	Inge II Bårdsson
1217–63	Håkon IV Håkonsson

1263–80	Magnus VI Håkonsson the Lawmender (Magnus Lagabøte)
1280–99	Eirik II Magnusson
1299–1319	Håkon V Magnusson
1319–55	Magnus Eriksson
1343–80	Håkon VI Magnusson
1381–87	Olav IV Håkonsson
1388–1412	Margrete Valdemarsdotter
1412–1814	Interim period, Norway is under the Danish crown. See the list of Danish regents from Erik of Pomerania through Frederik VI.
1814	Christian Frederik
1814–1905	Interim period, Norway is in union with Sweden. See the list of Swedish regents from Karl XIII through Oscar II.
1905–57	Haakon VII
1957–91	Olav V
1991–	Harald V

Sweden

The Swedish monarchy traces its history back to the later Viking Age, to about 970, when Erik was king. During the Middle Ages the regent was elected by the land-holders, and as we can see from the list below, the duration of the various reigns is sketchy until the thirteenth century. In 1544 the hereditary monarchy was introduced by Gustav I Vasa. Under the provisions the eldest son of the monarch inherited the throne, and neither a daughter nor her sons could inherit it. The first female regent, Margrete (Margareta in Swedish), was queen of Norway, Denmark, and Sweden; it was made possible for a woman to become regent during this period. The Swedish law was also adjusted a couple of times to allow Queen Kristina to succeed the throne in 1632 and Queen Ulrika Eleonora in 1718. In 1980 a new law was passed that gave women equal rights to the Swedish throne. At the time, King Carl Gustaf had two children, Victoria (b. 1977) and Carl Philip (b. 1979). At the time they were born, Prince Carl Philip was the heir apparent, but the law was made retroactive so that Princess Victoria became the crown princess.

In the Middle Ages, the kings bore typical Swedish names: Erik, Olof, Anund, Halsten, Inge, Ragnvald, Sverker, and Karl. Karl is of special interest here, as it is the most frequently used royal name in Sweden. In the list below, Karl VII Sverkersson (1161–67) is the first Karl mentioned, but since he is number seven, we assume that the name had been in use in the Swedish royal family long before the twelfth century. It is possible that this name came into fashion in Sweden as homage to Charlemagne (Karl the Great). But "karl" means "free man" in Swedish, and may have originally been a nickname, so it is also a genuine Swedish name.

Another name of note is Gustaf, which came into use with Gustaf Vasa. Gustaf is also used in its Latinized form Gustavus (such as Gustavus Adolphus College in Saint Peter, Minnesota), and means "staff of the Goths." Perhaps it was originally a nickname given to leaders, a kind of honorary name reserved for important people. But by the late eighteenth century the name had become quite popular among ordinary citizens. It has, however, retained its royal status; the last three Swedish kings have all been named Gustaf.

By the late fifteenth century the influence from Christian names becomes evident. Kings named Kristian and Hans (Johan) arrive on the scene. The three women regents were named Margrete (Margareta), Kristina, and Ulrika Eleonora, and all bore names that reflected foreign influences. Margrete and Kristina show the Christian influence; Ulrika, a feminine form of Ulrik, is originally a German name; and Eleonora is used by queens and nobility elsewhere in Europe. But all told, the foreign influence on regents' names is much less than in Denmark.

As in the Danish royal family, a child is given more names at the christening ceremony than he or she uses in the official capacity. Swedish princes and princesses are christened with a number of names to honor family members. The present king Carl XVI Gustaf has four names: Carl Gustaf Folke Hubertus, and he and Queen Silvia have also given each of their three children four names. Crown Princess Victoria's full name is Victoria Ingrid Alice Désirée, her brother Prince Carl Philip was christened Carl Philip Edmund Bertil, and their sister, Princess Madeleine, Madeleine Thérèse Amelie Josephine. Several names in the youngest generation are French, particularly in the case of Princess Madeleine. Perhaps this is to honor the French roots of the Bernadotte family, which ascended the Swedish throne in 1818. At that time, a French soldier-diplomat named Jean-Baptiste Jules Bernadotte was chosen to succeed Karl XIII, who was childless. His wife was Désirée, which is one of the names of Princess Victoria. The name Victoria comes from her great-grandmother Queen Victoria, consort of Gustaf V.

The name Oskar is also worthy of note. The son and great-grandson of King Karl Johan were both named Oskar. Oskar I was born in Paris, before his father came to Sweden. The name Oskar was chosen by none other than Napoleon Bonaparte, who had once been engaged to marry Oskar's mother Désirée. The name was popularized by *The Poems of Ossian*, published in the 1760s and claimed by its author James Macpherson to be translated poems from an old manuscript written by a poet named Ossian. This work was a major impetus to the Romantic Movement in European literature. One of the heroes in the poems was named Oscar, and this name became enormously popular in many countries, including the United States. In Sweden this name experienced immediate popularity after the announcement in 1810 that Jean-Baptiste Jules Bernadotte had been chosen to succeed Karl XIII. The first Oskar was christened in Sweden only a few weeks later, the parents having been charmed by a portrait of the ten-year-old son of the future monarch.

The Swedish Royal Family on Valborg's Mass, April 30, 2006, during the celebrations for the king's sixtieth birthday. Princess Madeleine (b. 1982), King Carl XVI Gustaf (b. 1946), Queen Silvia (b. 1943), Prince Carl Philip (b. 1979), and Crown Princess Victoria (b. 1977; heir to the throne). (photo by Jonas Ekströmer / Scanpix, used by permission)

Advice on Using Swedish Royal Names

If you are thinking of naming your child after a Swedish monarch, you have a number of good Swedish names to choose from. Most of the royal names in Sweden are solidly anchored in Swedish culture, but Karl and Erik in particular are very common and will not necessarily be interpreted as kingly. Nor will Oskar be a Swedish identifier. A much more distinctive choice would be Sten, Sverker, Gustaf, or Inge. The first three will do fairly well pronounced by English speakers, whereas Inge will not. It will not be a good idea to spell it "Inga," as this name will readily be identified with the girls name Inga. A better choice would be Ingemar or another Swedish name beginning with *Ing*. Gustaf may be spelled "Gustav," but we would not recommend "Gustave," as this spelling will lead to incorrect pronunciation of the last part. The double name Karl Gustav is a regal sounding name, easily recognized as Swedish. We would not, however, recommend Gustav Adolf, as Adolf will still be associated with Adolf Hitler.

As for female names, Margareta is a good Swedish marker, as is Kristina. Ulrika is a better marker of a German background. Victoria will also not be recognizable as a Swedish name.

Recommended Swedish Royal Names (with adjusted spelling)

For Boys	For Girls
Birger	Astrid
Gustav	Hedvig
Erik	Gunilla
Karl	Ingeborg
Knute	Karin
Magnus	Katarina
Sten	Kristina
Sven	Margareta
Sverker	Sigrid

Swedish Regents from Erik Segersäll to Carl XVI Gustaf (list somewhat simplified)

ca. 970–995	Erik VII the Victor (Erik Segersäll)
ca. 995–1022	Olof Skötkonung
ca. 1022–50	Anund Jakob
ca. 1050–60	Emund the Old (Emund den Gamle)
ca. 1060–66	Stenkil
ca. 1067–70	Halsten
ca. 1079–83	Inge Stenkilsson the Elder (Inge den Äldre)
ca. 1083–85	Sven the Sacrificer (Blot-Sven)
ca. 1085–1110	Inge Halstensson the Younger (Inge den Yngre)
ca. 1110–18	Inge and Filip
ca. 1118–20	Inge the Younger
mid-1120s	Ragnvald Buttonhead (Ragnvald Knaphövde)
ca. 1125–30	Magnus Nilsson
ca. 1130–56	Sverker I the Elder (Sverker den Äldre)
ca. 1156–60	Erik, Saint Erik (Erik den Helige)
ca. 1160–61	Magnus Henriksson
ca. 1161–67	Karl VII Sverkersson
ca. 1167–95	Knut Eriksson
ca. 1195–1208	Sverker II Karlsson
ca. 1208–16	Erik Knutsson
ca. 1216–22	Johan I Sverkersson
ca. 1222–29	Erik Eriksson the Lame Lisper (Erik Läspe och Halte)
ca. 1229–34	Knut Långe
1234–50	Erik Eriksson the Lame Lisper
1250–75	Valdemar Birgersson

1275–90	Magnus Birgersson the Barnlocker (Magnus Ladulås)
1290–1318	Birger Magnusson
1319–64	Magnus Eriksson
1364–89	Albrekt of Mecklenburg
1389–96	Margrete (Margareta)
1396–1439	Erik of Pomerania
1441–48	Christoffer of Bavaria
1448–57	Karl VIII Knutsson the Farmer (Karl Knutsson Bonde)
1457–64	Kristian I
1464–65, 1467–70	Karl VIII Knutsson the Farmer
1470–97	Sten Gustafsson Sture (Sten Sture den äldre)
1497–1501	Hans (Johan II)
1501–3	Sten Gustafsson Sture
1504–12	Svante Nilsson Sture
1512–20	Sten Sture the Younger (Sten Sture den yngre)
1520–21	Kristian II
1521–60	Gustav I Eriksson Vasa
1560–68	Erik XIV
1568–92	Johan III
1592–99	Sigismund
1599–1611	Karl IX
1611–32	Gustav II Adolf
1632–54	Kristina
1654–60	Karl X Gustav
1660–97	Karl XI
1697–1718	Karl XII
1719–20	Ulrika Eleonora
1720–51	Fredrik I
1751–71	Adolf Fredrik
1771–92	Gustav III
1792–1809	Gustav IV Adolf
1809–18	Karl XIII (in Norway Karl II)
1818–44	Karl XIV Johan (in Norway Karl III Johan)
1844–59	Oskar I
1859–72	Karl XV (in Norway Karl IV)
1872–1907	Oskar II
1907–50	Gustav V
1950–73	Gustaf VI Adolf
1973–	Carl XVI Gustaf

A Scandinavian Name for Your Baby

Are you looking for a Scandinavian name for your baby? Of course, you are free to choose any name in this book, but some of them will work better in English than others. We will therefore recommend a number of names. The main considerations here are how the names will sound in English, and whether they are readily associated with a Scandinavian heritage. International names, even though they enjoy high frequency in Scandinavia, are therefore not included, as they are not markers of a Scandinavian identity.

We have divided the recommended names into two categories, the first one (Tables 1 and 3) consisting of names that when pronounced in English will sound more or less the same as in a Scandinavian language. The second category (Tables 2 and 4) consists of names that when pronounced by English speakers will have an acceptable, though not genuine Scandinavian, pronunciation.

In the tables below, we have left out a number of very common names prevalent in Scandinavia, such as Anna, Ida, and Elisabeth for girls, and Albert, Christoffer, and Martin for boys. Even though these names are very common, they are international and not obvious markers of a Scandinavian identity. You will, however, find a good many of these names in the dictionary section. Please refer to that section if you are interested in such a name.

In choosing a name, it is important to think about your child's future comfort level with his or her name. This will be related to how English speakers with no particular knowledge of a Scandinavian language will pronounce it. In the international world in which we live, where great numbers of people migrate to new cultural areas, this problem is not unique to those with a Scandinavian background. It must be said that there are many people living in an English language setting who have roots in other languages and cultures that are much more "foreign" than the Scandinavian ones ever will be in an English language context. However, it may be tiresome for a child if he or she time and again has to correct the pronunciation of his or her name. To what extent a name is a problem or not is something that parents and their children will have to decide for themselves. But we hope our recommendations will heighten the level of awareness and facilitate a good choice.

Particularly in the recommendations for boys names, we have included a good many names that are quite rare in Scandinavia today. Since our main consideration is pronunciation, there is no reason not to include these names. In addition, we are convinced that some parents are looking for a distinctive marker name that is not borne by a large number of people, and here they will find many alternatives. Many of these names go back to the Viking Age, and such names may be attractive for just that reason.

Please refer to the dictionary section of this book for information on pronunciation, meaning, and prevalence of each name, and whether it is primarily used in Denmark, Norway, or Sweden.

Recommended Girls Names

The names in Table 1 should not be a problem for English speakers to pronounce, and at the same time they will be distinctive markers of a Scandinavian identity. The names in Table 2 will sound all right, even though the English pronunciation will differ from the Scandinavian. These names also are markers of a Scandinavian identity.

Many girls names have alternative spellings ending in *a* or *e*. In order to ease the pronunciation in English, it will be advisable to spell these names ending in *a*. Note that the names Helle and Mette are not spelled with an *a* ending in Scandinavia, as

Maren Anne, born in 2008 in Oregon. This state has a significant Scandinavian American population. In 2008, 7 other girls born in Oregon were named Maren, as were 118 girls born there from 1961 to 2008. In Scandinavia as of 2008 there are a good many more: Denmark, 1,802; Norway, 6,103; Sweden, 148. (photo by Nancy L. Coleman)

Marika, born in 1984 in Hawaii, with her mother Martha, born in 1948 in New York State. Martha is named after her Norwegian great-great-grandmother, who immigrated to the United States in 1862. Marika is actually a German diminutive form of Maria, and thus not a traditional Scandinavian name, but Martha found it in a Norwegian name book and liked it. She gave Marika the Norwegian farm name Stokset as a middle name. Marika is rare in Denmark and Norway but fairly common in Sweden. Bearers in 2008: Denmark, 212; Norway, 140; Sweden, 5,790. (photo by Nancy L. Coleman)

they are most common in Denmark, where such names almost always end in *e*. But there is no reason why they cannot follow the pattern of other similar names, and we recommend the adapted spelling if you want to use these names in an English-language setting.

It will also be noted that only one name beginning with *A* is included in Table 1. This is due to the fact that the English pronunciation will normally give a different sound to the *A*. Sometimes, but not always, the English pronunciation will be close to the Danish one, but most often it will not be comparable to the Norwegian or Swedish. For the same reason, a great many names containing *a* will not be found here, but rather in Table 2. (In English there are two pronunciations for Karen/Karin; for a Scandinavian pronunciation, pronounce the 'a' as in 'father.' Maren rhymes with Karen when the *a* is pronounced as in 'father.') The same is true for the other vowels, as *e, i, o,* and *u* all usually have a different pronunciation than in English. There are no names beginning with *J* in either list, as the pronunciation of *j* is normally like *y* in English. We also do not recommend using names beginning with Ø, Ö, Å, or *Au*. The spelling of these names may be adapted, such as Oshild for Åshild, Osa for Åse, or Owd for Aud. But using an adapted spelling will often mean that the name no longer is recognizable as Scandinavian, or the spelling may give rise to unpleasant associations in English (Owd). But there may also be good reasons to choose a name containing one of these letters, so we leave this question for you to decide.

Table 1: Girls Names Easily Pronounced in English

Arnhild	Hedda	Martina
Benta or Bente	Hedvig	Metta
Berit	Helga	Nilla
Birgit or Birgitta	Hella or Helle	Nora
Bodil	Hild(a)	Oda
Borghild	Inga	Oletta
Brit(t) or Britta	Ingeborg	Pia
Brynhild	Inger	Runa
Cecilia	Ingrid	Selma
Christina or Kristina	Ingvild	Signy
Ebba	Kaia	Sigrid
Edda	Karen or Karin	Sigvor
Edvarda	Ki(e)rsten	Silja
Eldrid	Kristin(a)	Siri
Elisa	Laila	Sissel(a)
Ellisiv	Linn	Solvor
Elsa	Lisa	Svanhild
Embla	Lisbet	Sylvi
Emma	Lona or Lone	T(h)ora
Fredrikka	Lotta	Tirill
Freya	Lovisa	Torborg
Freydis	Magrit	Tordis
Frida	Maia	Torfrid
Frigg	Maren	Torhild
Gro	Margit	Tova or Tuva
Gunilla	Marika	Vigdis
Halldis	Marta	

Table 2: Girls Names with an Acceptable English Pronunciation

Agneta	Andrina	Dagny
Alfhild or Alvhild	Astrid	Elena
Alida	Bergit	Elin or Elen
Alma	Berta	Eva
Alva	Carrie or Kari	Gerda
Amalia	Christiana or Kristiana	Gertrud
Amanda	Clara or Klara	Greta
Andrea	Dagmar	Gudrun

Gunnhild	Linnea	Oleanna
Gunnvor	Liv	Pernilla
Guro or Goro	Liva	Ragna
Herborg	Magda	Ragnhild
Herdis	Magdalena	Rannveig
Idunn	Malena	Saga
Ingunn	Margareta	Sigrun
Kari	Mari	Siv
Klara	Marianna	Solveig
Kristiana	Nanna	Turid
Lena	Norunn	

Recommended Boys Names

The names in Table 3 should not be a problem for English speakers to pronounce, and at the same time they will be distinctive markers of a Scandinavian identity. The names in Table 4 will sound all right, even though the English pronunciation will differ from the Scandinavian. These names also are markers of a Scandinavian identity.

Leif Rangnar, born in 2006 in Oregon. Rangnar is an adjusted spelling of Ragnar. Leif's mother is of Norwegian ancestry, and she wished to honor her heritage. Between 1961 and 2008, 193 boys in Oregon were given the name Leif. In Scandinavia the names Leif/Leiv and Ragnar are popular: Denmark, Leif 18,352, Leiv 4, Ragnar 133; Norway, Leif 15,203, Leiv 1,410, Ragnar 5,314; Sweden, Leif 68,852, Leiv 20; Ragnar 18,575. (photo by Martha Pederson Anderson)

Names beginning with *A* may cause some problems, as the *a* sounds different in most Scandinavian words than it does in English. For this reason, most of these names appear in Table 4. But names beginning with *Ar* or *Arn* fit fairly well into English, and are therefore placed in Table 3. Sometimes, but not always, the English pronunciation of *a* will be close to the Danish one, but most often it will not be comparable to the Norwegian or Swedish. For the same reason, a great many names containing *a* will also be found in Table 4. The same is true for the other vowels, as *e, i, o,* and *u* all usually have a different pronunciation than in English.

There are no names beginning with *J* in either list, as the pronunciation of *j* is normally like *y* in English. There is one name beginning with *J* that we might recommend despite the pronunciation differences: Jens. The patronymic Jensen is fairly well known in English, and using the given name Jens may be a good option in some families.

There are a good many Scandinavian boys names ending in *e*, such as Arve, Atle, Bjarne, Endre, Folke, Gisle, Inge, Ove, Rune, and Tore. Even though these names are excellent and distinctive Scandinavian names, they are not included in the list because the bearers will usually have to teach people to pronounce their names at every turn in the road. But whether or not it is a good idea to use such a name is a

Eric, born in 1978 in Minnesota, and his sister Ingrid, born in 1975. Their father is of Norwegian American descent. Eric is currently popular in the United States; 5,322 boys were named Eric in 2008. For statistics on Eric, see page 111. Ingrid ranked number 561 in the United States in 2008. Bearers in Scandinavia in 2008: Denmark, Ingrid 10,799, Ingri 8; Norway, Ingrid 24,806, Ingri 406; Sweden, Ingrid 122,919, Ingri 88. (photo by Larry Carpenter, used by permission)

choice parents will have to make, and we leave it up to your discretion. A few names ending in *e* in modern Danish, Norwegian, and Swedish have been included using the older forms (Old Norse) that end in *i*, including Bragi, Helgi, Hogni, and Snorri. These names are known from Norse mythology, and the forms used here are the ones used in English translations of Old Norse literature. Note that not all names ending in *e* in modern Scandinavian ended in *i* in Old Norse, so it is not a good idea to make up your own forms by changing a final *e* to *i*! Nor is it a good idea to change the *e* to *a*, as we have recommended for girls names. We base this on the fact that many English speakers associate a name ending in *a* with a feminine name.

We also do not recommend using names that contain *ø* or *ö*, *æ* or *ä*, or *å*. Boys names beginning with these special Scandinavian vowels are fairly rare, and several of them present additional problems when pronounced by English speakers. A few names containing these letters may be otherwise desirable. The name Bjørn/ Björn, for example, thanks to sportsmen and entertainers like Björn Borg, Bjørn Dæhlie, and Björn Ulvaeus, has become a recognizable boys name in the English-speaking world with the spelling Bjorn. Bjørn is also a frequent second element in boys names: Asbjørn, Herbjørn, Sigbjørn, Torbjørn, and so forth. These names do not appear in either list, but some parents may want to use them despite difficulties in pronunciation, and based on the success of Bjorn, they may not turn out to be a problem spelled Herbjorn, Sigbjorn, and Torbjorn. We leave it up to you to decide whether or not Asbjorn is a problem!

Table 3: Boys Names Easily Pronounced in English

Arnfinn	Carl	Eldar or Eldor
Arni	Carsten	Ellev or Ellef
Arnstein	Christen	Elling
Arnulf or Arnulv	Christer	Embret or Embrik
Arvid	Christian	Engelbert
Balder	Clement or Clemens	Engelbrekt or Engelbregt
Bendik(t)	Colben	Engelhart
Bengt or Benkt	Detlef, Ditlef, or Detlof	Esben or Espen
Birger	Dreng	Finn
Bo	Edmund or Edmond	Flemming
Bodvar	Edvard	Folkvard
Borger or Borgar	Eigil	Fred(e)rik
Botolv or Botolf	Einar	Freystein
Bragi	Einvald	Frodi
Brigt or Brikt	E(i)rik	Gard or Gardar
Bror	Eivind	Geir

Geirmund
Gorm
Greger(s)
Grim
Gustav or Gustaf
Hartvig
Hein
Helgi
Hellik, Hellek, or Helleik
Helmer
Hemming
Henning
Henrik
Hilmar or Hilmer
Hogni
Holger
Ib
Ingar(d)
Ingebret or Ingebrigt
Inggeir
Ing(e)mar
Ingo
Ingolf or Ingolv
Ing(e)vald
Ingvar(d)
Kai
Karl
Karste(i)n
Keld
Klement, Klemet, or
    Klemens
Kleng
Kolbe(i)n
Kristen
Krister
Kristian
Kurt
Lars
Leidulf or Leidulv
Leif or Leiv

Lennart
Loren(t)s
Markus
Mika(e)l
Mikkel
Mogens
Mons
Ni(e)ls
Norman(n)
Oddmar
Oddmund
Oddvar
Odin
Ogmund
Ola or Ole
Olaf or Olav
Olof or Olov
Oluf
Ommund
Ordin
Orm
Orvar
Osmund
Osvald
Ottar
Petter
Povel
Reidar
Reidulf or Reidolv
Rein
Reinert
Rolf or Rolv
Runar
Semming
Sigfred
Siggeir
Sigleif or Sigleiv
Sigmar
Sigmund
Sigstein

Sigtor
Sigurd
Sigvald
Sigvard or Sigvart
Sigvid
Sixten
Snorri
Solmund
Sondolv
Stein
Steinar
Steingrim
Steinulf or Steinulv
Stillef or Stillev
Sturla
Svein or Sven(d)
Sveinung
Svenning
Tellef or Tellev
T(h)or
Tollak
Torben
Tord
Torfinn
Torge(i)r
Torgils
Torgny
Torgrim
Torkil(d)
Torleif
Torolv or Torolf
Torstein or Torsten
Torvald
Tron(d)
Valdemar
Viggo
Vigleik
Volmer

Table 4: Boys Names with Acceptable English Pronunciation

Agnar or Agner

Aksel or Axel

Alf or Alv

Algot

Almar or Almer

Alvar

Amund

Anders

Anker

Annar

Anund

Arnt

Ari

Arild

Asge(i)r or Asgar

Ask

Askild or Askell

Aslak

Asmund

Bergsve(i)n

Bertil or Bertel

Birger or Berger

Bjorn, Bjørn, or Björn

Dag

Dagfinn

Dan

Didrik

Egil

Erland or Erlend

Erling

Ernst

Evald

Eystein

Eyvind

Gerhard

Greger(s) or Gregor

Gudbrand or Gulbrand

Gudmund

Gunnar, Gunder, or

   Gunner

Gunnleif or Gunnleiv

Gunnste(i)n

Gunnvald

Guttorm

Haftor or Havtor

Hakon

Halfdan or Halvdan

Haldor

Hallgeir

Hal(l)stein

Hallvard, Halvar, or

   Halvor

Hans

Harald

Hauk

Helmut

Herbrand

Hergeir

Herleif, Herleiv, or

   Herlof

Hermod

Hermund

Ivar or Iver

Ketil, Kittel, or Kittil

Kla(u)s

Knute

Levar(d) or Levor

Mads or Mats

Magnar

Magnus

Marius

Matti(a)s

Maurits

Njord

Peder

Per

Ragnar

Randolf or Randolv

Randulf or Randulv

Rasmus

Regin

Roald

Roar

Rodgeir

Rune or Runi

Severt

Sigfus

Sigvat

Staffan

Ste(e)n

Stener or Stenar

Stian

Stig

Tallak

Tarald

Tormod

Truls

Vegard

Vemund

Viking

Definitions

Diminutive—used in connection with names implies smallness, either referring to a small person or as a token of affection.

Element—in our context, a part of a name. In contrast to a prefix or suffix, an element is a word that can stand by itself, or be combined with other elements to produce different names, e.g., Bjørn, Bjørnhild; Alf, Alvin, Alfhild.

Matronymic—a name derived from the given name of one's mother, with the suffix meaning 'son' or 'daughter' attached to it, e.g., Ingridsson, Astridsdotter. In theory, such a name might be a primary or secondary matronymic (see *patronymic*, below), but examples of such a practice are certainly rare, if they exist at all.

Middle Ages—in European history, a period of about a thousand years beginning with the fall of the Roman Empire in the fifth century and ending with the beginning of the modern period in the sixteenth century. In Scandinavian history, the Middle Ages usually refers to the period following the Viking Age, ca. 1050–1536. This period coincides with the introduction of Christianity (the Catholic Church) around the year 1000, and ends with the Reformation, which split the Church into Catholic and Protestant branches. The period is usually divided into three parts. A comparison of the Middle Ages in European and Scandinavian history is shown in the table below.

Period Name	European Middle Ages	Scandinavian Middle Ages
Early Middle Ages	500–1000	1050–1200
High Middle Ages	1000–1300	1200–1400
Late Middle Ages	1300–1536	1400–1536

Nordic countries—the preferred term for Scandinavia in the Northern European region, consisting of Denmark, Finland, Iceland, Norway, Sweden, the Faroe Islands, Greenland, and Åland. Recently, Estonia, usually considered a Baltic country, has made claim to belonging to the Nordic region. The claim is based on its language, which is related to Finnish, and the fact that it was under either Danish or Swedish rule during much of its history.

Norse—adjective referring to the language and culture of Scandinavia during the Viking Age (ca. 750–1050) and for another three hundred years into the Middle Ages.

Norsemen—the people living in present-day Norway, Denmark, and Sweden, and in the colonies belonging to this area during the Viking Age.

Norse mythology—the literature (beliefs, myths, and legends) based on the pre-Christian religion in the North Germanic area, including the Scandinavian countries.

Old Norse—the language in Norway and its colonies, the Faroe Islands, Iceland, and Greenland, ca. 700–1350. Note that whereas the terms Norse, Norsemen, and Norse mythology also include Denmark and Sweden, the language Old Norse does not. Old Danish and Old Swedish refer to Viking Age Danish and Swedish.

Patronymic—a name derived from the given name of one's father, with the suffix meaning 'son' or 'daughter' attached to it, e.g., Nilsson, Nilsen; Nilsdotter, Nilsdatter. Such a name may be a *primary* or *secondary* patronymic. A primary patronymic changes with each generation, as it is always based on the father's name. A secondary patronymic is one that originally was a primary patronymic, but has been passed on to the grandchildren of the original father, and on down through the generations.

Prefix—a group of letters added to the beginning of a word, thus forming a new word and changing its meaning. Common prefixes in English are *re*, *ex*, and *anti*.

Scandinavia—strictly speaking, the geographical area encompassing the Scandinavian peninsula (Norway and Sweden) and Denmark. The word *Scandinavia* is probably derived from the name Skåne, the southernmost part of the Scandinavian peninsula and now in present-day Sweden. Scandinavia is usually construed to include the rest of the countries in this area that have similar languages and/or cultures: Iceland and Finland, as well as the remaining colonies, the Faroe Islands and Greenland. A more correct term for the whole area is the Nordic countries.

Suffix—a group of letters added to the end of a word, thus forming a new word and changing its meaning. Common suffixes in English are *ly*, *less*, and *ful*.

References

Name Books

Brandt, Mogens Severin. *Hvad skal barnet hedde*. Copenhagen: Politikens Forlag, 1992.

Dictionary of American Family Names. Edited by Patrick Hanks. Vols. 1–3. Oxford: Oxford University Press, 2003.

DUDEN: Das große Vornamenlexikon. Edited by Rosa and Volker Kohlheim. Mannheim: Dudenverlag, 2003.

Kruken, Kristoffer, and Ola Stemshaug. *Norsk personnamnleksikon*. 2nd ed. Oslo: Det Norske Samlaget, 1995.

Kvaran, Guðrún, and Sigurður Jónsson frá Arnarvatni. *Nöfn Íslendinga*. Reykjavik: Heimskringla, 1991.

Meldgaard, Eva Villarsen. *Den store navnebog*. Copenhagen: Aschehoug Dansk Forlag, 1994.

Norsk personnamnleksikon. Edited by Ola Stemshaug. Oslo: Det Norske Samlaget, 1982.

Otterbjörk, Roland. *Svenska förnamn: Skrifter utgivna av Svenska språknämnden 29*. Stockholm: Almqvist and Wiksell, 1979.

Oxford Dictionary of First Names. Edited by Patrick Hanks, Kate Hardcastle, and Flavia Hodges. 2nd ed. New York: Oxford University Press, 2006.

Saarikalle, Anne, and Johanna Suomalainen. *Suomalaiset etunimet: Aadasta Yrjöön*. Jyväskylä: Gummerus, 2007.

Søndergaard, Georg. *Danske for- og efternavne: Betydning, oprindelse, udbredelse*. Copenhagen: Askholms Forlag, 2000.

———. *Danske efternavne: Popularitet, betydning, oprindelse*. Copenhagen: Det Ny Lademann, 1991.

Veka, Olav. *Namneboka*. Oslo: Det Norske Samlaget, 1991.

———. *Norsk etternamnleksikon: Norske slektsnamn—utbreiing, tyding og opphav*. Oslo: Det Norske Samlaget, 2000.

Name Data

1880 United States Federal Census. www.ancestry.com. Accessed April 9, 2010.

Danmarks Statistik. Navne. http://www.dst.dk/Statistik/Navne.aspx. Accessed 2007–9.

Hagstofa Íslands. Nöfn. http://www.hagstofa.is/Hagtolur/Mannfjoldi/Nofn. Accessed 2007–9.

Oregon Government, Center for Health Statistics. Oregon Baby Names. http://www.dhs.state.or.us/dhs/ph/chs/babyname/index.shtml. Accessed 2007–9.

Social Security Administration. Popular Baby Names. http://www.ssa.gov/OACT/babynames/. Accessed 2007–9.

Statistics Denmark. How many have the name? http://www.dst.dk/HomeUK/Statistics/Names/HowMany.aspx. Accessed 2007–9.

Statistics Iceland. Names. http://www.statice.is/Statistics/Population/Names. Accessed 2007–9.

Statistics Norway. Name Statistics. http://www.ssb.no/navn_en/. Accessed 2007–9.

Statistics Sweden. Name Search. How many are named? http://www.scb.se/Pages/NameSearch
_____259070.aspx. Accessed 2007–9.
Statistisk sentralbyrå. Namnestatistikk. http://www.ssb.no/emner/00/navn/. Accessed 2007–9.
Svenska namn. Namnstatistik Sverige. http://www.svenskanamn.se/statistik/sverige. Accessed
2007–9.
U.S. Census Bureau, Population Division. Genealogy Data: Frequently Occurring Surnames from
Census 2000. http://www.census.gov/genealogy/www/data/2000surnames/index.html. Ac-
cessed 2009.

Other Literature

Haugen, Einar. *The Norwegian Language in America: A Study in Bilingual Behavior.* 2 vols. Philadel-
phia: University of Pensylvania Press, 1953.
Lindal, V. J. *The Icelanders of Canada.* Winnipeg: National and Viking, 1967.
Løken, Gulbrand. *From Fjord to Frontier: A History of Norwegians in Canada.* Toronto: McClelland
and Stewart, 1980.
Lovoll, Odd S. *Norwegian Newspapers in America: Connecting Norway and the New Land.* Minne-
apolis: Minnesota Historical Society Press, 2010.
Mørkhagen, Sverre. *Farvel Norge: Utvandringen til Amerika 1825–1975.* Oslo: Gyldendal, 2009.
The Saga of Gunnlaugur Snake's Tongue: With an Essay on the Structure and Translation of the Saga.
Translated and edited by E. Paul Durrenberger and Dorothy Durrenberger. Cranbury, N.J.: As-
sociated University Presses, 1993.
Sawyer, Birgit. *The Viking Age Rune-Stones: Custom and Commemoration in Early Medieval Scandi-
navia.* Oxford: Oxford University Press, 2000.
Singh, Balkaran. "Bruker feriene på skolebenken." *Aftenposten,* July 2, 2004.
Snorres kongesoger. Translated by Steinar Schjøtt. Oslo: Gyldendal, 1964.
Svanevik, Anne. "Norske fornavn i Amerika—angloamerikanske fornavn i Norge." *Norsk språk i
Amerika/Norwegian Language in America. Papers Read at a Conference on the 19th of November
1987, Blindern, Oslo, Norway.* Edited by Botolv Helleland, 193–220. Oslo: Novus, 1991.
Østrem, Nils Olav. *Norsk utvandringshistorie.* Oslo: Det Norske Samlaget, 2006.

Web Resources

Anderson, Alan. "Norwegian Settlements." Encyclopedia of Saskatchewan. University of Regina
and Canadian Plains Research Center, 2007. http://esask.uregina.ca/entry/norwegian_settle
ments.html. Accessed March 4, 2010.
———. "Scandinavian Settlements." Encyclopedia of Saskatchewan. University of Regina and Canadian Plains Research Center, 2007. http://esask.uregina.ca/entry/scandinavian_settlements
.html. Accessed March 4, 2010.
Anderson, Alan, and Joan Eyolfson Cadham. "Icelandic Settlements." Encyclopedia of Saskatchewan. University of Regina and Canadian Plains Research Center, 2007. http://esask.uregina
.ca/entry/icelandic_settlements.html. Accessed March 4, 2010.
Blanck, Dag. "A Brief History of Swedish Immigration to North America." Swenson Swedish Immigration Research Center, Augustana College, Fall 2005. http://www.augustana.edu/x14897
.xml. Accessed February 9, 2008.
Brittingham, Angela, and G. Patricia de la Cruz. "Ancestry: 2000." U.S. Census Bureau, June 2004.
http://www.census.gov/prod/2004pubs/c2kbr-35.pdf. Accessed November 18, 2007.
"Census 2000: First, Second and Total Responses to the Ancestry Question by Detailed Ancestry Code." U.S. Census Bureau, January 22, 2007. http://www.census.gov/population/www/
ancestry/anc2000.html. Accessed November 18, 2007.

Christianson, J. R. "Danes." The Electronic Encyclopedia of Chicago. Chicago Historical Society, 2005. http://www.encyclopedia.chicagohistory.org/pages/363.html. Accessed November 25, 2007.

Danish American Heritage Society. Ames, Iowa. http://www.danishamericanheritagesociety.org/. Accessed February 3, 2007.

Danish Immigrant Museum. Elk Horn, Iowa. http://www.dkmuseum.org/. Accessed February 3, 2008.

"Det løfterike landet: Norsk utvandring til Amerika og norsk-amerikansk historie 1825–2000." Norsk utvandrermuseum og Nasjonalbiblioteket, 2000–2006. http://www.nb.no/emigrasjon/. Accessed February 3, 2008.

Granquist, Mark S. "Swedish Americans." Multicultural America, 2006. http://www.everyculture.com/multi/Sr-Z/Swedish-Americans.html. Accessed February 3, 2007.

Hale, Christopher S. "Danes." The Encyclopedia of Canada's Peoples. Multicultural Canada. http://www.multiculturalcanada.ca/Encyclopedia/A-Z/d1. Accessed March 4, 2010.

———. "Swedes." The Encyclopedia of Canada's Peoples. Multicultural Canada. http://www.multiculturalcanada.ca/Encyclopedia/A-Z/s13. Accessed March 4, 2010.

"Immigration by Country, 1820–1998." Scholastic Inc. http://teacher.scholastic.com/activities/immigration/pdfs/mulit_column.pdf. Accessed November 25, 2007.

"Inn- og utvandring, oversjøisk utvandring og utvandring til USA. 1821–1948." Statistisk sentralbyrå, 2000. http://www.ssb.no/emner/historisk_statistikk/aarbok/ht-020220-051.html. Accessed November 25, 2007.

"The Lost Names of 1880." Nameberry. http://nameberry.com/blog/2009/11/18/the-lost-names-of-1880. Accessed April 2010.

Lovoll, Odd S. "Norwegian Americans." Multicultural America, 2006. http://www.everyculture.com/multi/Le-Pa/Norwegian-Americans.html. Accessed February 3, 2007.

Løken, Gulbrand. "Norwegians." The Encyclopedia of Canada's Peoples. Multicultural Canada. http://www.multiculturalcanada.ca/Encyclopedia/A-Z/n4. Accessed March 4, 2010.

Nielsen, John Mark, and Peter L. Petersen. "Danish Americans." Multicultural America, 2006. http://www.everyculture.com/multi/Bu-Dr/Danish-Americans.html. Accessed December 8, 2008.

Norsk utvandrermuseum. http://www.museumsnett.no/emigrantmuseum/emigrant.html. Accessed February 3, 2008.

Ockerstrom, Lolly. "Icelandic Americans." Multicultural America, 2006. http://www.everyculture.com/multi/Ha-La/Icelandic-Americans.html. Accessed February 3, 2008.

Spiegel, Taru. "The Finns in America." Library of Congress. November 26, 2007. http://www.loc.gov/rr/european/FinnsAmer/finchro.html. Accessed January 9, 2008.

"Svenska namnsdagar från 2001." http://stjarnhimlen.se/ndag/ndag2001.html. Accessed November 25, 2007.

"Swedish namedays." http://stjarnhimlen.se/ndag/namedays.html. Accessed November 25, 2007.

Zetterberg, Seppo. "Main Outlines of Finnish History." Virtual Finland, 2005. http://finland.fi/public/default.aspx?contentid=160058&contentlan=2&culture=en-US. Accessed February 3, 2008.

Index

Scandinavian given names that are mentioned in *both* the dictionary and guide sections appear in the index. See the dictionary section for Scandinavian given names not mentioned in the guide section. Page numbers for the dictionary section appear in bold type.

Aaboe, 91
Aasen, Ivar, 132; Ivar, **33**
ABBA, 140; Agneta, **3**; Anni, **4**
Adolphus, 55, 106, 107, 169; Gustav, **30**
Agnes, Saint, 127–29
Agnet(h)a/Agnete, **3**, 129, 140, 150, 176
Ahlef, **22**, 87, 92
Albert, **22**, 85–86, 87, 88–89, 92, 93, 106, 152, 155, 173; Alberta, **3**; Albrekt, **22**; Anders, **23**; Andreas, **23**
Alf, **22**, 106, 107, 130, 143, 150, 154, 181, 183; Alva, **3**
alliteration, 86
Alva, **3**, 86, 97, 99, 137, 144, 155, 176
Amerikan Suomalainen Lehti, 57
Amerikan Suomalaisen Kirjallisuuden Seura, 57
Anders, xii, **23**, 72, 74, 82–84, 85, 87, 88, 91–92, 93, 106, 107, 109, 110, 113, 116, 117–18, 119, 141, 143, 157, 181; Per, **41**
Andersen, 72, 79, 82–83, 85–86, 87, 89, 90, 93, 109, 112, 118, 136; Hans, **31**; Hjalmar, **32**; Kristian, **36**; Pelle, **41**
Andersson, 70, 72, 77, 78, 79, 89, 93, 109, 140; Anders, **23**
Andres, **23**, 92, 106, 107–8, 116, 118
Andrew, 87, 91–92, 93, 106–7, 109, 113, 118; Anders, **23**; Andreas, **23**
Ane, **4**, 88, 127
Anna, xi, xiii, xv, **4**, 77, 82–84, 85, 87, 88, 92, 96, 102–3, 113, 127, 133, 140, 144–45, 154, 157, 173; Ane, **4**; Anita, **4**; Anja, **4**; Anne, **4**; Anni, **4**; An(n)ika, **4**; Hanna, **9**; Karina, **12**; Maria, **14**; Nanna, **15**; Nina, **15**; Oleanna, **16**
Anna, mother of Virgin Mary (Saint Ann), 127, 140
Anne, x, **4**, 53, 85–86, 88, 96, 102, 127, 133, 140, 144, 154, 165, 174; Ane, **4**; Anna, **4**; Anne, **4**; Karianne, **12**; Liv, **13**; Marian(n), **14**; Marie, **14**; Stina, **18**
Annelise, 117
Annie, **4**, 19, 96, 102, 131
An(n)ika, **4**, 46, 113, 115, 116, 152
approved names, 135–38
Ari, **23**, 116, 117, 181

Arne, **23**, 93, 106, 107, 110, 122, 125, 132, 133, 141, 155; Christer, **36**; Geir, **29**; Kjell, **35**; Veslemøy, **20**
Arthur, 114, 131; Oluf, **40**
Arvid, **23**, 56, 106, 107, 143, 152, 155, 179
Ásgarðr (Asgard), 148
Ask, **24**, 143, 146, 148, 154, 181; Embla, **7**; Odin, **39**
Astrid, **4–5**, 82, 97, 99, 104, 115, 122–24, 132, 140, 144, 152, 157, 166, 171, 176; Asta, **4**; Birk, **25**; Emil, **27**; Estrid, **7**; Karl, **35**; Linda, **13**; Ronja, **17**; Åsta, **21**
Augustana College, 55
Augustana Synod, 55
Austin, 95, 106, 114, 119

Baardsen, Gjest, 121; Gjest, **29**
Bakken, 76
Balder, **24**, 132, 146, 148, 179; Nanna, **15**; Odin, **39**
Beata, **5**, 117, 157
Bee, The, 58
Bergkvist, 77
Bergman, 77; Bo, **25**; Ingmar, **33**, 117; Ingrid, **11**; Linn, **13**; Monica, **15**; Pia, **16**
Bergsjö, 77
Bergsvein, **24**, 123
Berit, **5**, 93, 104, 117, 127, 129, 137, 156, 176
Bernadotte, House of, 169
Bernadotte, Jean-Baptiste, 169
Berta/Bertha, **5**, 84, 88, 97, 98, 101, 107, 115, 151, 155, 176; Börta, **6**
Bethany College, 55
Biblical names, 127; Ask, **24**; Eli, **7**; Embla, **7**; Eva, **7**; Gabriel, **29**; Hulda, **10**; Judith, **11**; Magdalena, **14**; Ruth, **17**; Susanna, **18**
Bien (The Bee), 58
Birch Hills, Saskatchewan, 66
Birgitta, Saint, 127–29
Birgitta/Birgitte, **5**, 127–29, 137
Birk, **25**, 119
Birt(h)e, **5**, 129, 135, 137, 144
Bjarne, **25**, 88, 92–93, 110, 125, 141, 152, 154, 178
Bjorn, **25**, 110, 116, 179, 181
Bjug, **25**, 124

Bjørg, ix, xii, xiii, **5**, 124, 133, 137, 140, 153
Björk, **5**, 72; Birk, **25**; Sindre, **45**
Björkman, 77
Bjørnson, Bjørnstjerne, 132; Arne, **23**; Arnljot, **23**;
    Bergljot, **5**; Synnøve, **19**
Bluetooth, 115, 121–22, 159; Gorm, **29**; Harald, **31**
Blöndal, 72
Bo, **25**, 137, 141, 143, 153, 154, 179
Bonaparte, Napoleon, 169
bondkomik, 55
Brage, **25**, 125, 132, 143, 148; Odin, **39**
Brit(t)/Brit(t)a, **5**, 117, 128–29, 144, 154, 176; Mai, **14**;
    Ulla, **20**
Brommeland, 82
Bror, **25**, 137, 143, 156, 179; Syster, **19**
Brønla, 87, 90–91, 124; Brynhild, **5**
Bure Stone, 123
Buringrud, 75, 85
bygdelag, 60

California Lutheran University, 55
Canute, 90, 159, 162; Knud, **36**
Carl, ix, **25–26**, 56, 88, 100, 105–10, 116–17, 119, 130,
    137, 141, 143, 165, 168–72, 179
Carl XIV Johan, king of Sweden, 130, 169, 172;
    Johan, **34**
Carl XVI Gustaf, king of Sweden, 168–72, 172; Carl,
    25; Gustav, **30**
Carla, 97, 100, 117
Carolus Magnus, 139; Magnus, **37**
Carrie, **6**, 90, 94, 97–99, 101, 102–4, 115, 176; Kari, **12**
Carsten, xii, **26**, 116, 119, 141, 179
Catherine, Saint, 127–29
Cecilia, Saint, 127–29
Charlemagne, 126, 139, 168; Magnus, **37**
Christen, **26**, 104, 110, 179; Kristen, **36**
Christer, **26**, 137, 151, 179; Krister, **36**
Christian (given name), ix, xii, xiv, **26**, 58, 92, 106–8,
    110, 116, 119, 127, 133, 141, 143, 160–64, 165, 168, 180;
    Espen, **28**; Hans, **31**; Kristian, **36**; Olav, **40**
Christian II, king of Denmark-Norway, 160, 163
Christian IV, king of Denmark-Norway, 58; Kris-
    tian, **36**
Christian IX, king of Denmark, 159, 164
Christian names, 120, 126–28, 129, 131, 140, 169
Christian saints, 127–29, 139
Christina, queen of Sweden, 54
Christina/Christine, ix, xii, **6**, 97, 98, 103, 104, 115, 116,
    130, 144, 165, 176
Christoffer/Christopher, **26**, 109, 112; Kristoffer, **36**
Clara, **6**, 88, 97–98, 100, 107, 176; Klara, **12**
Clausen, Claus L., 58
Consumers' Co-operative Society, 68

Dag, xiii, **26**, 119, 125, 155, 156, 181; Dag-, **6**
Dagmar, **6**, 97, 99, 117, 156, 162, 176
Dagny, **6**, 117, 155, 176

Dana, **6**, 97, 99–100, 114–15
Dana College, 58
Dane, **26**, 106, 108, 115, 116, 117
Danica/Danika, **6**, 97, 102, 113, 114–15
Danish American press, 58
Danish Evangelical Lutheran Association, 58
Danish Evangelical Lutheran Church in America, 58
Danish Pioneer, The, 58
Danish West India and Guinea Company, The, 57
Decorah-Posten, 59; Kristian, **36**
Depression, 63
Désirée, 130, 153, 161, 165, 169
Dickens, Charles, 131
Doll's House, A, 116; Nora, **15**
Dort(h)e, **6**, 137
Dynna Stone, 122–23

Easthouse, 76, 91
Eielsen, Elling, 59; Egil, **27**; Elling, **27**
Einar, xiv, **27**, 71, 93, 106, 110, 125, 141, 143, 156, 179
Eirik, **27**, 92, 110, 111–12, 119, 125, 143, 153, 165–68;
    Gunnhild, **9**; Jerker, **34**. *See also* Erik
Eirik the Red, 72, 111; Eirik, **27**; Erik, **28**; Frøydis, **8**
Eklund, 77, 89, 93
Eldar, **27**, 119, 154, 179
Elizabeth, Saint, 127–29
Ellemann-Jensen, Uffe, 74; Uffe, **49**
Elling Eielsen's Synod, 59
Embla, **7**, 146, 148, 154, 176; Ask, **24**; Eva, **7**; Odin, **39**
Emigranten, 59
Endre, xiii, **27**, 74, 81–82, 93, 119, 146, 156, 178
English names, 120, 130–31
Erica/Ericka, **7**, 92, 97
Eric/Erich/Erick, 92–93, 106–8, 110–11, 116, 119, 178.
    See also Erik
Erik, xv, **28**, 72, 88, 92–93, 100, 106–12, 116, 119, 133,
    139, 141, 143, 144, 153, 160–63, 168, 170–72; Eirik,
    27; Erica, **7**
Erika, **7**, 92, 97, 100, 102–5, 115, 117, 144, 150, 153
Erikson, Leif, 53, 72, 108, 111; Leiv, **37**; Rasmus, **42**
Erik the Red, 72, 111; Eirik, **27**; Erik, **28**; Frøydis, **8**
Erling, **28**, 93, 106–7, 119, 125, 141, 154, 156, 181; El-
    ling, **27**
Erlinga, 114
Espen, **28**, 137, 150, 153, 179
ethnic names, 73, 96, 102–3, 105, 108–12; Dane, **26**
ethnic names revival, 102–3, 105, 108–9, 112
Etholén, Arvid Adolf, 56
Etolin, 56
Evinrude, 76; Ole, **40**

farm names, 74–76, 78, 82, 89, 175
Faroe Islands, 60, 63, 120, 183, 184; Grim, **29**; Olav,
    40; Regin, **42**; Roe, **43**
Fartein, 123
fashions in naming, 3, 73, 113, 139, 149
Finland, Pennsylvania, 55

Finlandia University, 57
Finland Society, 57
Finn, **28**, 141, 156, 179
Finnish American press, 57
Finnish Civil War, 67
Finnish Literature Society, The (Amerikan Suomalaisen Kirjallisuuden Seura), 57
Finn's Point, 55
Finntown, 65
Fisketjon, 76
Flagstad, Kirsten, 101; Kirsten, **12**
Fleming, Klaus, 54, 55
Flemming, **28**, 137, 156, 159
Flora Danica, 113
Forsberg, 78
Forsell, 77, 78
Forsgren, 78
Forslund, 78
Forsman, 78
Forstrom, 78
Fort Christina, 54
Fossum, 76
Fox River settlement, 59
Frederik, crown prince of Denmark, 160; Fredrik, **28**
Frederik VII, 159, 164
Frederik IX, 160, 164; Fredrik, **28**
French names, 120, 130
Freya, **8**, 115, 117, 119, 146–48, 176; Saga, **17**
Frida, 7, 97, 101, 104, 144, 151, 156, 176
Fride, 123
Frigg, 7, 132, 146, 148, 176
Friis, 73; Laila, **13**
"Frithiofs saga," 132; Fridtjov, **28**
Frode, **28**, 125, 137, 151; Are, **23**
Frøydis, **8**, 148, 151
Furuhjelm, Johan Hampus, 56
Fältskog, Agnetha, 140; Agneta, **3**

Gaspé Peninsula, 65
Geir, **29**, 137, 153, 179
Gerd, xiii, **8**, 124, 133, 137, 140, 146, 148, 152
Gerhardsen, Einar, 71; Einar, **27**
German names, 120, 128–30
giants, 148
Gitte, x, xi, **8**, 89, 129, 137, 144, 152; Gunilla, **8**
Gjertrud, xii, **8**, 114, 152
Gjest, **29**, 121, 125
Glücksborg, House of, 159
Golden Horns, 120–21
Gorm the Old, 115, 122; Gorm, **29**
Grand View College, 58
Green County, Wisconsin, 76
Greenland, vii, 60, 111, 120, 183, 184; Eirik, **27**; Frøydis, **8**
Greta, xv, **8**, 97, 99, 104, 115, 129, 151, 154, 176
Grundtvig, Nikolai F.S., 58; Nikolaus, **39**
Gunilla, **8**, 137, 150, 171, 176

Gunnar/Gunder/Gunner, xii, xv, **30**, 72, 94, 106, 108, 110, 116, 119, 122, 125, 132, 133, 141, 143, 150, 181
Gust, 94, 106–7
Gusta, **9**, 97, 99
Gustav/Gustaf, **30**, 92, 106–7, 137, 169, 170, 180; Gusta, **9**
Gustav I Vasa, 168
Gustav III, 130, 172
Gustavus Adolphus College, 55, 169; Gustav, **30**
Gyllenhammar, 77
Göran, xiv, **30**, 137, 152; Örjan, **49**
Gösta, xv, **30**, 137, 153

Haakon, **30**, 94, 119, 165, 166
Haakon Magnus, crown prince of Norway, 166; Håkon, **33**; Magnus, **38**
Hagia Sophia, 122
Haglund, Ivar, 112; Ivar, **33**
half-god, 148; Loki, **37**; Narve, **38**
Halvorsen/Halvorson/Halvorsson, 77
Hanakam, 74, 82–83
Hanna(h), **9**, 97–99, 144–45, 150; Anna, **4**
Hans, **31**, 72, 73, 94, 105, 106–8, 128–30, 133, 134, 139, 141, 143, 154, 155, 161, 163, 169, 172, 181; Johannes, **34**; Peter, **42**
Hanseatic League, 130
Hansen/Hanson, 72, 73, 79, 119
Harald Bluetooth, 115, 121–22, 159, 162; Gorm, **29**; Harald, **31**
Harald Fairhair, 164, 167; Gyda, **9**; Harald, **31**; Åsa, **21**
Harold, **31**, 106–8, 162, 166
Harstad, 76
Haug, 76
Haugen, Einar, 88, 97; Einar, **27**
Haugli, 76
heathen names, 131
Hedvig/Hedwig, **9**, 97–99, 130, 156, 171, 176
Hege, **9**, 137, 156
Helga, xii, **9**, 71, 74, 82, 85, 92, 97, 99, 125, 132, 144, 156, 157, 176; Hege, **9**; Helge, **9**; Helle; **10**; Olga, **16**
Helgason, 73
Helga the Fair, 71; Helga, **9**
Helge, **31**, 53, 94, 122, 125, 132, 143, 156; Helga, **9**
Helland, 76, 82–83, 87, 89, 90–91, 93, 136
Helle: boys name, **31**; girls name, **10**, 137, 144, 157, 174, 176
Hellström, 77
Helsinki of America, 56
Hemlandet, 55
Hemstad, 76
Henie, Sonja, 100, 116; Sonja, **18**
Henning, **31–32**, 137, 153, 180
hereditary surnames, 73, 75, 77
Herseth, 76
Hilda, **10**, 97–100, 104, 117, 144, 150, 157
Hildur, **10**, 97–99
Hill, 91

History of the Norwegian Kings, 124, 126, 132; Magnus, 37
Holst, 73
Hulda(h), 10, 97–99
hyphenated last names, 136
Håkon, 32–33, 60, 125, 132, 143, 154, 165–68, 181; Haakon, 30; Hågen, 32; Kristina, 12–13
Håland, 74, 82

Ibsen, Henrik, 132; Eiolv, 27; Greger, 29; Hedda, 9; Hedvig, 9; Henrik, 32; Hjalmar, 32; Nora, 15; Osvald, 41; Peer, 41; Solveig, 18; Terje, 47; Åse, 21
Icelandic sagas, 124, 132. *See also* Saga, Old Norse-Icelandic
Idun(n), 10, 125, 146–48, 150
Ildjarnstad, 76
Inga, 10, 97–99, 104
Inge: boys name, 33, 126, 143, 151, 167, 168, 170–71, 178; girls name, 10, 104, 139, 144, 157; Ingo, 33
Ing(e)mar, 33, 126, 137, 143, 153, 158, 170
Ingrid, 11, 69, 97, 100, 101, 104, 115, 132–33, 139–40, 144, 151, 156, 161–62, 165–66, 169, 176, 178; Inga, 10; Pia, 16
Ingstad, Anne Stine, 53; Stina, 18
Ingstad, Helge, 53; Helge, 31
Ivar/Iver, xi, xiii, 33, 92, 94, 112, 119, 126, 143, 150, 181
Ivar's Fish Restaurants, 112; Ivar, 33

Jacobson, 75
Jelling Stone, 121–22
Jens, x, 34, 72, 94, 110, 128–29, 133, 134, 139, 141, 143, 152, 156, 178; Jensina, 11; Sina, 18
Jensen, 72, 73–74, 79, 112, 119, 135, 136, 178; Carsten, 26; Georg, 29; Jens, 34; Johannes, 34
Jesper, 34, 137, 141, 153, 154; Kasper, 35
Jette, 11, 137, 144
Johansson, 72, 77, 78–79; Ingemar, 33; Johan, 34
Johnson, 78
John the Baptist (Saint John), 127–29
Jon, 34, 72, 92, 106–7, 109, 129, 133, 134, 141, 154, 155; Jo, 34; Johannes, 34; Jone, 35
Jón Jónsson, 72
Joran/Jöran, 35, 119
Jorun(n), 11, 125, 137, 154
Joséphine, 130
Jotunheimen, 147
Jussi, 119, 129
Jytte, x, 11, 137
Järsberg Stone, 121

Kajsa, xiv, xv, 11, 137, 155; Kaia, 11
Kalm, Pehr, 55–56
Kalmia, 56
Kárason, 73
Karen, x, 12, 92, 94, 96–100, 102–4, 115, 116, 128–29, 133, 140, 144, 155, 175–76
Kari, xii, 12, 90, 94, 97, 101, 102–4, 115–16, 128–29, 137, 157, 176–77; Carrie, 6; Gunilla, 8; Solveig, 18

Karin, 12, 92, 97–101, 104, 129, 133, 144, 155, 171, 175–76; Kajsa, 11; Karina, 12
Karl, x, 35, 72, 88, 94, 100, 105–8, 110, 116–17, 119, 137, 141, 150, 168, 170–71, 180
Karl III Johan, king of Norway, 130, 172
Karla, 97, 100, 117
Karlsson, 72, 77, 79; Karl, 35
Karsten, xiv, 35, 116, 119, 141, 153
Katrina/Katrine, 12, 97, 100, 103–4, 115–16, 129; Cathrina, 6; Kari, 12; Karin, 12; Trine, 20
Kaupang, 89, 93
Kensington Rune Stone, 53
Kirsten/Kirstin, 12, 97, 100–101, 104, 115–16, 140, 144, 157; Kirsti, 12
Kittel, 35, 83, 87, 181
Kittelson, 90
Kjell, xii, 35, 119, 133, 143, 154; Keld, 35; Kittel, 35
Kjetil, 35, 94, 126, 137, 154; Ketil, 35; Kittel, 35; Kjell, 35
Knut the Great, 90, 159, 162, 167; Knud, 36
Koch, 73
Kongsberg, 130
Kristen: boys name, 36, 83, 110, 115, 127, 153, 180; girls name, 97, 100, 103–4, 127
Krister, xv, 36, 137, 157, 180
Kristi, 12, 97, 100–104, 154
Kristian, 36, 82–83, 92, 100, 106, 108, 110, 116, 119, 127, 141, 143, 153, 157, 180; Carsten, 26; Karsten, 35; Kristen, 36; Krister, 36; Kristiana, 12; Stian, 45
Kristin, xiii, 12, 97, 100–104, 115–16, 127, 144, 154, 166, 176; Kristina, 12
Kristina/Kristine, xv, 12, 82–84, 97, 99, 100–104, 115–17, 127, 133, 144, 154, 169–71, 176; Kine, 12; Kirsten, 12; Kjersti, 12; Kristi, 12; Nina, 15; Stina, 18; Tina, 19
Kristin Lavransdatter, 100; Erland, 28; Kristin, 12; Lavrans, 37
Kristoffer/Kristopher, 36, 109–10, 112, 141, 143, 151, 158
Kuparinen, Aleksanteri, 56

Landnámabók, 124
L'Anse aux Meadows, 53; Helge, 31; Stina, 18
Lapland, 55
Lapp, 63; Arnfinn, 23; Dagfinn, 26; Finn, 28; Laila, 13; Torfinn, 48
Lars, x, 37, 72, 74, 77, 82, 85, 92, 94, 110, 116, 128, 129, 139, 141, 143, 155, 180; Lasse, 37; Laura, 13; Laurits, 37; Lavrans, 37; Lorents, 37
Lawrence, Saint, 127–29
Laxness, 72
Lee, 76, 90, 114
Leiv/Leif, 37, 94, 106, 108, 110, 111, 116, 133, 141, 143, 152, 156, 177, 180
Lena, 13, 97–98, 104, 115, 116, 145, 155, 156, 177; Helen, 9; Ole, 40
Lidén, 77
Lindberg, 77–78, 89

Lindgren, Astrid: Astrid, **4**; Birk, **25**; Emil, **27**; Karl, **35**; Ronja, **17**
Lindholm, 77
Lindstrom/Lindström, 78; Lars, **37**; Pia, **16**
Linn, Charles, 56
Liv/Live/Liva, **13**, 105, 115, 117, 118, 124, 125, 133, 144, 152, 156, 177
Loke/Loki, **37**, 119, 143, 148; Narve, **38**
Lone, xi, **13**, 137, 144, 151, 176
Lundgren, 77
Luther College, 60

Macpherson, John, 92, 169; Orla, **41**; Oskar, **41**; Selma, **17**
Mads, x, **37**, 181; Mats, **38**
Magnus, **37–38**, 110, 114, 116, 126, 137, 139, 141, 143, 152, 155, 162, 165–68, 171–72, 181; Håkon, **33**; Mogens, **38**; Mons, **38**; Roland, **43**
Malin, xv, **14**, 117, 144, 154, 157
Maren, **14**, 95, 105, 115, 144, 151, 174, 175, 176
Margaret, Saint, 127–29
Margareta, **14**, 117, 129, 133, 145, 154, 168–71, 177; Grete, **8**; Margreta, **14**; Marta, **14**; Merete, **15**; Mette, **15**; Märta, **15**; Rita, **17**
Margit, **14**, 95, 117, 129, 144–45, 153, 154, 176; Maia, **14**; Marit, **14**
Margrete I, queen of Norway, Denmark, and Sweden, 163, 165, 168, 172; Margreta, **14**
Margrethe II, 160–64; Margreta, **14**; Torhild, **19**
Mari, **14**, 85, 88, 97, 100–101, 117, 137, 144, 152, 177; Marian(n), **14**
Maria/Marie, **14**, 88, 96, 99, 101, 114, 127, 130, 133, 140, 144–45, 151, 152, 175; Björk, **5**; Dina, **6**; Maia, **14**; Mali, **14**; Mari, **14**; Marianne, **14**; Marie, **14**; Marika, **14**; Marius, **38**
Marika, **14**, 117, 156, 175, 176
Marit, **14**, 117, 128, 129, 153, 154, 165–66; Mette, **15**
marker names, 102, 107–8, 117
Markland, 61
Marttinen, 55
Mary, the Virgin, 127
Mats, **38**, 119, 128, 143, 151, 181; Mads, **37**
Medelsvensson, 77
Mellin, 77
metronymic, 70–71, 135, 136, 183; Gunnhild, **9**
Mette, **15**, 97–100, 117, 129, 140, 144, 151, 174, 176
Mette-Marit, crown princess of Norway, 165–66; Mette, **15**
Minneapolis Tidende, 59
Modér, 77
Moen, 76
Mogens, **38**, 137, 141, 180; Magnus, **37–38**
Morgenstern, 77
Mormons, 58, 60
Morton, John, 54, 55
Mount Furuhelm, 56
Munch, Peder Andreas, 132
Munk, Jens, 58

mythological names, 146; Helge, **31**; Signe, **17**; Signy, **17**. *See also* Norse mythology
Møller, 73
Mårtenson, 55

namesake, 80–84, 85, 115
name types: Anders, **23**; Christian (names of Catholic saints), 120, 126–28, 129, 131, 140, 169; Denmark, 73–74; Egil, **26–27**; English, 120, 130–31; ethnic, 73, 96–102, 102–5, 105–8, 108–12, 112–13, 113–19; farm, 74–75, 75–76, 78, 82, 89, 175; French, 120, 130; German, 120, 128–30; Hans, **31**; heathen, 131; hereditary surnames, 73, 75, 77; Iceland, 72–73; Jens, **34**; Johan, **34**; Karl, **35**; Kittel, **35**; matronymic, 70–71, 135–36, 183; Niels, **38**; Nils, **39**; Norway, 74–76; occupational, 73, 78, 99, 100; Ola, **39**; Olav, **40**; ornamental, 77–78; patronymic, 69, 70–79, 82, 89–90, 107, 118–19, 135, 178, 184; Per, **41**; Pål, **42**; Sweden, 77–78
Napoleon Bonaparte, 169
Narve, **38**, 95, 148, 158
National Romanticism, 132
Nels, **38**, 85–86, 89–90, 95, 106, 107, 119; Nils, **39**
Nelson, 79, 85–86, 93, 107, 112, 119; Knud, **36**; Nels, **38**
New Denmark, 67
New Iceland, 61, 66
New Netherland, 54
Newport tower, 53
New Sweden, 54, 55
Niall, 119; Njål, **39**
Nicholas, Saint, 129
nicknames, 77, 131, 158, 168–69; Erland, **28**; Fleming, **28**; Svante, **46**; Sverre, **46**
Nielsen, Brigitte, 89
Nielsen/Nilsen/Nilsson, 70, 72, 73, 78, 79, 89, 93, 112, 171–72; Niels, **38**; Nils, **39**; patronymic, 184; Torstein, **48**
Nils/Niels, xi, **38**, **39**, 72, 95, 110, 119, 128, 129, 137, 139, 141, 143, 156, 157, 163; Nels, **38**; Nikolaus, **38–39**; Nilsine, **15**
Njord, **39**, 132, 146, 148, 181
Nora, **15**, 98–99, 115–16, 144, 152, 176
Nordisk Tidende, 59
Nordlyset, 59
Nordmann, 107; Kari, **12**; Ola, **39–40**
Nordstjernan, 55
Norman, **39**, 106–8, 110, 116–17, 153, 180; Danica, **6**
Norse mythology, 81, 124, 132, 146–48, 179, 183; Ask, **24**; Balder, **24**; Embla, **7**; Frigg, **7**; Frøy, **8**; Frøya, **8**; Gun(n), **8**; Hermod, **32**; Idunn, **10**; Magne, **37**; Nanna, **15**; Narve, **38**; Odin, **39**; Regin, **42**; Saga, **17**; Siv, **18**; Tjalve, **47**; Tor, **47**; Trym, **48**; Unn, **20**; Yngve, **49**; Ægir, **49**
Norstedt, 77
Northern Light, 59
North Park University (Chicago), 55
Norwegian American Genealogical Center, 59
Norwegian American Lutheran Church, 59

Norwegian American press, 59–60
Norwegian-American Weekly, 59–60
Nova Dania, 58
Nya Vasa, 55
Nyman, 77

occupational names, 73, 78, 99, 100
Oda, xv, **15**, 98, 152, 176; Ottilia, **16**
Odd, xv, **39**, 126, 133, 137, 152
Odin, **39**, 110, 112, 116, 119, 132, 143, 146, 148, 152, 180;
    Balder, **24**; Hermod, **32**
Oehlenschläger, Adam, 132; Kjartan, **35**; Signe, **17**
Ola/Ole, xi, **39–40**, 72, 82, 85, 92, 95, 106–7, 142–43,
    152, 154, 180; Jens, **34**; Kari, **12**; Lena, **13**; Olea, **16**;
    Oleanna, **16**
Olaf, **40**, 88, 90, 92, 95, 106–7, 110, 119, 132, 133, 142,
    166, 180; Ahlef, **22**; Olav, **40**
Ólafur Ragnar Grímsson, 72; Olafur, **40**; Ragnar, **42**
Olav, **40**, 70, 82, 90, 92, 95, 110, 126, 133, 137, 142–43,
    154, 165–66, 180; Ola, **39**; Olafur, **40**; Olava, **16**;
    Olavus, **40**; Ole, **40**; Oleiv, **40**; Olof, **40**; Oluf, **40**
Olav, Saint, 126, 142, 167; Olav, **40**; Åsta, **21**
Olav Tryggvason, 159; Olav, **40**; Trygve, **48**; Tyra, **20**
Olav V, 164–66, 168; Olav, **40**; Ragnhild, **16**
Old Danish, 120, 161, 183
Oldenburg, House of, 159
Old Norse, xvii, 69, 70–71, 120, 124, 129, 132, 140, 148,
    179, 183
Old Swedish, 120, 183
Ole and Lena, 116; Lena, **13**; Ole, **40**
Olga, **16**, 114, 152, 157
Olof, xv, **40**, 110, 133, 137, 142–43, 154, 168, 180
Olsen/Olson, 71–72, 76, 79, 89, 93, 107, 112; Nels, **38**;
    Ola, **39**; Olav, **40**
Order of Runeberg, The, 57
ornamental names, 77–78
Osa/Osie, **16**, 70, 98–100, 175; Åsa, **21**
Oscar, **41**, 88, 92–93, 95, 106, 114, 141, 169; Amanda, **4**
Oscar I, 130
Ossian, 92, 157, 169; Orla, **41**; Oskar, **41**; Selma, **17**
Ostebee, 76, 91
Östen/Østen/Øystein, xiii, **50**, 95, 106, 114, 119, 126,
    133, 150, 155, 165, 167; Esten, **28**; Eystein, **28**

Pacific Lutheran University, 60; Bjug, **25**
patronymic, 69, 70–79, 82, 89–90, 107, 118–19, 135,
    178, 184; Anders, **23**; Denmark, 73–74; Egil, **26**;
    Hans, **31**; Iceland, 72–73; Jens, **34**; Johan, **34**; Karl,
    35; Kittel, **35**; Niels, **38**; Nils, **39**; Norway, 74–76;
    Ola, **39**; Olav, **40**; Per, **41**; Pål, **42**; primary, 71–78,
    184; secondary, 71–75, 77–79, 184; Sweden, 77–78
Paul, Saint, 127–29
Peder, **41**, 72, 110, 129, 155, 181; Per, **41**
Peer Gynt, 132; Peer, **41**; Solveig, **18**; Åse, **21**
Peerson, Cleng, 58; Kleng, **36**
Per, **41**, 95, 110, 128–29, 133, 139, 141, 143, 154, 155, 181;
    Peder, **41**; Peer, **41**; Pelle, **41**; Pär, **42**

Pernille, **16**, 137, 153; Nille, **15**
Peter, Saint, 127–29
Petraeus, 77
Pettersson/Peterson, 78
Pia, **16**, 137, 144, 151, 157, 176
Poul, **42**, 129, 133, 137, 141, 143
Preben, xi, **42**, 137, 153
Proto-Nordic, 120–21; Olav, **40**

Quakers, 58
Quebec, Canada, 65–66

Randi, xii, **16**, 82, 98, 100–101, 115, 151
Rask, 77; Rasmus, **42**
Rasmussen, Anders Fogh, 74
Red Finns, 67
Reformation, 128–30, 149, 167, 183
Reidun, **17**, 137, 153, 154
Rennesø, 105
replacement names, 85–86, 106, 109, 113, 118
Restaurationen, 58; Kleng, **36**
Romantic Movement, 132, 169
Ronja, **17**, 137, 151; Birk, **25**
Ronning, 91
Rood, 76, 90, 93
Royal Family: Denmark, 159–64; Norway, 164–68;
    Sweden, 130, 168–72
Rud, 76
Rune (boys name), **43**, 133, 137, 141, 153, 157, 178, 181;
    Runa, **17**
rune stone, 53, 71, 121–23, 127
Røros, 130

Sabo(e), 70, 91
Saga (girls name), **17**, 137, 144, 177
Saga, Old Norse-Icelandic, 53, 71, 124, 127, 132; Agnar,
    22; Brynhild, **5–6**; Bue, **25**; Didrik, **26**; Egil, **26**–
    27; Fridtjov, **28**; Gisle, **29**; Gudrun, **8**; Helga, **9**;
    Njål, **39**; Orvar, **41**; Signy, **17**
Saga of Gunnlaugur Snake's Tongue, The, 71; Helga, **9**
Saga of the Volsungs, The: Brynhild, **5–6**; Gudrun, **8**;
    Signy, **17**
Saint Olaf College, 60; Olaf, **40**
Saints' Days, 149
Sámi, 63
Sandbakke, 76
Sandmo, 76
Sawyer, Birgit, 71
Scandinavia, Manitoba, 67
Scandinavian Canadian press, 67
Scandinavian Names Renaissance, 120, 131–33
Scandinavian names revival, 102–5, 108–12
Serena, **17**, 90, 98–99, 115
Sevareid, 91; Erik, **28**
Sibelius, 77
Sigfast, **44**, 123
Sigmund, **44**, 106–7, 126, 141, 143, 150, 180

Signe, **17**, 125, 155, 176
Sigrid, **17**, 88, 90, 95, 98–100, 105, 122, 125, 133, 144, 153, 155, 171, 176
Silverstjärn, 77
Sissel, **18**, 83, 129, 137, 157, 176; Cecilia, **6**; Sidsel, **17**
Siv, **18**, 105, 124, 132, 137, 146–48, 151, 155, 177
Sjödahl, Carl, 56
Skandinaven, 59
Sloopers, The, 58
Solveig, xiii, **18**, 117, 125, 133, 136, 137, 144, 153, 155, 177; Sol, **18**; Sylvi, **18**
Sonja, **18**, 98–100, 115, 116, 153, 157, 164, 166
Sonja, Queen of Norway, 116, 164; Sonja, **18**
Sons of Norway, 60
Soren/Søren, xi, **45**, **47**, 108, 117, 137, 141, 156
Stark, 77
Statute of Westminster, 66
Stéfansson, 72–73
Stein/Sten, xi, **45**, 110, 124, 126, 157, 180
Stockholm, Saskatchewan, 67
Stokset, 85
Sture, **46**, 137, 155, 156
Sturluson, Snorri, 124, 126, 132, 164; Gyda, **9**; Magnus, **37**; Snorre, **45**
Suomi College, 57
Suomi-Seura, 57
Suomi Synod, 57
Svea, **18**, 55, 132, 137, 144, 150; Danica, **6**; Nora, **15**
Svein, **46**, 95, 110, 126, 137, 157, 165–66, 180; Sveinke, **46**; Sveinung, **46**; Svend, **46**
Sven/Svend, **46**, 110, 133, 137, 141, 143, 157, 160–63, 171, 180; Svante, **46**
Svenska Amerikanaren, 55
Svenska Amerikanska Posten, 55
Svensson, 77–79
Svithiod Order, 55
Swedish American press, 55
Swedish capital of Canada, 67
Sweyn Forkbeard, 159, 162; Svend, **46**
Söderberg, 77
Søndenå, 74, 81

Tage, **47**, 110, 119, 143, 155, 156; Hasse, **31**
Terje, **47**, 137, 156
Thelma, **19**, 98–101, 144
Thor, **47**, 69, 81, 92, 95, 110, 112, 146–48, 180. *See also* Tor
Thora/Tora, **19**, 105, 117, 125, 151, 156, 176
Thorsen/Thorson, 112
Thorvald, **48**, 112, 126, 143, 154, 155, 180
Thygesen, 74
Thyra Danebod, 121
Thyra/Tyra, x, xi, **20**, 115, 121, 125, 132, 144, 152, 155, 161–62, 166

Tjalve, **47**, 148
Tor, xi, xiii, **47**, 69, 92, 95, 110, 112, 132, 143, 146–48, 155, 156, 180; Tor-, **19**
Torben, **47**, 112, 137, 141, 153, 180
Torbjorn/Torbjørn/Torbjörn, **47**, 112, 126, 151, 179
Tore, **48**, 95, 110, 112, 156, 178; Ture, **48**
Torfinn, **48**, 53, 95, 112, 150, 180; Tue, **48**
Torgrim, **48**, 112, 126, 154, 180
Torkil(d), **48**, 112, 157, 180; Terkel, **47**; Toke, **47**; Tyge, **48**
Torsen/Torson, 112
Torsten, **48**, 110, 112, 119, 122, 126, 180
Torvald, **48**, 112, 126, 143, 154, 155, 180
Tove/Tova, xi, **19**, 105, 117, 121, 125, 145, 151, 157, 162, 176; Tuva, **20**
Travels into North America, 56
Trym, **48**, 143, 147–48, 155
Tufteskog, 76
Tyler, Liv, 117–18; Liv, **13**

Ulla, xv, **20**, 137, 154
Ullmann, Liv, 117–18; Liv, **13**; Linn, **13**
University of Wisconsin, 60

Valborg's Mass, 170
Valdemar, **49**, 126, 143, 152, 160–63, 165, 168, 171, 180; Volmer, **49**
valkyrie, 124, 132, 136; Brynhild, **5–6**; Gunn, **8**
Vanaheim, 148
Vasa Order, 55
Veka, 82
Vetrhus, 76, 83, 90–91
Victoria, crown princess of Sweden, 168–70; Victoria, **20**
Viking Age, 60, 70, 120–26, 134, 146, 159, 161, 164, 168, 174, 183
Viking Order, 55
Vinland, 53
Vinland Map, 53
von Fersen, Count Axel, 54

Wallace, Birgitta, 53
Western Viking, 59
White Finns, 67
Wickmann, William, 60
Winterhouse, 76, 91
Work People's College, 57

Ylva, xv, **20**, 137, 152

Ægir/Ägir, **49**, 148
Åbø, 91
Åland, 63, 183
Ås/Åsen, 91

929.7 Co   1065852 $27.95